# First Language Lessons
## for the Well-Trained Mind

# by Jessie Wise
### Illustrations by Sarah Park

Peace Hill Press
Books for the Well-Trained Mind
Charles City, VA 23030

# Publisher's Cataloging-in-Publication

Wise, Jessie.
   First Language Lessons for the well trained mind / by Jessie Wise ;
illustrations by Sarah Park.
   p. cm.
   Includes bibliographical references and index.
   LCCN 2002108374
   ISBN 0-9714129-2-8

   1. English language--Grammar--Study and teaching.
2. English language--Rhetoric--Study and teaching.
I. Park, Sarah. II. Title.

PE1112.W57 2002           428'.007
                    QBI33-613

Cover photo by Colonial Photography
Cover design by Andrew J. Buffington

Printed in the U.S.A. in 2006

ISBN: 0-9714129-2-8

For children everywhere—
and for my grandchildren especially.

# Table of Contents

# SECOND GRADE

# Acknowledgments

I am grateful to my daughter, Susan Wise Bauer, for giving me a vision for this book, and then sharing her time, computer expertise, and research experience to make it a reality.

I am indebted to Sara Buffington for her editing work polishing the many revisions of the manuscript, for her contributions of poetry and prose, and for her adapting traditional stories to fit my format.

I am also indebted to Sherrill Fink for her skillful proofreading and for her excellent suggestions that improved the first manuscript. I take responsibility for errors that may appear in this final version.

I am especially thankful for my husband, Jay, for his encouragement, for his help with household chores, and for his taking care of the business end of publishing.

# How To Use This Book

I believe we underestimate what young children are capable of learning. Our ideas are influenced by the school model, which aims most of its instruction at what it considers the largest population—the "average child." But when we teach to the average, we train our children to be…average! Instead, we can grow children who exceed the average by exposing them to above-average content—as long as that content is taught patiently, frequently, and consistently, and is reviewed often.

## General Thoughts on Teaching Language

Learning rules without practical application is a sterile activity. Absorbing grammar incidentally without the guidance of rules is inefficient. By combining simple rules with continued "real life" use of those rules in language, the teacher lays the foundation for a child's application of appropriate rules to his own work in the future.

Children are natural imitators. This book provides you with examples of correctly spoken and written English in order to train the child's ear and hand. Then his original ideas can have form and beauty when they are expressed.

Every time a child speaks or writes correctly, that pattern is imprinted on his mind; the same is true for patterns that are incorrectly practiced. It is better to do less work, and do it correctly, than to practice errors. Then the child doesn't have to spend time unlearning and relearning.

So don't hurry through these lessons just to finish. Take the time to have the child answer in complete sentences. Take the time to frequently repeat rules until the child knows them. Take the time to have the child write correctly. Take the time to allow the child to make corrections immediately. If you require him to correct his mistakes, you will not damage his self-esteem. Compliment the correction and you will build his confidence.

Do not wait until a child is reading to expose him to good literature. Likewise, do not wait until a child is writing to expose him to proper use of our language. This is why I encourage the use of oral exercises while the child is young. Speech patterns are developed early. The longer a child uses incorrect language, the harder it will be to teach him correct speech and writing.

This early exposure is the purpose of my introducing young children to what some may consider advanced material. But this early introduction is not intended to result in mastery; mastery comes later.

I suggest you file the child's work in a notebook. This will serve as a way to organize all of his language work—narrations that you write for him, his copy work and dictations, his exercises, and copies of the letters he writes to real people.

## The Method of This Book

*First Language Lessons for the Well-Trained Mind* combines the best of traditional content with examples and illustrations meaningful to present-day children. The scripted lessons focus on training the child in the proper use of standard English. They are not intended to be read by the child—instead, they aim to give you some idea of how to teach these skills. Appropriate answers that the child should give to your questions are suggested, but the child should certainly not be required to give those answers word-for-word! Do remember, though, to require all answers in complete sentences. If the child answers with a single word or phrase, reword the answer as a complete sentence, repeat it to the child, and ask him to repeat it back to you. This will begin to train his ear to recognize complete sentences.

This book covers grammar and writing skills for grades 1–2. You will also need to provide a phonics/spelling program and formal penmanship instruction.

## Goals for Grades 1–2

1. To train the child's ear by allowing him to listen to correctly-spoken language.
2. To train the child's speech by practicing correctly spoken grammar with him.
3. To train the child's attention by reading aloud to him and having him narrate back to you the content or story line, using proper grammar.
4. To teach beginning skills in correct writing:
    a) by copying short sentences, using correct capitalization and punctuation
    b) by writing short sentences from dictation, using correct capitalization, punctuation, and spelling
5. To give the child opportunity to practice these skills in writing.

Remember: exposure, not mastery, is the goal at this level!

# The Tools Used in This Book: the "Four Strand" Approach

This book teaches rules, usage, and beginning writing skills by using four different tools.

## Strand 1: Memory work

The child is assigned simple memory work—short poems and brief rules and definitions to learn by heart. The poems instill the beauty and rhythm of correct language in the child's mind. The rules and definitions may not be completely understood when they are first committed to memory, but they will be a resource for the child as he continues to exercise his growing language skills.

## Strand 2: Copying and dictation

The student is asked to copy sentences in first grade and to take sentences from dictation in second grade. This early training in writing uses correct models to shape the child's writing skills, and allows children to practice proper writing technique without forcing them to come up with original ideas. Although first and second graders may choose to write original stories and compositions, they should never be required to do so. They are still learning the "code" of written language and should be allowed to focus on the technicalities of this "code" without simultaneously producing original content! This approach makes it possible for children to absorb more grammar content earlier than is expected in programs that require young children to produce original writing. Ideas come slowly for many young children, and getting those ideas on paper is difficult before adequate skills are acquired.

Copying allows the student to store in his mind (and muscle memory) the look and feel of properly written language. Dictation, done after the student has had plenty of practice in copying, teaches the student to picture a sentence in his mind before putting it down onto paper. Both steps are necessary before the student is required to do original writing. File copywork and dictations in a three-ring binder so that the child can view his progress.

## Strand 3: Narration

While the student is learning correct mechanics through copying and dictation, he is also practicing the producing of original content *orally*. This will prepare him for "real writing." By third or fourth grade, the student will have learned through copying and dictation how to put written language down on paper. Through narration, he will have learned how to formulate his thoughts into complete sentences. At this point, he will be ready to do original written compositions.

Two types of narration are used; both are intended to train the child in attention, observation, and expression, so that as he matures he will be able to share his own thoughts with eloquence.

a. Picture narration

Some of the lessons ask the student to look at and describe a picture. This allows him to practice observation skills as well as proper language use—always encourage the child to describe the picture in complete sentences!

b. Story narration

In other lessons, you will read a short story to the child and then ask him to tell it back to you in his own words. This type of narration helps the child to listen with attention, to comprehend spoken language, and to grasp the main point of a work.

### *Strand 4: Grammar*

The rules of grammar bring order to the chaos of words in the child's mind. Think of the study of formal grammar as the building of a room. The essentials—nouns and verbs—are the floor, walls, and ceiling. The room is decorated with adjectives and adverbs. The relationships between the different pieces of furniture in the room are demonstrated through prepositions and conjunctions. And sometimes the people in the room show intense emotion—with interjections!

The student is taught the correct definitions of grammatical terms from the very beginning. Much of this grammar is done orally, so that more advanced grammar can be covered while the child is improving his writing skills through the practice of copying, dictation, and narration. Lessons in oral usage are also provided so that the instructor can pinpoint any areas of difficulty in the child's use of language.

The lessons are planned to give an adequate foundation for every child. I assume that many children will not be ready to do a great deal of pencil-work in first and second grade. For children who are physically capable of doing more writing, I have provided "enrichment activities." But it is not necessary—or expected—that most children will do these enrichment exercises!

Even if your child can already write, plan on doing the first 45 exercises orally.[1] Lessons in copying begin with Lesson 42. The first 100 lessons are intended for first-grade students; dictation exercises begin in second grade, Lessons 101–200.

This book is designed as a two-year study. Lesson 100 is the last lesson in the first year of study. Do not take three months off before continuing with Lesson 101! Even if you move into a "summer break," continue to do at least one lesson per week until you "start school" again. Two is better! If you do only one lesson per week, you should also plan on reviewing previous lessons as necessary, since the child may not remember material covered earlier. Young children forget more between the first grade and second grade years than in any other interval. Try to avoid a long break!

## Using the Lessons

Suggested wording for the instructor is in traditional print.

⇨   Notes to the Instructor are in smaller, traditional print and are bulleted.

*Suggested wording for child is in italics.*

Suggested wording that the child is to read or follow is in larger traditional print.

**Definitions and terms are in larger bold print.**

If you wish to gather all your materials for first grade in advance, you will need a map of your state, business size envelopes and stamps, a family calendar and a child's personal calendar, scissors, drawing supplies, crayons, highlighter markers, a tape recorder, colored construction paper, old magazines to cut up, a flower seed catalog, and some family mail. Materials for second grade are listed on page 173.

---

[1] **A note on inclusive pronouns:** I studied advanced traditional grammar in the 1950s as part of my training in teacher certification. I learned that the pronouns "he" and "him" were generic pronouns, used to refer to both men and women. Although I understand why some users would prefer to see an alternate use of "he" and "she," I find this style of writing awkward; my early training shapes my usage! So I have used "he" and "him" to refer to the child throughout. If you prefer, simply change these pronouns to "she" and "her."

# First Grade

# Lesson 1

-Introducing nouns

Instructor: Everything has a name. I will read the definition of a noun aloud to you three times.

⇨ Note to Instructor: Repeat the following sentence three times.

**A noun is the name of a <u>person</u>, place, thing, or idea.**

Instructor: We will talk about persons first. You are a person. Are you a boy or a girl?

⇨ Note to the Instructor: Encourage the child to answer in complete sentences.

*Child: I am a _____.*

Instructor: "Boy" and "girl" are naming words that are common to a lot of persons, so we call them **common nouns**. Other naming words that are common to a lot of persons are words like "mother," "father," "sister," "brother," "grandmother," "grandfather," "aunt," "uncle," and "cousin."

⇨ Note to Instructor: Repeat definition of a noun three more times, emphasizing the word person: "A noun is the name of a <u>person</u>, place, thing, or idea."

# Lesson 2

-Introducing poem memorization: "The Caterpillar"
* The child will need art supplies for the enrichment activity

⇨  Note to Instructor: Read the poem to the child and discuss it before working on memorization.  As a helpful technique to assist in memorization, try the following: On the first day that the poem is assigned, read the poem aloud to the child three times in a row. Repeat this triple reading twice more during the day, if possible. After the first day, read the poem aloud three times in a row once daily. (It may be more convenient to read the poem into a tape recorder three times, and then have the child replay the tape.)  On the second day, and every day thereafter, ask the child to try to repeat parts of the poem along with you (or the tape recorder). When he can say the poem along with you, encourage him to repeat it first to a stuffed animal, then to himself in a mirror, and finally to "real people."

⇨  Note to Instructor: Today, read "The Caterpillar" aloud three times in a row.  Repeat twice more during the day.  Don't forget to say the title and author as part of each repetition!


The Caterpillar
*Christina G. Rossetti*

Brown and furry
Caterpillar in a hurry;
Take your walk
To the shady leaf, or stalk.

May no toad spy you,
May the little birds pass by you;
Spin and die,
To live again a butterfly.

## Enrichment Activity

Ask the child to illustrate the poem.

# Lesson 3

-Common nouns
     -Family relationships
-Poem review: "The Caterpillar" (Lesson 2)


⇨   Note to Instructor: Don't forget to review "The Caterpillar" today!

Instructor: I will read the definition of a **noun** to you:

**A noun is the name of a person, place, thing, or idea.**

Try to say as much of it as you can with me, as I say this definition slowly three times more:

Together: **A noun is the name of a person, place, thing, or idea.**

⇨   Note to Instructor: Repeat this definition three times along with the child.

Instructor: The first part of the definition is "A noun is the name of a person…" You are a person. Are you a boy or a girl?

*Child: I am a_____.*

Instructor: "Boy" and "girl" are naming words that are common to a lot of persons, so we call them **common nouns**. The words "mother," "father," "sister," and "brother" are also **common nouns**. They name persons in families. Let's talk about persons in families. Families start with mothers and fathers. Everyone has a mother and a father. I will help you answer the following questions:

⇨   Note to Instructor: Help the child answer each question in a complete sentence. Give the child plenty of help!

Instructor: What do we call two girls who have the same mother and father?

*Child: Two girls who have the same mother and father are called "sisters."*

Instructor: What do we call two boys who have the same mother and father?

*Child: Two boys who have the same mother and father are called "brothers."*

Instructor: Sisters and brothers are persons who have the same mother and father! Do you know what your mother's mother is called?

*Child: My mother's mother is my grandmother.*

Instructor: What is your father's mother called?

*Child: My father's mother is my grandmother.*

Instructor: "Grandmother" is the **common noun** that names the mother of your mother or father! Do you know what your mother's father is called?

*Child: My mother's father is my grandfather.*

Instructor:  What is your father's father called?

*Child: My father's father is my grandfather too.*

Instructor:  "Grandfather" is the **common noun** that names the father of your mother or father!  Remember: Mother, father, sister, brother, and grandfather are persons in families.  Aunts, uncles, and cousins are also persons in families.  An aunt is the sister of your mother or father.  Do you have any aunts?

*Child:  My aunt is Aunt _____.*

Instructor:  An uncle is the brother of your mother or father.  Do you have any uncles?

*Child:  My uncle is Uncle _____.*

Instructor:  Uncle and aunt are **common nouns** for the brother and sister of your mother and father!  A cousin is the child of your aunt or uncle.  Do you have any cousins?

*Child:  My cousins are _____.*

Instructor:  Mother, father, sister, brother, grandfather, aunt, uncle, and cousin are all **common nouns** that name people.

# Lesson 4

-Proper nouns

      -First names

-Poem review: "The Caterpillar" (Lesson 2)

\* The instructor will need a pencil and paper for the lesson. The child will need a pencil and paper for the enrichment activity.

⇨ Note to Instructor: Remember to review "The Caterpillar" today! Remember that one of your goals is to teach the child to answer in complete sentences. Encourage the child to use the words of the question in his answer.

Instructor: I will read the definition of a **noun** to you. **A noun is the name of a person, place, thing, or idea.** Try to say as much of this definition of a noun as you can along with me. I will say it slowly three times more.

Together (three times): **A noun is the name of a person, place, thing, or idea.**

Instructor: The first part of the definition is: "A noun is the name of a person…"

What is your name?

*Child: My name is_____ .*

Instructor: You are not just any boy or girl. You are _____ [use child's proper name]. This is your own special "proper" name. **Proper names** are the same as **proper nouns. Proper nouns** begin with capital letters.

⇨ Note to Instructor: Write the child's name and show him the capital letter.

Instructor: What is your mother's name?

*Child: My mother's name is_____ .*

⇨ Note to Instructor: Either a proper name or "Mommy" is acceptable!

Instructor: She is not just any mother—she is your special mother with a special name.

⇨ Note to Instructor: Print the special name of the child's mother. Point and show that the name begins with a capital letter.

Instructor: **Proper names** begin with a capital letter. What is your father's name?

*Child: My father's name is_____ .*

Instructor: He is not just any father, he is your special father with a special name.

⇨ Note to Instructor: Print the special name of the child's father. Point and show that the name begins with a capital letter.

Instructor: **Proper names** begin with a capital letter. "Sister" and "brother" are naming words that are common to a lot of sisters and brothers in lots of families. Do you have a sister or brother? If you do, that sister or brother is one special person with a special name. What are the names of your sisters and brothers?

⇨   Note to Instructor: If the child doesn't have sisters and brothers, you can substitute "friend" in the exercise below.

*Child: My sister's name is* _____ . *My brother's name is* _____ .

⇨   Note to Instructor: Print the name as the child gives it. Point to the first letter.

Instructor: This is a capital letter. Proper names begin with a capital letter. These are the **proper names** of your brother and sister. These names tell you that they are not just any brother or sister. These names are special to them. These special, **proper names** begin with a capital letter.

## Enrichment Activity

If the child is already writing easily, you may have him copy family names using correct capitalization.

# Lesson 5

-Introducing story narration: "The Rabbit and the Turtle"
* The instructor will need a pencil and paper.

⇨ Note to Instructor: Narration is a skill to be learned through practice. In narration, the child simply tells back a story in his own words. There are two common difficulties in learning to narrate.

> 1. The child gives every detail of the story, making the narration too long to write down.

> 2. The child doesn't know how to start or what to say.

For both problems, try the following procedure:

Pick the first two sentences and read them to the child. Then ask the child to condense them into one sentence. Suggest phrases that will help shorten the narration. Ask him to repeat after you. A child who has difficulty in narrating often can't think of a different way to repeat information. Practice this skill by offering the child one phrase at a time and by helping him to find synonyms for the words used in the story.

When he is able to do two sentences at a time, add a third. Suggest to him that he can leave out some of the information completely. When you add a fourth sentence for him to narrate, you can allow his narration to be two sentences long. Keep on using this process, adding one sentence at a time from the story until the child can summarize the entire selection.

If the child uses verbal "fillers" such as "uh," "like," or "you know," encourage him to stop and think in silence until he is ready to speak the sentence. When these "fillers" slip back into the narration, simply repeat what the child has said, omitting the useless word; then have him repeat after you.

There is no rush! This is a skill to be learned. You are training the child in thinking skills, so that he can grasp and retain more knowledge in his later stages of education. Narration exercises train the mind to grasp what is central—an essential skill for note-taking later on.

⇨ Note to Instructor: Read the following Aesop's Fable aloud to the child, and then ask the child to tell it back to you. If necessary, encourage him with the "starter questions" provided. When the child is able to summarize the story in three or four sentences, write these sentences down for him in neat printing (or in writing that he can easily read). Read his version back to him, and then file it in his notebook.

## The Rabbit and the Turtle

One day a rabbit made fun of a turtle. "How short your feet are! And how slowly you move!" he said. "Does it take you all day to walk to the table for breakfast?"

"My feet may be short," the turtle said, "but I can still beat you at a race!"

The rabbit laughed. He was sure that the little turtle could not possibly win! So he proposed that they run a race.

"All right," said the turtle, "but we need someone to declare the winner."

"Let's ask the fox," said the rabbit.

So they asked the fox to watch the race and decide on the winner. The fox said, "Ready, set, go!" And the race was on.

The turtle and the rabbit started out. The rabbit went leaping ahead in huge jumps and bounds. Soon he was far, far out of sight. The turtle plodded slowly along, so slowly that you could barely see him move.

The rabbit looked behind him. The turtle was nowhere in sight! And he was tired from all that leaping and bounding. So he decided to lie down beside the road and take a nap.

While he was sleeping, the turtle plodded right past him! When the rabbit woke up, he could just see, far in the distance, the turtle heading across the finish line.

He jumped up and ran as fast as he could. But before he could catch up, the turtle had crossed the line and won the race.

"The turtle is the winner!" the fox declared.

"Wait! Wait!" the rabbit cried. "I'm the faster runner!"

"That may be so," the fox said. "But the turtle has won *this* race. Remember: it is much better to be slow and steady than to be fast and lazy."

Moral: "Slow and steady wins the race!"

⇨ Note to Instructor: Use these questions to help the child summarize the story.
What did the rabbit and turtle decide to do? *The rabbit and turtle decided to run a race.*
Who watched the race for them? *The fox watched them.*
Who was winning at first? *At first the rabbit was winning.*
Then what did the rabbit do? *He decided to take a nap.*
What did the turtle do while the rabbit was sleeping? *The turtle crossed the finish line while the rabbit was sleeping.*
What is the moral of this story? *Slow and steady wins the race!*

# Lesson 6

-Proper nouns
     -First names
-Poem review: "The Caterpillar" (Lesson 2)
* The instructor will need a pencil and paper.

⇨   Note to Instructor: Remember to review "The Caterpillar" today.

Instructor:  Do you remember what a grandmother is?

*Child: My grandmother is my mother's mother or my father's mother.*

Instructor: Your grandmothers have special names.  What are your two grandmothers' special names?

*Child: My grandmothers' special names are _____.*

⇨   Note to Instructor:  Either a given name or the grandmother's "family" name— Grammy, Maw-Maw, Granny, etc.— is acceptable.

Instructor:  I will write those names down for you.  Can you point to the capital letters that begin those names?  These are the **proper names** of your grandmothers.

⇨   Note to Instructor:  Write the names down and help the child point to the capital letters that begin them.

Instructor:  Do you remember what a grandfather is?

*Child: My grandfather is my mother's father or my father's father.*

Instructor: What are your grandfathers' special names?

*Child: My two grandfathers' special names are _____.*

Instructor:  I will write those names down, too.  These are the **proper names** of your grandfathers.  Can you show me the capital letters that begin them?

⇨   Note to Instructor:  Write the names down and help the child find the capital letter at the beginning of each.

# Lesson 7

-Common and proper nouns

* The child will need a pencil and paper for the enrichment activity.


Instructor: Repeat the definition of a **noun** with me three times.

Together (three times): **A noun is the name of a person, place, thing, or idea.**

Instructor: **A noun is the name of a person, place, thing, or idea.** We have talked about different kinds of people—mothers, fathers, sisters, brothers, grandmothers, grandfathers. All of these words are nouns, because they are the names of kinds of people. We call these **common nouns** because these words don't name a particular person. There are many mothers, fathers, sisters, brothers, grandmothers, and grandfathers in the world! Here are some other **common nouns** for kinds of people: firefighter, farmer, teacher, engineer, doctor, and nurse. Can you think of other **common nouns** for kinds of people?

⇨ Note to Instructor: Help the child to think of other common nouns that name occupations.

Instructor: Every firefighter, farmer, teacher, doctor, and nurse also has a special name. If the special name of the person is used, it is called a **proper noun.**

⇨ Note to Instructor: Read the following pairs of sentences aloud to the child, pointing out common and proper nouns.


The fire was put out by the firefighter.

Jonathan Mendel put out the fire.

Instructor: "Firefighter" is a **common noun** because it doesn't name any special firefighter. "Jonathan Mendel" is a **proper noun** because it names one special firefighter.


The doctor wore a white coat.

Susanna Wright wore a white coat.

Instructor: "Doctor" is a **common noun** because it doesn't name any special doctor. "Susanna Wright" is a **proper noun** because it names one special doctor.


## Enrichment Activity

Have the child copy one of the above pairs of sentences, using correct capitalization.

# Lesson 8

-Common and proper nouns
-Poem review: "The Caterpillar" (Lesson 2)
* The child will need a pencil and paper for the enrichment activity.

⇨ Note to Instructor: Remember to review "The Caterpillar" today.
Instructor: Repeat the definition of a **noun** with me three times.
Together (three times): **A noun is the name of a person, place, thing, or idea.**
Instructor: Now can you say this definition all by yourself?
*Child: A noun is the name of a person, place, thing, or idea.*
Instructor: A noun is the name of a person, place, thing, or idea. A **common noun** is the name of a kind of person. A **proper noun** is a person's special, particular name. Let's talk some more about **common and proper nouns**.
⇨ Note to Instructor: Read the following pairs of sentences aloud to the child, pointing out common and proper nouns.

The teacher went to the store for some milk.
Maria Santilli went to the store for some milk.
Instructor: "Teacher" is a **common noun** because it doesn't name any special teacher. "Maria Santilli" is a **proper noun** because it names one special teacher.

The farmer grows corn.
Mark Elder grows corn.
Instructor: "Farmer" is a **common noun** because it doesn't name any special farmer. "Mark Elder" is a **proper noun** because it names one special farmer.

My mother ate cereal for breakfast.
_____ ate cereal for breakfast.
⇨ Note to Instructor: Fill in the proper name of the child's mother.
Instructor: "Mother" is a **common noun** because there are many, many mothers in the world. But _____ is the special, **proper name** of your own mother. There is only one of those!

## Enrichment Activity
Have the child copy one of the above pairs of sentences.

# Lesson 9
-Introducing picture narration: "In the Kitchen"

⇨   Note to Instructor: Ask the following questions to help the student describe the picture. *Always wait for the child's answer*, and then follow up with the scripted dialogue. Use the scripted answers to affirm the child (ex. "Yes, the family is making cookies." or "Yes, they are baking. They are making cookies.") or to gently correct the child (ex. "Actually, they are making cookies."). The most important thing is to acknowledge the child's responses as this encourages participation. Remember to encourage the child to answer in complete sentences.


Are there any people in the picture? Yes, there are many people in this picture. They are a family. What do you think they are doing? They are making cookies. The children love to eat warm cookies. Do you like cookies?

Are there any mothers or fathers in the picture? Can you point to them? There is a grandmother in the picture. Can you point to her? She is measuring sugar for the cookies.

Are there any sisters or brothers in the picture? Can you point to them? I see the baby sister. She is sitting in her father's lap. How many brothers does she have? Yes, she has two brothers. The baby can't really help with the cookies, but she loves to play with the dough. She is making a mess!

Everyone else is helping to make the cookies. Do you see the older brother sitting down? What is he doing? He is rolling out the cookie dough. What is the father doing? He is using the cookie cutter to cut the dough into shapes. What shapes do you see? I see a heart and a star. The mother has a piece of paper in her hands. It is the recipe; it tells how to make the cookies. The younger brother is asking his grandmother a question. He is saying, "May I please have a little cookie dough to eat?"

Everybody in the family also has a special, **proper name**. I think the grandmother's special, proper name could be Marie. What do you think is the special, **proper name** of the mother? What is the special, **proper name** of the younger brother? What are the special, **proper names** of everyone else?

# Lesson 10

-Proper nouns
   -Writing the child's proper name
-Poem review: "The Caterpillar" (Lesson 2)
* Both the instructor and the child will need a pencil and paper.

⇨ Note to Instructor: Review "The Caterpillar" today. Ask the child to say as much of it as he can alone. He should be able to repeat most or all of the poem from memory for you.

Instructor: I will read the definition of a **noun** aloud to you. Then, you say it with me when I say it again. **A noun is the name of a person, place, thing, or idea**. Now let's say that together.

Together: **A noun is the name of a person, place, thing, or idea.**

Instructor: Are you a person?

*Child: I am a person!*

Instructor: Are you just any person or are you one special person?

*Child: I am one special person.*

Instructor: What is your special name?

*Child: My name is _____.*

⇨ Note to Instructor: The child can simply give his first name. Print the child's name. Point to the capital letters beginning his name.

Instructor: This is your name. It is a special name, so it is called a **proper noun.** With what kind of letters do names begin?

*Child: Names begin with capital letters.*

Instructor: Let's say that together three times.

Together (three times): Names begin with capital letters.

⇨ Note to Instructor: Have the child copy his first name today.

Instructor: Your name is a special, **proper noun** because it names one special person—you!

# Lesson 11

-Proper nouns

    -Writing first names

\* Both the instructor and the child will need a pencil and paper.


Instructor: Let's review our definition of what a **noun** is. Repeat it with me two times: "**A noun is the name of a person, place, thing, or idea. A noun is the name of a person, place, thing or idea.**" Now, can you repeat that definition alone?

⇨   Note to Instructor: Prompt the child, if necessary.

Instructor: Nouns that name many different persons are called **common nouns**. Are you a boy or a girl?

*Child: I am a _____.*

Instructor: There are many boys and girls in the world! But what is your special name?

*Child: My name is _____.*

⇨   Note to Instructor: Remember to prompt the child to answer in complete sentences!

Instructor: Your special name says that you are not just any boy or girl. We call your special name a "**proper noun.**" You have a mother and a father (and a sister and/or a brother and/or a friend). They all have **proper names** too! Let's write down the special names for all of these people.

⇨   Note to Instructor: Print the proper names of each person in the child's family. Point out that each name begins with a capital letter. Then ask the child to copy his own first name twice, neatly. Remind him that it begins with a capital letter.


## Enrichment Activity

Ask the child to copy the first names of other family members.

# Lesson 12

-Story narration: "The Lion and the Mouse"
* The instructor will need a pencil and paper.

⇨ Note to Instructor: Read the following Aesop's Fable aloud to the child, and then ask the child to tell it back to you in his own words. If necessary, encourage him with the "starter questions." When the child is able to summarize the story in three or four sentences, write these sentences down for him in neat printing (or in writing that he can easily read). Read his version back to him and then file it in his notebook.

## The Lion and the Mouse

One hot afternoon, a great lion lay sleeping in the shade. A little mouse, going back to his cool home underneath the roots of a nearby tree, accidentally ran across the lion's outstretched tail. The lion woke at once and grabbed the little creature with his huge paw.

"How dare you disturb my nap!" he growled. "I'll eat you for that!"

"Please, please don't eat me!" begged the little mouse. "Let me go, and I'll repay the favor one day—I'll help you when *you* need help!"

The lion laughed. "How could a tiny thing like you ever help a huge lion like me?" he chuckled. But he was so amused by the mouse's promise that he let the mouse go. The mouse skittered away to his little house, and the lion lay back down to finish his nap.

Several weeks later, the lion was hunting when he stepped into a great net, spread by hunters! The net closed over him at once. He struggled and struggled, but the strands only wrapped more tightly around him. Finally, he threw back his huge head and roared in distress.

From far away, the little mouse heard the lion's anguished roar. He ran as quickly as he could until he saw the lion's plight.

"Now it is my turn to help you!" the mouse exclaimed. He climbed up onto the lion's back and began to gnaw the thick ropes with his tiny teeth. One by one, the ropes gave way. Before long, the lion was free! He shook his mane with relief.

"Little mouse," he said, "I was wrong. I thought that you couldn't help me because you are so small. But you have saved my life. How glad I am that I spared you when you stepped on my tail!"

36

Moral: "Even a little one can help in times of trouble!"

⇨ Note to Instructor: Use these questions to help the child summarize the story.

Which two animals were described in the fable? *The animals described in the fable were a lion and a mouse.*

What did the mouse do that made the lion wake up? *The mouse ran across the lion's tail.*

What did the lion think about doing? *The lion wanted to eat the mouse.*

What did the mouse promise? *The mouse promised to help the lion if the lion would let him go.*

Did the lion let the mouse go? *Yes, the lion let the mouse go.*

How did the lion get into trouble? *He was trapped in a net by hunters.*

How did the mouse set him free? *The mouse chewed the net apart with his teeth.*

Was the lion grateful? *Yes, the lion thanked the mouse for helping him.*

## Enrichment Activity
Have the child copy the moral of the story.

# Lesson 13

-Proper nouns
      -Family names
-Poem review: "The Caterpillar" (Lesson 2)
\* Both the instructor and the child will need a pencil and paper.


⇨ Note to Instructor: Remember to review "The Caterpillar" today.
Instructor: I will read the definition of a **noun** to you. **"A noun is the name of a person, place, thing, or idea."** Can you say that definition by yourself?

⇨ Note to Instructor: Prompt the child, if necessary, to use the exact words of the definition.

Instructor: First names are special names given to each person. Last names are names that you share with other members of your family. What is your first name?

*Child: My first name is* _____.

Instructor: What is your last name—your family name?

*Child: My last name is* _____.

Instructor: Family names are **proper nouns**, too. Your family is not just any family—it has its own special name! What are the first and last names of other members of your family?

⇨ Note to Instructor: Talk with the child about various family members' first and last names. Then, let the child watch as you write his first and last name. Ask the child to copy his first and last name. Help him put his finger between the two names to space them properly.


## Enrichment Activity

Have the child copy the first and last names of other family members.

# Lesson 14

-Proper nouns

    -Middle names

\* Both the instructor and the child will need a pencil and paper.


Instructor: Say the definition of a **noun** with me three times: **A noun is the name of a person, place, thing, or idea.** We've talked about **proper names**—first and last names. What is your first name?

*Child: My first name is_____.*

Instructor: What is your last name—your family name?

*Child: My last name is _____.*

Instructor: Most people also have a middle name. A middle name is another, special name given to a child. What is your middle name?

*Child: My middle name is_____.*

Instructor: Let's write your middle name now.

⇨ Note to Instructor: Write the child's middle name. Point out the capital letter. Have the child read his own middle name. Then add the child's first and last name on either side of the middle name.

Instructor: What is your mother's middle name?

⇨ Note to Instructor: Tell the child the answer, if necessary.

*Child: My mother's middle name is _____.*

Instructor: What is your father's middle name?

*Child: My father's middle name is _____.*

⇨ Note to Instructor: Write out the full names of the child's mother and father. Point out the first, middle, and last names. Then have the child copy his own full name. Show him how to space the words by putting his finger between each name.


## Enrichment Activity

Have the child copy the full names of family members.

# Lesson 15

-Poem memorization: "Work"

⇨ Note to Instructor: Read the poem aloud to the child three times now. Repeat this triple reading twice more during the day. Remember to read the title and author. Tell the child that "Anonymous" means we don't know who wrote the poem.

"Work"
*Anonymous*

Work while you work,
Play while you play;
This is the way
To be happy each day.
All that you do,
Do with your might;
Things done by halves
Are never done right.

# Lesson 16

-Proper nouns
        -Full names
-Poem review: "Work" (Lesson 15)
* The instructor will need a pencil and paper.


⇨   Note to Instructor: Have the child repeat the poem "Work" three times before beginning today's lesson.

Instructor:  Can you say the definition of a **noun** for me?

⇨   Note to Instructor:  If necessary, prompt child to use the exact words: "A noun is the name of a person, place, thing, or idea."

Instructor: First names and middle names are special given names to children.  Last names are family names.  All of these names are **proper nouns**. Let's talk about the first, middle, and last names of people in our family.

⇨   Note to Instructor:  Have the child tell you the full name of each family member.  Supply names, if necessary!  Don't forget grandparents; include aunts, uncles, and cousins if you wish.  Write each name as the child says it. Point out the capital letters.

Instructor: Now practice writing your own full name.

⇨   Note to Instructor:  Write the child's full name.  Have the child copy it, again showing him how to space the words by putting his finger between each name.


## Enrichment Activity

Have the child write his own name from memory.

# Lesson 17

-Common nouns
   -Names of places
-Poem review: "Work" (Lesson 15)
* The child will need a pencil and paper for the enrichment activity.


⇨  Note to Instructor: Remember to review "Work" today!

Instructor: Say the definition of a **noun** with me.

Together: **A noun is the name of a person, place, thing, or idea.**

Instructor: We have learned about names of people. Now let's learn about names of places. What room are we in?

*Child: We are in the _____.* (kitchen, living room, etc.)

Instructor: This room is a place. This room is in a house (or apartment). This house (or apartment) is also a place. And this house (or apartment) is in a city (or town, or county). Words like "kitchen," "bedroom," "house," "apartment, " "city," "town," and "county" are **nouns** because they name places. All of these names are **common nouns**. There are lots of kitchens, bedrooms, houses, cities, and towns! We call all of these words **common nouns** because they could be naming any kitchen, bedroom, house, city, or town. Other words that name common kinds of places are words like "mountain," "hill," "yard," "street," "road," "sidewalk," "museum…" Let's name some other places together.

⇨  Note to Instructor: Prompt the child to think of other names of places. Look out of the window, use pictures, or walk around the house or yard. Remember to prompt the child for common nouns that name places.

Instructor: All of these names tell us about places. They are all **common nouns**. Remember: **A noun is the name of a person or place**.


## Enrichment Activity

Have the child copy the first two lines of the poem "Work."

# Lesson 18

-Proper nouns
    -Places
       -Your city and state
-Poem review: "The Caterpillar" (Lesson 2) and "Work" (Lesson 15)
* The instructor will need a pencil and paper.


⇨ Note to Instructor: Today, review both "The Caterpillar" and "Work." Don't be surprised if the child has forgotten some of "The Caterpillar." Allow him to read it or listen to you recite it in order to refresh his memory.

Instructor: Say the definition of a **noun** three times with me.

Together (three times): **A noun is the name of a person, place, thing, or idea.**

Instructor: What room are you in?

*Child: I am in the* _____.

Instructor: This room is in a house (or apartment). This house (apartment) is in a city (town, county). Do you know the name of this city (town, county)?

*Child: This city* (town, county) *is* _____. (Tell child the name, if necessary!)

Instructor: (Name of city, town, or county) is not just any place. It is one special place where you live! This name is the special, **proper name** of your city (town, county). We call names like this **proper nouns**. I will write the **proper name** of the place where you live.

⇨ Note to Instructor: Write the proper name of the place where your child lives. Show him that it begins with a capital letter.

Instructor: Your city (town, county) is in a special state. That state is _____. It is not just any state—it is one special state, with its own name. This special name is also a **proper noun**. When you write the name of your city (town, county), you write the name of the state next to it.

⇨ Note to Instructor: Write out the name of the state next to the city (town, county). Put a comma between the two names (Chicago, Illinois; Austin, Texas; Louisa County, Virginia). Point out the capital letters. Ask the child to repeat the place name and state together three times.


## Enrichment Activity

Have the child copy the proper name of the place where he lives. Remind him to put a comma between the town and the state.

# Lesson 19

-Proper nouns
    -Places
-Poem review: "Work" (Lesson 15)
* The child will need a pencil and paper for the enrichment activity.


⇨   Note to Instructor: Be sure to review "Work" today! You will need a map of your state for today's lesson.

Instructor: Say the definition of a **noun** for me.

*Child: A noun is the name of a person, place, thing, or idea.*

Instructor: We have been talking about names of places—**common names**, like town, city, county, state, bedroom, kitchen, and **proper nouns**, like _____ (use name of child's city, town, or county). We also talked about the **proper name** of your state. Do you remember your city (town, county) and state?

*Child: I live in* _____. (Prompt child to use "I live in"; also remind him of the proper names of his city and state, if necessary)

Instructor: (City and state) are **proper nouns**. They are the special names of the city (town, county) and state where you live. There are many other places in your state. There are mountains, rivers, parks, hills, streets, roads, valleys, cities, and towns. All of these **nouns** name places. They are all **common nouns**. But most of these places also have special names—**proper names**. Let's look on a map of our state and find some of these **proper names**.

⇨   Note to Instructor: Look at a map of your state together. Help the child identify mountains, rivers, and other geographical features. Read together the proper name of each place. Remind the child that each proper name is a noun. Point out the capital letters at the beginning of each proper name. Explain to the child that to make things clear in a crowded place, maps often print important names in <u>all</u> capital letters.


## Enrichment Activity

Ask the child to practice writing the name of his city and state from memory, placing a comma between the city and state.

# Lesson 20

-Proper nouns

    -States

\* The child will need a pencil and paper for the enrichment activity.

⇨ Note to Instructor: Have the child copy his name before beginning today's lesson.

Instructor: Do you remember the **proper name** of the state in which you live? *Child: I live in* _____.

Instructor: That is only one state. But there are fifty states in the United States! "State" is a **common noun**—it could refer to any of those states. But each state has its own special name. Those names are **proper nouns**. Let's look at some of the state names together.

⇨ Note to Instructor: Point to the different state names on the following page and practice saying them. Remind the child that each one begins with a capital letter. Explain to the child that to make things clear in a crowded space, maps often print important names in <u>all</u> capital letters. Be sure to identify states where different family members and friends may live or where the child has visited for vacations. Print some states with only the first letter capitalized for the child to see.

## Enrichment Activity

The child may practice writing names of the states where friends and family live. Remind the child that these are proper names and should begin with capital letters.

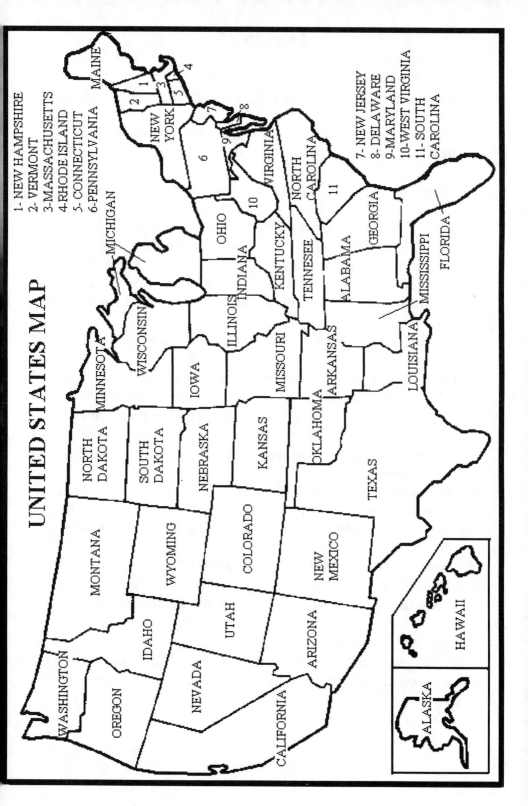

# UNITED STATES MAP

1- NEW HAMPSHIRE
2- VERMONT
3- MASSACHUSETTS
4- RHODE ISLAND
5- CONNECTICUT
6- PENNSYLVANIA

7- NEW JERSEY
8- DELAWARE
9- MARYLAND
10- WEST VIRGINIA
11- SOUTH CAROLINA

WASHINGTON
OREGON
CALIFORNIA
NEVADA
IDAHO
MONTANA
WYOMING
UTAH
ARIZONA
NEW MEXICO
COLORADO
NORTH DAKOTA
SOUTH DAKOTA
NEBRASKA
KANSAS
OKLAHOMA
TEXAS
MINNESOTA
WISCONSIN
IOWA
MISSOURI
ARKANSAS
LOUISIANA
MICHIGAN
ILLINOIS
INDIANA
OHIO
KENTUCKY
TENNESEE
MISSISSIPPI
ALABAMA
GEORGIA
FLORIDA
MAINE
NEW YORK
VIRGINIA
NORTH CAROLINA
ALASKA
HAWAII

47

# Lesson 21

-Proper nouns
    -Your address

-Poem review: "The Caterpillar" (Lesson 2) and "Work" (Lesson 15)

* The instructor will need a pencil and paper for the lesson. The child will need a pencil and paper for the enrichment activity.

⇨ Note to Instructor: Be sure to review "The Caterpillar" and "Work" today!

Instructor: Do you remember the name of your city and state? (Prompt child, if necessary. Ask child to repeat the city-state combination several times.) You live on _____. (Provide name of the child's street or road.) That is your street's special name. It is a **proper noun**, so we write it with a capital letter. I will write it down for you.

⇨ Note to Instructor: Write the name of the child's street. Point out the capital letter.

Instructor: You aren't the only person who lives on this street. Your house has a special number that goes with it. This number doesn't belong to any other house on the street! The number of your house, along with the street name, is your street address. When we write down your street address, your city, and your state, we have written your full address.

⇨ Note to Instructor: Let the child watch you write out his entire address except the zip code (do not abbreviate state). Zip codes will be done later. Both of you read the address, pointing to each capital letter. As you write, point to each capital letters and say:

Instructor: Addresses are names of special places, so we call them **proper nouns. Proper nouns** begin with capital letters.

⇨ Note to Instructor: Have the child repeat his address three times.

## Enrichment Activity

Child may write from memory the name of his city and state, placing a comma between the city and state. Child may also copy his own address.

# Lesson 22

-Story narration: "The Little Girl Who Wanted To Be Dirty"
* The instructor will need a pencil and paper.


⇨   Note to Instructor: Read the following old tale aloud to the child, and
then ask the child to tell it back to you in his own words. If necessary,
encourage him with the "starter questions." When the child is able to
summarize the story in three or four sentences, write these sentences down
for him in neat printing (or in writing that he can easily read). Read his
version back to him and then file it in his notebook.


### The Little Girl Who Wanted to be Dirty

There once was a little girl who cried and screamed every time
her mother wanted to give her a bath. " I like being dirty, and I hate to
take baths!" was the little girl's reply each time her mother made her
bathe. Her mother told her often, "If you don't bathe, you will be as
dirty as a pig!" But the little girl wanted to be dirty—and she thought
that she would love to be as dirty as a pig.

One night the little girl lay thinking about pigs. "I wish I were
living in a pig pen," she thought. "I could wallow and play in soft cool
mud all day. And at night I could just snuggle right down in the mud
and sleep. I would never have to wash again!"

Suddenly she looked around. She wasn't in her clean white bed
anymore. She was lying in the middle of a pigpen! The sun was
shining down on her. It was warm and beautiful outside. She sat up.
Mud dripped down the back of her neck. It felt wonderful! Mud
squished between her fingers and her toes. There were three cute little
pigs in the pen. They ran up to her and pushed at her with their noses.
They wanted to play!

She jumped up and played tag with the pigs. They splattered
mud all over each other! Then they played pig-in-the-middle and
stuck-in-the-mud. When they were tired of playing, they all piled up
into a big muddy heap for a rest.

Soon the little girl heard a voice calling, "Supper!" She was
hungry from all that play. She jumped up and ran to the pig trough.
But all she found there was slop! Old corncobs, bits of leftover sandwiches, tops of tomatoes, broken half-eaten cookies, and rotten potatoes. Her pig friends were eating happily. But the little girl began to
cry. This wasn't her idea of a good supper! The sun was going down,

and her fingers and toes were wet and cold. Mud had dried in her hair, and it made her head itch. Mud was smeared all down her face and neck. Her clothes were stiff with mud.

"I want to go home!" she said. So she crept out of the pigpen, down the road, until she got to her own house. She sneaked in the back door of her house, up the stairs and into the bathroom. Then she ran a tub of clean warm water with bubbles. She scrubbed off all of the dirt, put on fresh flowered pajamas, and sank into her soft bed, snuggling her head on her favorite pillow.

When she awoke the next morning, she ran to her mother to tell her all about it. "You have had a dream," said Mother.

"Oh, Mother," said the little girl, "it was a good dream because it made me want to be clean!"

⇨    Note to Instructor: Use these questions to help the child summarize the story.

Did the little girl know that she was having a dream? *No, the little girl thought she was really in a pigpen.*

Did she like the pigpen at first? *Yes, the little girl liked the pigpen.*

Why did she like it? *The little girl got to squish in the mud and to play with the pigs.*

What did she get for supper? *The little girl got old rotten food, like the pigs.*

Did she still like the mud? *No, the little girl wanted to be clean.*

How did the little girl get clean? *She went home and took a bath.*

Did the dream change the way she thought about baths? *Yes, the dream made the little girl want to have a bath.*

# Lesson 23

-Common nouns

    -Things

* The child will need a pencil and paper.

⇨ Note to Instructor: Ask the child to practice writing his name before beginning today's lesson.

Instructor: Let's say the definition of a **noun** together.

Together: **A noun is the name of a person, place, thing, or idea.**

Instructor: We have talked about names of people— **common names** like boy, girl, mother, father, firefighter and teacher. These names are **common nouns**. We have also talked about **proper names**—the special names that each person has. These are **proper nouns**. We've also talked about names of places. These are **nouns**, too. Do you remember some **common nouns** that are places? [Prompt the child: kitchen, bedroom, town, city, river, mountain, etc.] Most places also have a special name—a **proper noun**. Do you remember any of the special names for these places? (Prompt the child with the proper names of places you have discussed.) Now we will talk about the third kind of **noun**: things. **Nouns** are also the names of things.

⇨ Note to Instructor: Ask the child to name things he can see in the house and outside. Ask him to name things he uses for school, things he eats, and things he wears.

Instructor: All of these names are **common nouns**. They are **nouns** because they are names of things. They are **common nouns** because you can find these things in many different places. Remember: **A noun is the name of a person, place, thing, or idea**. Now can you recite the definition of a **noun** for me?

*Child: A noun is the name of a person, place, thing, or idea.*

⇨ Note to Instructor: Help, if necessary, by saying the definition with the child and by ending with a sincere compliment.

# Lesson 24

⇨   Note to Instructor:  Start off the day by having the child copy his full name.

How many people are in this picture?  There are two people in this picture.  They are a mother and a son.  The mother's special **proper name** is Mrs. Norris.  The son's special **proper name** is Julian.  What room are they in?  They are in the bathroom.  How did you know?

What is Mrs. Norris doing?  She is helping Julian dry off.  He has just taken a bath.  Do you see any toys he played with in his bath?  Yes, I see a rubber ducky.   It is resting on the edge of the bathtub.  Can you see two bottles of shampoo?  Julian washed his hair with shampoo.

You see, Julian was very dirty.  How might he have gotten so dirty?  He could have stomped in mud puddles, or built a racetrack for his toy cars out of dirt and sticks, or planted some seeds for a garden. I will tell you what really happened.  Julian was playing in his back-yard fort with his friend Justin.  He and Justin were jumping in leaf piles, hiding under bushes, and collecting sticks to build a barricade.  They were pretending to be guards defending their fortress.  By the time Mrs. Norris called Julian in for supper, he was covered in dirt from head to toe.

That is why Julian had to take a bath.  He had to scrub behind his ears and between his toes.  Now he is drying off, and telling his mother about the adventures of the afternoon.  But he still has a few more things to do before he can have his supper.  Do you see a comb in the picture?  Julian needs to comb his hair.  See how messy his hair is?  There is a piece that is sticking up!  Julian also needs to change into his pajamas.  Do you see his pajama shirt?  Point to it.  How many buttons can you see on his pajama shirt?  There are two buttons on his pajama shirt that you can see.

When Julian is clean and dressed, he will go to dinner.  He will be excited, because Mrs. Norris has made Julian's favorite meal: macaroni and cheese. What is your favorite meal?

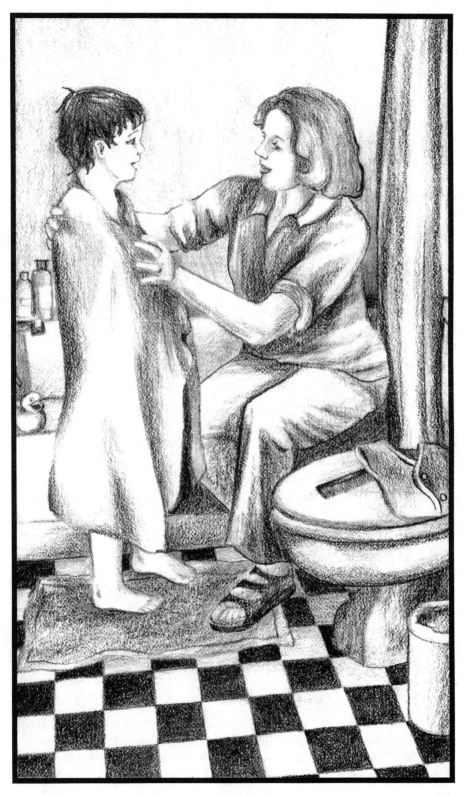

# Lesson 25

-Proper nouns

     -Aunts and uncles

-Introducing oral usage: "Avoiding Ain't"

-Poem review: "The Caterpillar" (Lesson 2) and "Work" (Lesson 15)

\* The instructor will need a pencil and paper for the lesson.  The child will need a pencil and paper for the enrichment activity.


⇨ Note to Instructor: Review "The Caterpillar" and "Work" today. Lessons 25–26 are about the family relationship of uncles, aunts, and cousins. You should feel free to omit any part of these lessons if the child does not have uncles, aunts, or cousins to talk about.

Instructor: Say the definition of a **noun** with me three times.

Together (three times): **A noun is the name of a person, place, thing, or idea.**

Instructor: The words "aunt" and "uncle" name kinds of persons. What are aunts?

*Child: My aunt is my mother's (or father's) sister.*

Instructor: Do you have an aunt? (Does your mother or father have a sister?)  What is your aunt's name?

*Child: My aunt's name is* _____.

⇨ Note to Instructor: If your child has more than one aunt, repeat the exercise until all aunts are named.  After you have done this oral work, you should write out the answers in sentences and show this to the child ("My aunt's name is_____.")  Remind the child that this is not just any aunt, but names one special aunt,  and so the aunt's name begins with a capital letter.

Instructor: What are uncles?

*Child: <u>Uncles</u> are brothers of my mother or father.*

Instructor: *Do you have an uncle? What is your uncle's name?*

*Child: My uncle's name is_____. (Example: Don)*

My other uncles are_____.

⇨ Note to Instructor:  Write for the child, "My uncle's name is ____." Show the child that this is not just any uncle, but one special uncle, and so the uncle's name begins with a capital letter.


## Oral Usage Exercise

⇨ Note to Instructor Concerning Oral Usage: Beginning with this lesson, oral practice in correct usage will be included in some lessons.  The rules cited in the "Note to the Instructor" are for the instructor's information. They are not to be "taught" to a young child.  Rather, the child's ear should be trained to recognize correct usage.

⇨ Note to Instructor: Most usage problems occur with state-of-being verbs (am, is, are, was, were, be, being, been) and helping verbs (have, has, had, do, does, did, shall, will, should, would, may, might, must, can, could). At this level we will be practicing only correct usage; we are not yet ready to define "state of being" and "helping." This first oral usage practice avoids the use of "ain't," which is now used only in dialect or illiterate speech. Standard English uses *"am not," "are not," "is not," "has not,"* or *"have not."* If the child uses an incorrect form, give him the correct form and ask him to repeat it.


Instructor: I will ask you a question. I want you to answer the question starting with the word, "No."
Isn't Aunt Lucy coming today?
*Child: No, she isn't coming today.*
Instructor: Isn't Uncle Hector coming tomorrow?
*Child: No, he isn't coming tomorrow.*
Instructor: Isn't your cousin Davis coming this summer?
*Child: No, he isn't coming this summer.*

## Enrichment Activity

Ask the child to copy the names of aunts and uncles. Children enjoy practicing their writing skills by using the names of familiar people! You might consider mailing the child's practice to the aunt or uncle named—you can address the envelope as the child watches.

# Lesson 26

-Proper nouns

    -Cousins

-Poem review: "The Caterpillar" (Lesson 2) and "Work" (Lesson 15)

\* The instructor will need a pencil and paper for the lesson. The child will need a pencil and paper for the enrichment activity.

⇨ Note to Instructor: Review "The Caterpillar" and "Work" today.

Instructor: Last lesson we talked about uncles and aunts. Do you remember whom we talked about? Today we are going to talk about the children of those aunts and uncles. Children of your aunts and uncles are called your cousins. The word "cousin" doesn't name any particular person, so the word "cousin" is a **common name** for lots of people. But if we name the name of a particular, special cousin, that name is a **proper noun**. Do you have any cousins? What are their names?

⇨ Note to Instructor: As the child gives the names of real cousins, write down their first, middle, and last names in a complete sentence. If the child can read, have him read it aloud to you.

*Child: (\_\_\_\_ \_\_\_\_ \_\_\_\_) is my cousin.*

⇨ Note to Instructor: Point out to the child which are first, middle, and last names. If they were named for other family members, tell the child about that. Do this exercise for two or three cousins—more if there is time and interest.

Instructor: Who are cousins?

*Child: Cousins are children of my aunts and uncles.*

## Enrichment Activity

Ask the child to write the names of his cousins. Then have the child copy or write sentences showing relationships, for example, "My cousin Mary Jane is Aunt Joan's daughter."

# Lesson 27

-Poem memorization: "Hearts Are Like Doors"

⇨ Note to Instructor: Read this new poem aloud to the child two times in a row now, and three more times at some point later in the day.

"Hearts Are Like Doors"
*Anonymous*

Hearts, like doors, will open with ease,
To very, very little keys,
And don't forget that two of these
Are "Thank you, sir" and "If you please!

## Enrichment Activity

Ask the child, "What do you think the poem means when it says "Hearts will open with ease?" (A possible answer: People will like you.) We talk about liking and loving people with our hearts. When people like you, we say they "open their hearts" to you. When you are polite and grateful for what they do for you, they "open their hearts" to you.

# Lesson 28

-Common and proper nouns
  -Family relationships
  -Places

* The instructor will need a pencil and paper.


⇨   Note to Instructor: Read the poem "Hearts are Like Doors" out loud to the child three times in a row.

Instructor:  Say with me the definition of a **noun**.

Together:  **A noun is the name of a person, place, thing, or idea**.

Instructor:  Remember that special **proper names** of persons and places begin with a capital letter.  Your **address** and the addresses of where other people live are special **proper names** of those places, so they are written with  capital letters.  I am going to write your **address** and the address of (choose another person the child knows). These are special, particular places—**proper nouns**, and so we write them with capital letters.

⇨   Note to Instructor:  Write the addresses as the child watches.  Point out the capital letters in the special "proper" names.

Instructor:  Remember how we talked about **common names** of people like mother, father, sister, brother, grandmother, grandfather, aunt, uncle, cousin. These words could mean people in anyone's family. Let's name the special **proper names** of these people in our family.

⇨   Note to Instructor:  Let the child watch you write the "proper name" as you say the sentence.  Example: "My mother's name is _____; My father's name is _____."

## Enrichment Activity

The child may copy the full name of his mother or father (or other family names).

# Lesson 29

-Proper nouns
    -Your address and zip code
-Poem review: "Hearts Are Like Doors"
* The instructor will need a pencil and paper for the lesson as well as an envelope for the enrichment activity.


⇨   Note to Instructor: Have the child repeat the poem "Hearts Are Like Doors" three times in a row today.

Instructor: Last lesson we talked about **common names** of people like mother and father. Then I showed you the special, **proper name** of those people. Today we are going to talk about sister and brother. These words could mean people in anyone's family. Let's name the special **proper names** of these people in our family.

⇨   Note to Instructor: Let the child watch you write the "proper name" as you say the sentence. (Example: My sister's name is_____; My brother's name is_____.)

Instructor: Now let's talk about something a little different. We already learned your address. But there's one more part of it you need to know. In an address, a zip code is a number after the state that tells the post office what part of the country you live in. Your zip code is_____.

⇨   Note to Instructor: Write your zip code and read it to the child. Practice having him say it with you.

Instructor: What is name of the street (or road) on which you live?
*Child: I live on _____ .*

⇨   Note to Instructor: Have the child watch as you write his address. Write the number of his street or road , the name of his street or road, and on the next line, write his town, state (full spelling), and zip code. Abbreviations will be studied later.

Instructor: This is your address. All the words in an address begin with capital letters. They are **proper nouns** because they name a special, particular place.

⇨   Note to Instructor: Read the address with the child, pointing to the capital letters as you say the following reminder:

Instructor: <u>Names</u> of streets, roads, cities, towns, counties, and states begin with capital letters. They are special, particular places. Say with me the definition of a **noun**.

Together: **A noun is the name of a person, place, thing, or idea.**

Instructor: Can you say that alone?

⇨  Note to Instructor:  Have the child repeat the definition of a noun to you.

## Enrichment Activity

Let the child watch you address a real envelope with the child's name and complete address, including zip code. Have the child draw a picture or write a message to be mailed back to him.  Mail the letter!

# Lesson 30

-Common and proper nouns

\* The instructor will need a pencil and paper for the lesson as well as drawing supplies for the enrichment activity.

- Instructor:  Say with me the definition of a **noun**.

Together: **A noun is the name of a person, place, thing, or idea.**

Instructor:  Look around the room and name common things you see that don't have special names.

⇨    Note to Instructor: Prompt child, if necessary—curtain, paper, rug, window, or table.

Instructor:  We have already talked about **common names** of people like mother, father, sister, brother, grandmother, and grandfather. These words could mean people in anyone's family. But these people also have **proper names**. Today we are going to name the special **proper names** of your grandmother and grandfather.

⇨    Note to Instructor:  Let the child watch you write the proper name as you say the sentence. (Example:   My grandmother's name is _____; My grandfather's name is _____.)

## Enrichment Activity

Draw a picture of things in a room.  Label the things.  Entitle the picture: "Common Nouns."

# Lesson 31

- Common nouns
    - Living things
-Oral usage: "Was/Were"
-Poem review: "Hearts Are Like Doors" (Lesson 27)

⇨   Note to Instructor: Don't forget to review the poem "Hearts Are Like Doors" today.

Instructor: Let's say the definition of a **noun** together.

Together: **A noun is the name of a person, place, thing, or idea.**

Instructor: We have talked about names of people, places, and things. Did you know that names of animals are **nouns**, too? The names of all living things are **nouns**. Insects are living things. Can you name some insects for me? (flies, mosquitoes, bees).

Fish and sea life are living things. Name some things that live in the water (crabs, gold fish, stinging nettles, sharks).

Plants are living things. Name some trees (maple, oak, pine). Name some vegetables (tomatoes, potatoes, lettuce). Name some fruit (apples, oranges, grapes). Name some nuts (pecans, walnuts).

Flowers are living things. Name some flowers (tulips, roses).

Animals are living things!  Name some animals (cats, hamsters, dogs). All of the words we talked about today are **nouns** because they tell what the living things are *named.*

## Oral Usage Exercise

⇨   Note to Instructor: Use "was" and "were" to tell about something that happens in the past. Use "was" to tell about one person or thing. Use "were" to tell about more than one person or thing. Always use "were" with the word "you."

Instructor: I will ask you a question. I want you to answer the question starting with the word, "Yes."

Instructor: Was the kitten too little to walk?
*Child: Yes, the kitten was too little to walk.*
Instructor: Were the kittens grey and black?
*Child: Yes, the kittens were grey and black.*
Instructor: Were you cuddling the kittens?
*Child: Yes, I was cuddling the kittens.*
Instructor: Was I feeding the kittens?
*Child: Yes, you were feeding the kittens.*

# Lesson 32

-Common and proper nouns
    -Family relationships
    -Living things

\* The instructor will need a pencil and paper for the lesson. The child will need a pencil and paper for the enrichment activity.

Instructor: Names of animals are common nouns. But some animals have special **proper names**, too! If you give a pet a special **proper** name, that name would be written with a capital letter. I am going to write some sentences for you to look at. They show the difference between **common and proper nouns** as names of pets.

⇨   Note to Instructor: Write sentences that include the common and proper names of pets ("My cat's name is Fluffy," or "Lily's mouse is named Chang"). If the child has a pet, or knows the name of someone else's pet, use those real names for this exercise.

Instructor: Remember how we talked about **common names** of people like mother, father, sister, brother, grandmother, and grandfather, aunts, uncles, and cousins? These words could mean people in anyone's family. Today, we are going to name the special **proper names** of these people in our family.

⇨   Note to Instructor: Choose any members of your family. Help the child to give the family member's proper name ("My aunt's name is_____ (either "Aunt Sabrina" or "Sabrina Cortez" is correct). Write out the sentence as you say it. Let the child watch you write. Point out that you are beginning proper names with capital letters.

## Enrichment Activity

If the child has a pet, ask him to write the common and proper name of the pet.

# Lesson 33

-Picture narration: "Pet Shop"

Look at all the animals! Do you like animals? This boy in the picture likes animals. What do you think is his special **proper name**? Yes, his name could be that. But his name is really Eric. Eric is in a store where pets are sold. There are many kinds of animals here at the store. What kinds of animals do you see? Can you point to the bird? "Bird" is a **common noun** because it is a name of an animal. This bird is not for sale. He belongs to the owner of the pet store. The owner named the bird. What do you think is its special **proper name**? Yes, it could be that. But the bird's name is really Tweets, because he goes "tweet-tweet-tweet" all day.

There are also fish. How many fish do you see? There are two fish. One is hiding behind the castle. The fish do not belong to anybody yet; they are for sale. "Fish" is a **common noun** because it is the name of a thing. I bet when someone buys the fish he will give them special **proper names**. What special **proper names** would you give the fish?

I don't think Eric will name the fish. He is interested in something else. In what animal is Eric interested? That's right, he is interested in the dog. "Dog" is a **common noun** because it is the name of an animal. The dog likes Eric. See how he is sniffing Eric's hand? Eric is petting him very gently. Eric is wishing that he could take this dog home to be his pet. Eric has already given this dog a special **proper name**. The dog's special **proper name** is Jack.

Jack has a sister. She is lying beside him. Can you point to Jack's sister? Jack's sister does not have a special **proper name** yet. What would you name her if you could? If I could give her a special **proper name**, I would call her Sally.

What is Sally doing? She is chewing on something. Maybe it is a special dog chew-toy or a piece of blanket. Do you see a blanket anywhere? Point to it. The blanket is in the box. It looks like a soft and cuddly blanket. Why do you think there is a blanket in the box? It is for the dogs. They can sleep in the box when they get tired.

Do you think Eric will be able to take Jack home? I don't know if he will be able to or not. He will have to ask his parents. I hope that Eric and Jack go home together. They already seem to be good friends.

# Lessons 34

-Proper nouns

  -Days of the week

-Poem review: "Work"(Lesson 15) and "Hearts Are Like Doors" (Lesson 27) and "The Caterpillar" (Lesson 2)

\* The instructor will need a calendar for the lesson as well as pencil, paper, and scissors for the enrichment activity.


⇨   Note to Instructor: Don't forget to review "Work" and "Hearts Are Like Doors" and "The Caterpillar" today.

Instructor: *Remember our definition of a noun? Say it with me.*

Together: **A noun is the name or a person, place, thing, or idea.**

Instructor: *Today we are going to name the days of the week.*

⇨   Note to Instructor: Use a real calendar and point to the days.  Some calendars begin with Sunday as the first day of the week; others begin with Monday.  Use a calendar that shows the day your family considers to be the first day of the week.

Instructor: There are seven days in a week—Sunday, Monday, Tuesday, Wednesday, Thursday, Friday, and Saturday.  These are not just any days.  Each day of the week has its own special proper name.  It begins with a capital letter.

⇨   Note to Instructor:  On your calendar, show the child the capital letters at the beginning of each day of the week.  If your calendar has the days in all capitals or abbreviations, you write the days of the week for the child, showing him that each name starts with a capital letter. Say the names of the days of the week aloud with the child three times, pointing to each name as you say it. Help the child to find today's day on the calendar.


**Enrichment Activity**

Instructor: On a sheet of lined paper, write the days of the week in a column, skipping lines.  Have the child cut them apart, mix them up, and then rearrange them in order. (If you save these names in an envelope, you can do this activity as often as needed, without having to rewrite them.)

# Lesson 35

-Poem memorization: "Days of the Week"
-Common and proper nouns
-Poem review: "Hearts Are Like Doors" (Lesson 27)
* The instructor will need a pencil and paper.

⇨ Note to Instructor: Review "Hearts Are Like Doors" today. Then read "Days of the Week" aloud to the child three times in a row. Repeat this triple reading twice more during the day.

Days of the Week
*Mother Goose rhyme*
*adapted by Sara Buffington*

Monday's child is fair of face,
Tuesday's child is full of grace;
Wednesday's child is ever so sweet,
Thursday's child is tidy and neat;
Friday's child is prone to a giggle,
Saturday's child is easy to tickle;
But the child that is born on restful Sunday
Is happy and cheerful, and loves to play.

Instructor: Today we are going to review **common and proper nouns. Common nouns** for persons are: girl, boy, man. Let's give a special **proper name** for each of these words.
⇨ Note to Instructor: Help the child select real people he knows. Write the common noun and the proper noun for each, as in the example that follows:
girl – Maria
boy – Jamal
man – Mr. Baxter
Instructor: **Common nouns** for places are: store, library, zoo, park. Let's give a special **proper name** for each of these places.
⇨ Note to Instructor: Write the common and proper nouns for each place, as in the example that follows:
store – (Name a store in which your child sees you shop.)
library – (Name the library you visit.)
zoo or park – (Name a zoo or park you have visited.)
Instructor: Other **common nouns** for things are: cereal, cookies,

toys, and books.  Let's give a special **proper noun** for each of these things.

Note to Instructor: Write the common and proper nouns for each thing, as in the example that follows:

cereal – Cheerios™

cookies – Oreos™

toys – Legos™

books – *Go, Dog, Go*

# Lesson 36

-Story narration: "The Hen and the Golden Eggs"
-Poem review: "Hearts Are Like Doors" (Lesson 27) and "Days of the Week" (Lesson 35)

⇨ Note to Instructor: Review "Hearts are Like Doors" and "Days of the Week" today. Then read aloud the Aesop's fable below. Have the child tell the story back to you. At the end of the story are suggested questions you can use if the child needs prompting.

## The Hen and the Golden Eggs

A man and his wife once had a hen which laid a little golden egg for them every day. They took good care of the hen, petted her, and fed her well. Every morning they would say to her, "Thank you, little hen, for your gift!" And every evening they would feed her a hot mash and say, "Sleep well, little hen!"

Finally, they saved enough golden eggs to build a nice little cottage in the forest. Then the little hen provided them with enough gold to buy food and clothes and to share with others who needed help. For many years, they were thankful to have the little hen with them.

But the more they had, the greedier they became! One day, the man said to his wife, "Why are we waiting to get one little egg of gold each day? Our hen must have lots of golden eggs inside her. Let's kill her and look! Then we can have all of the gold at once. We will be even richer!"

So the greedy man and his wife killed the hen and cut her open. But they were shocked to discover that the little hen was no different inside from other chickens. Day by day, they grew poorer without the eggs from the little hen. By trying to become rich all at once, they lost the only source of gold they had.

Moral: If you are greedy and harm others to get more, you may lose what you have.

⇨ Note to Instructor: Use these questions to help the child summarize the story.
Who owned the hen? *The farmer and his wife owned the hen.*
What was so special about the hen? *She could lay golden eggs.*
How did the farmer and his wife spend the gold? *They bought food*

*and clothes and helped other people.*

After a while, what did they do to the hen? *They killed the hen.*

Why did they kill the hen? *They were greedy and they wanted all the gold that they thought was inside her.*

Did the farmer find gold inside the hen? *No, the hen was just like every other hen.*

According to the moral of the story, what happens to those who harm others to get more? *They lose everything they have.*

# Lesson 37

-Nouns

    -Identifying Nouns in a Story

-Poem review: "Hearts Are Like Doors" (Lesson 27) and "Days of the Week" (Lesson 35)

* The child will need drawing supplies for the enrichment activity.


⇨   Note to Instructor: Review "Hearts Are Like Doors" and "Days of the Week" today.

Instructor: Say the definition of a **noun** with me.

Together: **A noun is the name of a person, place, thing, or idea.**

Instructor: I am going to read the story about the hen to you again, stopping at the end of each sentence. Tell me the words you hear that name persons, places, or things.

⇨   Note to Instructor: Have the child watch you run your finger under each word as you read. Stop at the end of each sentence and help the child find the nouns. If the child has trouble finding the nouns, encourage the child to listen for these words by pausing briefly when you say them. At this time, don't be concerned if the child does not name the nouns "morning," "evening," "years," and "day," since these are not concrete "things" that the child can see.

Paragraph 1: Man, wife, hen, egg, hen, morning, hen, gift, evening, mash, hen.

Paragraph 2: Eggs, cottage, forest, hen, gold, food, clothes, years, hen.

Paragraph 3: Day, man, wife, egg, gold, hen, eggs, gold.

Paragraph 4: Man, wife, hen, chickens, day, eggs, hen, gold.


## Enrichment Activity

On one sheet of paper, have child draw small pictures of nouns in the story. Label each little drawing, and title the picture "Nouns."

# Lesson 38

-Proper nouns

    -Days of the week

\* The instructor will need a pencil and paper for this lesson. The child will need a pencil, paper, and drawing supplies for the enrichment activity.

Instructor: Let's say the names of the days of the week together three times.

Together (three times): Sunday, Monday, Tuesday, Wednesday, Thursday, Friday, Saturday.

Instructor: I am going to write down each of these names of the days of the week. See, each one begins with a capital letter. Now, I am going to make a list of things we do each day.

⇨ Note to Instructor: If your family doesn't have a regular schedule, make a schedule for one special week. You may wish to post a schedule each week somewhere the child can see, so he will begin to see a family routine. Children find comfort in routine.

## Enrichment Activity

The child may make his own personal schedule by writing the names of the days of the week and drawing pictures for each day.

# Lesson 39

-Addresses
-Common and proper nouns
    -Aunts and uncles
-Poem review: "Days of the Week" (Lesson 35) and "The Caterpillar" (Lesson 2)
\* The instructor will need a pencil and paper for this lesson. The child will need a pencil and an envelope for the enrichment activity.

⇨   Note to Instructor: Review "Days of the Week" and "The Caterpillar" today. You will need the address of an aunt or uncle for this lesson.
Instructor: Our address tells people where we live. What is our address?
⇨ Note to Instructor: Write the address with zip code as the child dictates it to you. If the child is unsure of his address and zip code, repeat it five times together.
Instructor: Let's look at another address together. This is the address of your uncle/aunt. Can you show me the zip code?
⇨   Note to Instructor: Write the sentence, "My aunt/uncle lives in (city, state)" while the child watches.
Instructor: Remember, the words "uncle" and "aunt" could name anyone's uncle or aunt, so those words are not written with a capital letter. They are **common nouns**. But the name of a particular uncle or aunt is their **proper name** and it is written with a capital letter. Let us name particular uncles and aunts, and I will write their names for you.
⇨   Note to Instructor: Write out these sentences, following the examples below.
My mother's brother is Uncle_____.
My mother's sister is Aunt_____.
My father's brother is Uncle_____.
My father's sister is Aunt_____.

## Enrichment Activity
The child may copy his own address on an envelope and mail himself something!

# Lesson 40

-Proper nouns
     -Months of the year
-Oral usage: "See/Saw/Seen"
-Poem review: "Days of the Week" (Lesson 35)
* The instructor will need a highlighter marker and calendar for the lesson. The child will need a pencil and paper for the enrichment activity.


⇨ Note to Instructor: Review "Days of the Week" today.

Instructor: We have learned that each day of the week has a name. The months of the year also have names. There are twelve months in each year. Listen while I say the names: January, February, March, April, May, June, July, August, September, October, November, December.

⇨ Note to the Instructor: Give the child a calendar to browse and identify the names of the month. He can use a marker to circle the names.

Instructor: Let's say the first three months together, three times. Remember, those months are "January, February, March."

Together (three times): January, February, March.

Instructor: Now let's do the next three: April, May, June.

Together (three times): April, May, June.

Instructor: Now the next three: July, August, September.

Together (three times): July, August, September.

Instructor: And now the last three: October, November, December.

Together (three times): October, November, December.


## Oral Usage Exercise

⇨ Note to Instructor: "See" is the present tense of "to see." "Saw" is the past tense. "Seen" is also a past form of "to see," but must *always* be used with the helping verb "has" or "have."

Instructor: Repeat these sentences after me.

"I saw a bluebird in June."

"I have seen many birds in the summer."

"I saw snow in January."

"I have seen snow many times before."

"He saw beautiful flowers in April."

"He has seen tulips bloom in March."

"Have you seen red leaves in the fall?"

"Yes, I have seen beautiful red and yellow leaves."

**Enrichment Activity**

The spelling and pronunciation of "February" is difficult. Although dictionaries give acceptable pronunciations that leave out the sound of the first "r", you may wish to emphasize this syllable ("feb-**roo**-air-ee') as a game. This exercise will help prevent misspelling when writing February. Have the child practice copying "February" and then spelling it from memory.

# Lesson 41

-Proper nouns

     -Months of the year

-Poem review: "The Days of the Week" (Lesson 35)

\* The instructor will need a pen and a calendar for this lesson as well as paper and scissors for the enrichment activity.

&#8658;   Note to Instructor: Review "Days of the Week" today.

Instructor: I am going to say the months of the year: January, February, March, April, May, June, July, August, September, October, November, December. Let's practice again saying those months.

Instructor: Let's say the first three months together, three times. Remember, those months are "January, February, March."

Together (three times): January, February, March.

Instructor: Now let's do the next three: April, May, June.

Together (three times): April, May, June.

Instructor: Now the next three: July, August, September.

Together (three times): July, August, September.

Instructor: And now the last three: October, November, December.

Together (three times): October, November, December.

Instructor: Now let's look at a calendar together and find out what months are birthday months for our family.

&#8658;   Note to Instructor: Get a calendar and mark the birthdays of each person in the family. Mark the holidays your family celebrates. Give the child his own calendar, if possible, and mark for him birthdays and special holidays your family celebrates.

## Enrichment Activity

Instructor: Copy two lists of the months in order, skipping a line between each month. Have the child cut apart one list, mix them up, and rearrange them in order, using the uncut list to self-check.

# Lesson 42

-Introducing copywork: "My Name"

* The child will need a pencil and paper.

⇨ Note to Instructor: When beginning copywork, have the child do short amounts daily. (Later, as his physical writing ability matures, you should also ask the child to copy in other subjects like history and science.) By doing copywork, the child learns the look and feel of a correctly composed sentence that is properly spelled, spaced, and punctuated. Copywork engages both the visual and motor memory of a child. It gives the child correct models while he is still struggling with the basics of writing conventions: spaces between words, capital letters, punctuation, and spelling. In the beginning, it is helpful for some children to say the word aloud, sounding it out as they copy. You may wish to write out the copywork in your own handwriting for the child to see. Sit beside the child and correct him when he begins to copy incorrectly, rather than waiting until he is finished.

Instructor: Today we are going to start copying sentences, so that you can practice writing. We will also practice leaving proper spaces between words.

⇨ Note to Instructor: Three options will be given for each copywork. Choose the appropriate length for the child's skill. If the child lives in a "blended" family, use your discretion and substitute your own sentence for the third option.

My name is _____.(child's first name)
My full name is ___ _____ ___.(child's full name)
Family members have the same last name. My family name is

_____.

## Enrichment Activity

Copy names of family members that the child may not already write easily.

# Lesson 43

-Poem memorization: "The Months"
-Copywork: "My Birthday"
* The child will need a pencil and paper.


⇨ Note to Instructor: Read the poem aloud to the child three times now. Repeat this triple reading twice more during the day.

Instructor: The months are not the same length! Some months have more days that others. Most have 30 or 31 days, but February has only 28. And February is even stranger—once every four years February has one more day added. We call this year "Leap Year." I will read you a poem that will help you remember the number of days in each month. Remember that "four and twenty-four" is the same as "twenty-eight"!

## The Months
*Mother Goose rhyme*


Thirty days hath September,
April, June, and November;
All the rest have thirty-one,
Except for February alone,
Which has four and twenty-four
Till leap year gives it one day more.


Instructor: Now let's practice the poem together.
Together (three times): Thirty days hath September,
April, June, and November.
Together (three times): All the rest have thirty-one,
Except for February alone.
Together (three times): Which has four and twenty-four
Till leap year gives it one day more.
⇨ Note to Instructor: If the child inquires, an explanation might be given: Leap years were added to the calendar to make the calendar match the movement of the earth around the sun.

## Copywork

Choose appropriate length for child's ability:

1. _____(copy month of child's birthday)
2. My birthday is in_____ (month).
3. I have cake on my birthday in _____(month).

# Lesson 44

-Nouns
    -Ideas
-Copy lesson: "Love"
-Poem review: "The Months" (Lesson 43)
* The child will need a pencil and paper.


⇨   Note to Instructor: Repeat the poem "The Months" three times along with the child before beginning today's lesson.

Instructor:  Say the definition of a **noun** with me three times.

Together (three times): **A noun is the name of a person, place, thing, or idea.**

Instructor: An **idea** is something you think about in your mind, but cannot see or touch—like love, anger, energy, loneliness, or fear. You can name ideas, but you can't see them.

⇨   Note to Instructor: Read the following sentences aloud to the child. Move your finger under the words as you read, so the child can see the words. The underlined words are names for ideas.


The puppy gives me his <u>love</u>.
I felt <u>anger</u> when the boy teased my puppy.
I am full of <u>energy</u> when I get a good night's sleep.
<u>Kindness</u> makes people happy together.
There was no <u>peace</u> between the cat and the dog.
<u>Loneliness</u> comes when everyone leaves me.


Instructor: Can you see love?  Can you see energy?  No, but these are things that you feel and think about.  They are **ideas**.  Even though you can't see them, they are real.  These **idea** words are **nouns**.


## Copywork

Choose appropriate length for child:

1. I feel love for you.
2. My mother feels love for me.
3. The people in my family feel love for each other.


## Enrichment Activity

Copy another sentence from this lesson that contains a noun that names an idea (anger, energy, kindness, peace, loneliness).

# Lesson 45

-Noun review
-Copywork: "Four Types of Nouns"
-Poem review: "The Months" (Lesson 43)
* Both the instructor and the child will need a pencil and paper.


➭ Note to Instructor: Review "The Months" today.

Instructor: Let's review the definition of a **noun**.

Together: **A noun is the name of a person, place, thing, or idea.**

Instructor: Remember, **common nouns** name persons that could be lots of different people—like doctors, brothers, uncles, or teachers. But **proper nouns** name special, particular people, like Dr. Grove. Let's name some **common nouns** for persons and then name special, particular persons.

➭ Note to Instructor: Help the child think of the proper names for uncles, aunts, teachers, doctors, ministers, or baby-sitters.

Instructor: Remember, **common nouns** name places that could be lots of different places, but proper nouns name special, particular places like Plains, Arizona. Let's name some **common nouns** for places and then give a special, particular name for those kinds of places.

➭ Note to Instructor: Help the child think of the proper names for towns, rivers, mountains, stores, restaurants, ice-cream shops, etc.

Instructor: Now, let us name some **common nouns** for things and then give a special particular name for those things.

➭ Note to Instructor: Help the child to think of proper nouns for toys, songs, poems, cars, tractors, or books.

Instructor: What are some words that name ideas? We will only talk about **common nouns** for these. Today we will name those idea words that we think about in our mind, or feel, but can't see or touch like a thing can be felt or touched. Do you remember some we named in the last lesson? (love, anger, energy, kindness, peace, loneliness.)

➭ Note to Instructor: Feelings are the most immediate "ideas" for most young children. Help the child identify other feelings. If you think that he will understand, you can also discuss freedom, obedience, responsibility, patience, diligence, and other character qualities. These, too, are ideas.

## Copywork

Today the child will write some nouns of each kind. Title a sheet of paper "Nouns." Divide the paper into four horizontal sections, and title the sections "Persons," "Places," "Things," and "Ideas." Ask the child to think of a noun to go in each section. You write each word on another piece of paper, and ask the child to copy it onto his "Nouns" sheet. He should have at least one noun to go in each section.

## Enrichment Activity

The child may add words to the list, as many as appropriate for his writing ability.

# Lesson 46

-Introducing pronouns
    -I, me, my, mine
-Oral usage: "Ordering 'I' and 'Me'"
-Poem review: "The Months"

⇨ Note to Instructor: Review "The Months" today.

⇨ Note to Instructor: We will be covering these pronouns over the next five lessons. For your reference, here is the full list covered:

I, me, my, mine;

you, your, yours;

he, she, him, her, it, his, hers, its;

we, us, our, ours;

they, them, their, theirs.

Instructor: **A pronoun is a word used in the place of a noun.** Try to say the definition with me as I repeat it three times.

Together: **A pronoun is a word used in the place of a noun.**

Instructor: We have learned that a **noun** names a person, place, thing, or idea. Your own name is a **noun.** Today, we are going to talk about **pronouns** that can take the place of your name. These **pronouns** are I, me, my, mine. Let's repeat those together three times.

Together (three times): I, me, my, mine.

Instructor: What is your name?

*Child: My name is _____ .*

Instructor: Instead of saying "(Child's name) went out to play," you could say, "I went out to play." Repeat those two sentences for me.

*Child: (Child's name) went out to play. I went out to play.*

Instructor: The **pronouns** that stand for you are I, me, my, mine. We just used "I." Now let's use "me." Instead of saying, "Please give (child's name) a cookie," you could say, "Please give me a cookie." Repeat those two sentences for me.

*Child: Please give (child's name) a cookie. Please give me a cookie.*

Instructor: Now let's practice using "my." Instead of saying, "That is (the child's name)'s toothbrush, you could say, "That is my toothbrush." Repeat those two sentences for me.

*Child: That is (child's name)'s toothbrush. That is my toothbrush.*

Instructor: Now we have used I, me, my. Let's use "mine." Instead of saying, "That towel is (the child's name)'s," you could say, "That towel is mine." Repeat those two sentences for me.

*Child: That towel is (child's name)'s. That towel is mine.*

Instructor: I am going to say the definition of a **pronoun** again: **A pronoun is a word used in the place of a noun**. Say it with me again.

Together: **A pronoun is a word used in the place of a noun.**

Instructor: Now say the **pronouns** that can be used in place of your own name when you speak of yourself. We used them in sentences today: "I, me, my, mine."

Together: I, me, my, mine.

### Oral Usage Exercise

Instructor: When you are speaking of yourself and another person, always speak of the other person first. Say, "Charlie and I went fishing," not "I and Charlie went fishing." Repeat these sentences after me:

Jane and I are going with Mom.
My sister and I played soccer.
My father and I went to town.

Instructor: Say, "My mother drove Ellen and me to town," not "My mother drove me and Ellen to town. Here is a trick to help you remember: If you say "me" first, it will sound like "mean" Ellen! Repeat these sentences after me.

My sister invited Joy and me to her doll tea party.
The clown did a juggling trick for Lee and me.
My mother took my brother and me shopping.

### Enrichment Activity

If the child is reading easily, have him find and circle these four personal pronouns (I, me, my, mine) in newspaper or magazine articles.

# Lesson 47

-Pronouns

      -You, your, yours

-Copywork: "Pronoun List 1"

-Poem review: "The Months" (Lesson 43)

\* Both the instructor and the child will need a pencil and paper.


⇨ Note to Instructor: Review "The Months" today.

Instructor: Let's say the definition of a **pronoun** together three times.

Together: **A pronoun is a word used in the place of a noun.**

Instructor: Do you remember the **pronouns** that speak of yourself? Yes, they are "I, me, my, mine." Let's say those together three times.

Together (three times): I, me, my, mine.

Instructor: There are also pronouns that can take the place of the person to whom you are speaking. These pronouns are "you, your, yours." Let's say those together three times.

Together (three times): You, your, yours.

Instructor: Instead of saying, "(Instructor's name) is here with me," you can say, "You are here with me." Repeat those two sentences for me."

Child: "[Instructor's name] is here with me." "You are here with me."

Instructor: Instead of saying, "This is (instructor's name)'s book," you can say, "This is your book." Repeat those two sentences for me.

Child: "This is [instructor's name]'s book." "This is your book."

Instructor: Instead of saying, "This pencil is (instructor's name)'s," you can say, "This pencil is yours." Repeat those two sentences for me.

Child: "This pencil is [instructor's name]'s." "This pencil is yours."

Instructor: The pronouns you, your, and yours take the place of another person's name.


## Copywork

Today the child will begin to make his own list of pronouns. Title a sheet of paper, "Pronouns." Then write out in your own handwriting the two lists of pronouns we have learned: "I, me, my, mine" and "you, your, yours." Because the child has not learned commas, write these in vertical lists. Ask the child to copy these vertical lists of pronouns onto his own paper.

# Lesson 48

-Pronouns

      -He, she, him, her, it, his, hers, its

-Copywork: "Pronoun List 2"

-Poem review: "The Months" (Lesson 43)

\* Both the instructor and the child will need a pencil and paper.


⇨   Note to Instructor: Review "The Months" today.

Instructor: Let's say the definition of a **pronoun** together three times.

Together (three times) **A pronoun is a word used in the place of a noun.**

Instructor: We have learned that "I, me, my, mine" can be used in place of your own name. Let's say those together.

Together: I, me, my mine.

Instructor: We have learned that "you, your, yours" can be used in place of the name of someone to whom you are speaking. Let's say those together.

Together: You, your, yours.

Instructor: Now let's talk about the **pronouns** "he, she, him her, it, his, hers, its." Can you say those with me, three times?

Together (three times): He, she, him, her, it, his, hers, its.

Instructor: Instead of saying to you, "Jim is coming," I could say "<u>He</u> is coming." Repeat those two sentences for me.

*Child: Jim is coming. He is coming.*

Instructor: Instead of saying "Sara likes dessert," I could say "<u>She</u> likes dessert." Repeat those two sentences for me.

*Child: Sara likes dessert. She likes dessert.*

Instructor: Instead of saying "Wait for Ron," I could say, "Wait for <u>him</u>." Repeat those two sentences for me.

*Child: Wait for Ron. Wait for him.*

Instructor: Instead of saying, "I gave a cookie to Kim," I could say, "I gave a cookie to <u>her</u>." Repeat those two sentences for me.

*Child: I gave a cookie to Kim. I gave a cookie to her.*

Instructor: Instead of saying, "Bob found a worm," I could say, "Bob found <u>it</u>." Repeat those two sentences for me.

*Child: Bob found a worm. Bob found it.*

Instructor: Instead of saying, "This is Bob's pet worm," I could say, "This is <u>his</u> pet worm." Repeat those two sentences for me.

*Child: This is Bob's pet worm. This is his pet worm.*

Instructor: Instead of saying, "This strawberry shortcake is Lori's," I could say, "This strawberry shortcake is <u>hers</u>." Repeat those two sentences for me.

*Child: This strawberry shortcake is Lori's. This strawberry shortcake is hers.*

Instructor: Instead of saying, "The cat's bed is soft," I could say, "<u>Its</u> bed is soft." Repeat those two sentences for me.

*Child: The cat's bed is soft. Its bed is soft.*

## Copywork

Today the child will continue making his list of pronouns. Write out the pronouns "he, she, him, her, it, his, hers, its" in a vertical list. Ask the child to copy these pronouns onto his "Pronouns" page. If the list is too long for the child to do at one sitting, have him do half in the morning and half in the evening (or complete the list yourself).

# Lesson 49

-Pronouns
  -We, us, our, ours
-Copywork: "Pronoun List 3"
-Poem review: "The Months" (Lesson 43)
* Both the instructor and the child will need a pencil and paper.

⇨   Note to Instructor: Review "The Months" today.

Instructor: Let's say the definition of a **pronoun** together.

Together: **A pronoun is a word used in the place of a noun.**

Instructor: Here are the **pronouns** we learned in the first two **pronoun** lessons: I, me, my, mine, you, your, yours. Let's say those together three times.

Together (three times): I, me, my, mine, you, your, yours.

Instructor: Now let's review the **pronouns** we learned in the last lesson: He, she, him, her, it, his, hers, its. Let's say those together three times.

Together (three times): He, she, him, her, it, his, hers, its.

Instructor: Today we are going to say and write **pronouns** that mean more than one person. Those **pronouns** are we, us, our, ours. Let's say that together three times.

Together (three times): We, us, our, ours.

Instructor: Imagine that you and a person like cookies. Can you tell me that both of you like cookies? Start with "We..."

*Child: We like cookies.*

Instructor: Now ask me for some cookies for both of you. Start your sentence with, "Please give…"

*Child: Please give us some cookies.*

Instructor: If I give cookies to both of you, whose cookies are they? Start your sentence with, "The cookies are…"

*Child: The cookies are our cookies.*

Instructor: Whose cookies are they? Start with, "They are…"

*Child: They are ours.*

Instructor: "We, us, our, and ours" are **pronouns**. They take the place of the nouns that named you and the other person.

## Copywork

Write out the pronouns *we, us, our, ours* in a vertical list. Ask the child to copy these pronouns onto his "Pronouns" page.

# Lesson 50

-Pronouns
      -They, them, their, theirs
-Copywork: "Pronoun List 4"
* Both the instructor and the child will need a pencil and paper.


Instructor: Let's say the definition of a **pronoun** together three times.
Together: **A pronoun is a word used in the place of a noun.**
Instructor: These **pronouns** are also used in place of **nouns** that mean more than one person: they, them, their, and theirs. You use them when you are talking about a group of people that does not include you! Let's say "They, them, their, theirs" together three times.
Together (three times): They, them, their, theirs.
Instructor: Together, we'll read a sentence with a **noun** in it. Then you choose a **pronoun**—they, them, or their—to use in place of the **noun**. "Ducks swim on the pond." What **pronoun** can you use in place of "ducks"?
*Child: They swim on the pond.*
⇨ Note to Instructor: If child is unsure of answer, read the pronouns to him and allow him to choose.
Instructor: "We feed the ducks." What **pronoun** can go in the place of "ducks"?
*Child: We feed them.*
Instructor: "I like to watch ducks swim." Can you put a **pronoun** in place of "ducks"?
*Child: I like to watch them swim.*
Instructor: "Ducks' feet paddle fast." What **pronoun** can you use for "ducks' "?
*Child: Their feet paddle fast.*
Instructor: "The ducklings are the mother and father ducks'." What **pronoun** can you use for "mother and father ducks' "?
*Child: The ducklings are theirs.*
Instructor: Now let's review all of our **pronouns**! Say them after me. "I, me, my, mine."
*Child: I, me, my, mine.*
Instructor: You, your, yours.
*Child: You, your, yours.*
Instructor: He, she, him, her, it, his, hers, its.
*Child: He, she, him, her, it, his, hers, its.*

Instructor: We, us, our, ours
*Child: We, us, our, ours.*
Instructor: They, them, their, theirs
*Child: They, them, their, theirs.*

## Copywork

Write out the pronouns "they, them, their, theirs" in a vertical list. Ask the child to copy these pronouns onto his "Pronoun" page.

# Lesson 51
Story narration: "The Bundle of Sticks"

⇨   Note to Instructor: Read aloud the Aesop's fable below. Have the child
tell the story back to you; use the suggested questions at the story's end to
prompt the child, if necessary.


The Bundle of Sticks


A father had a family of six children: three boys and three girls.
They were very noisy children, for they spent most of each day quarrelling with each other. That day, the house was particularly noisy.

Jacob was angry with Emily for eating the last piece of toast.
"You already had two pieces of toast and I only had one piece. It is not
fair!" he complained.

"You always get whatever you want, Jacob. You never leave
anything for the rest of us!" she yelled back.

Sally stamped her feet because Martha was playing with Sally's
favorite doll. "You have the doll I always play with! You know that
she is my favorite, Martha! I refuse to play dolls with you if you keep
taking the best doll!"

"Well, I don't want to play dolls with you anyway," Martha
shouted back. "You are so bossy!"

Eric yelled at Simon because Simon was humming the same
tune over and over again. "I am trying to read," Eric complained, "and
you are humming just to annoy me. Stop humming, or I am going to
tell Dad!"

Simon gave Eric a mean look. "I will do whatever I want to
do," he snapped. "You are not Mom or Dad. You can't tell me what to
do!"

The children's father was sad that his children could not get
along. So he told them to come outside into their front yard. He asked
each of them to pick up a few sticks and bring them to him. He tied all
of the sticks into one bundle and gave the bundle to Eric. "Try to break
it in half," he commanded.

Eric tried with all his might, but he could not break the bundle.
The father gave the bundle of sticks to Martha, but she could not break
it, either. Each of the six children tried to break the bundle, but they
could not.

Then the father untied the bundle and divided the sticks among his children. "Now try to break the sticks one by one," he ordered. The children easily snapped the sticks in half.

"Children," their father said, "do you not see that when you agree with each other and get along together, our family will be impossible to break apart? The bundle of all the sticks was impossible to break. But the single sticks were easy to snap. When you argue and bicker and quarrel, you will be weak, like the single sticks. We cannot have a strong, happy family if each one of you is selfish and looks out only for his own interests. You must learn to agree with each other and help each other so that we may have a strong family. If you continue to fight and quarrel, you will be weak like one single stick."

⇨ Note to Instructor: Ask the child to tell you the story back in his own words. If the child has trouble remembering, use these questions:
What made the father sad? *His children were quarrelling with each other.*
What kinds of things were the brothers and sisters arguing about? *They were arguing about toys, food, and humming.*
What did the father ask his children to pick up once they were in the yard? *The father asked the children to pick up sticks.*
What did the father do with the sticks? *He tied them into a bundle.*
What did the father ask the children to do with the bundle? *He asked them to break it.*
Were the children able to break the single sticks? *Yes, the children were able to break the single sticks.*
What was the father trying to teach his children by having them try to break the bundle of sticks? *He was trying to teach them that they would be stronger if they agreed with each other instead of fighting.*

## Enrichment Activity
Pronoun Search: Have the child find all the personal pronouns in the story.
Paragraph 1: they, they
Paragraph 2: you, I, it, he
Paragraph 3: you, you, you, us, she
Paragraph 4: her, you, I, you, she, I, you, you
Paragraph 5: I, you, you
Paragraph 6: I, you, me, I
Paragraph 7: I, I, he, you, you, me
Paragraph 8: his, he, them, their, he, them, them, him, he, it, he

Paragraph 9:  his, he, she, it, they
Paragraph 10:  his, he
Paragraph 11:  their, you, you, our, you, you, we, you, his, you, we,
                you, you

# Lesson 52

-Introducing verbs

     -Action verbs

-Poem review: "Work" (Lesson 15)

\* The child will need a pencil and paper for the enrichment activity.


⇨    Note to Instructor:  Review "Work" today.

⇨    Note to Instructor: It isn't necessary for the student to understand state of being, linking or helping verbs while memorizing this definition—those will be covered at a later date.

Instructor: We have talked for many lessons about **nouns**, which name people, places, things, or ideas.  We have talked about **pronouns**, which can be used in the place of **nouns**.  Today we are going to talk about words that tell us what those **nouns** and **pronouns** do!  Those words are called "**verbs**."  I will read the definition of a **verb** aloud to you three times.

Instructor (three times): **A verb is a word that does an action, shows a state of being, links two words together, or helps another verb.**

Instructor: We will talk about **action verbs** today.  I am going to say some words that are action words: walk, stoop, run, laugh, write, erase, cry, skip, throw, catch, dance, and eat. These are all **verbs**. Can you think of more actions?

⇨    Note to Instructor: After the child tells you the ones he can think of, read the following list to him:

Run, skip, roll, fall, jump, eat, sing, sleep, jump, skate, talk, read, kick, hit, crawl, hop, bark, dance, play, look, paint, climb, swing, float, fly, open, close, move, race, smell, shout, yell, laugh, clean, bark, squeak, mew, roar, growl.

Instructor: Tell me as many of these action verbs as you can remember.

*Child: (repeats as many verbs as possible)*

Instructor: Remember, **a verb is a word that does an action**.

Let's say that part of the definition together three times.

Together (three times):  **A verb is a word that does an action.**


## Enrichment Activity

The child can title a sheet of paper, "Action Verbs," and make a list of as many action verbs he can remember. He can illustrate the list if he chooses.  He can also add to the list at any time.

# Lesson 53

-Pronouns
-Action verbs
-Copywork: "Label Nouns and Verbs 1"
* The child will need a pencil and paper.

⇨ Note to Instructor: Read the child the following list of pronouns three times. If the child can chime in with any of the pronouns, encourage him to do so, but he does not need to memorize the lists. *I, me, my, mine; you, your, yours; he, she, him, her, it, his, hers, its; we, us, our, ours; they, them, their, theirs.*

Instructor: I am going to say the definition of a **verb** three times for you.

Instructor (repeat three times): **A verb is a word that does an action, shows a state of being, links two words together, or helps another verb.**

Instructor: Now I want you to repeat parts of this definition after me: **A verb is a word that does an action.**

*Child: A verb is a word that does an action.*

Instructor: Now listen to the second part of the definition. **Shows a state of being.** Repeat that for me.

*Child: Shows a state of being.*

Instructor: **Links two words together.**

*Child: Links two words together.*

Instructor: **Or helps another verb.**

*Child: Or helps another verb.*

Instructor: We are going to practice using **action verbs** now. You name some family members. These names are **nouns**. Now think up **action verbs** for each family member. What can you imagine each person doing? For example, "The baby crawls." Say the sentences out loud and act out the action.

⇨ Note to Instructor: Suggest these verbs if the child has trouble coming up with his own: eats, drinks, sips, crawls, cries, swings, runs, walks, washes, works, laughs, drives, works, swims, yells, paints, swims.

## Copywork

Choose one of the following sentences of appropriate length for the child's ability. After he copies the sentence, tell him to print an "N" above the nouns and a "V" above the verbs in each sentence he copies.

Rabbit ran the race.

Ben and Sherri skipped and hopped.

The wind howled and the rain blew and the thunder roared.

## Enrichment Activity

The child may add more verbs to his "Action Verbs" sheet started in Lesson 52.

# Lesson 54

-Telephone numbers
-Addresses
-Poem review: "Hearts Are Like Doors" (Lesson 27)
* The child may need a new address book and a pencil for the enrichment activity.

⇨ Note to Instructor: Review "Hearts Are Like Doors" today.
⇨ Note to Instructor: If the child already knows his home telephone number, do the enrichment activity below in place of the lesson.

Instructor: Today, I want to be sure that you know what our family's home telephone number is. Our telephone number has ten numbers in it. The first three numbers are the area code. Our area code is _____. Say that with me three times.

Together (three times): (area code).

Instructor: An "area" is a certain amount of space. So the "area code" for our telephone is the same for a lot of people in the space near where we live. All telephone numbers from our area have the same first three numbers, but we have a telephone number at our home that no one else has! Our personal family telephone number has seven numbers. Those numbers are ___-____. Say that with me three times.

Together (three times): (telephone number).

Instructor: Our whole telephone number is (area code)____-_____.
We are going to say that together today TEN times! Let's hold up our fingers and fold one down every time say the number.

Together (ten times): (telephone number)

Instructor: Never give your telephone number to strangers, or give it out on the computer. Never, never, never! If someone asks for your telephone number, say, "Ask my parents!" Now, let's review who you are and where you live. What is your full name?

*Child: (Child gives first, middle, and last name.)*

Instructor: Where do you live?

*Child: (Child gives address. Encourage him to add the zip code.)*

Instructor: *What is your telephone number?*

*Child: (Child gives full telephone number.)*

## Enrichment Activity

Have child learn telephone numbers of trusted family members, neighbors, or friends. The child may start an address book with approved addresses and/or telephone numbers in it.

# Lesson 55

-Nouns
-Pronouns
-Action verbs
-Copywork: "Label Nouns and Verbs 2"
* The child will need a pencil and paper.

⇨ Note to Instructor: Read the child the following list of pronouns three times. He does not need to memorize the list now, but encourage him to chime in. *I, me, my, mine; you, your, yours; he, she, him, her, it, his, hers, its; we, us, our, ours; they, them, their, theirs.*

Instructor: Say the definition of a **noun** with me.

Together: **A noun is the name of a person, place, thing, or idea.**

Instructor: I will repeat the definition of a **verb** for you. **A verb is a word that does an action, shows a state of being, links two words together, or helps another verb.** Let's repeat the first part of that definition together three times: **A verb is a word that does an action.**

Together (three times): A verb is a word that does an action.

Instructor: Today we are going to talk about **nouns** that name animals and the **action verbs** that these animals can do. Can you give me the name of any animals along with an action these animals could do? For example, "The bird soared through the sky," or "The elephant crashed through the jungle."

⇨ Note to Instructor: Refer to verb list in Lesson 52 if needed. Allow the child to act out the action verbs. Remind him that if he can't *do* it, the word may not be an action verb!

## Copywork

Choose one, two, or three of the following sentences for the child to copy. Make sure that he skips a line between each sentence. After he copies the sentences, ask him to print an "N" above the nouns and a "V" above the verbs in each sentence.

The cat scratches.
The dog barks.
The hamster hides.
The lion roars.
The monkey climbs.

**Enrichment Activity**

The child may add more verbs to his "Action Verbs" sheet started in Lesson 52.

# Lesson 56

-Picture narration: "The Leaf Pile"

How many people are in this picture? There are four people in this picture. They are a family. Can you point to each person and say their common name? I will help you start. This is the mother.

⇨ Note to Instructor: Have the child point to each person and give their common name. "Brother" or "son" is acceptable.

This is the Williams family. The mother's special, proper name is Mrs. Jackie Williams. The father's special, proper name is Mr. Jason Williams. The older son's special, proper name is Jamal, and the younger son's special, proper name is Tyson. What is the Williams family doing? They are playing in the leaves. "Play" is a word that shows action. It is called an "**action verb**." The trees have all shed their red, orange, yellow, and brown leaves. It is the season of fall.

Do you think this is daytime or nighttime? It is nighttime. How could you tell? It is very dark outside. It is a Saturday night. The Williams have been at their neighbor's house for dinner. They had a lot of fun.

On their walk home, Tyson pointed to the leaves they had raked into a pile that day. He said, "Look at that big pile of leaves we raked today! I would love to jump into it." "Jump" is a word that shows action. It is an **action verb**. Mrs. Williams looked at her husband and smiled. "Look" is a word that shows action. It is an **action verb**. Mrs. Williams said, "I have an idea. Let's all play in the leaves." They all ran to the leaf pile and started scooping up the leaves and tossing them high into the air.

Look at Jamal, the older son. Do you see his face? What is he doing? He is laughing. "Laugh" is a word that shows action. It is an **action verb**. Look at Tyson. He has just thrown a handful of leaves into the air. "Throw" is a word that shows action. It is an **action verb**. Now look at Mr. Williams. He is catching the leaves as they fall to the ground. "Catch" is a word that shows action. It is an **action verb**.

It is getting close to Tyson and Jamal's bedtime. They will probably go into the house soon. I bet they will spend a few more minutes playing outside. They look like they are having a great time playing in the leaves.

# Lesson 57

-Cumulative poem review

Instructor: Today we are going to review all of the poems you have worked on so far. When we recite a poem, we begin with the title and author. I will read each poem to you, and then I want you to try to say the poem back to me. Remember: Stand up straight! Don't fidget while you're reciting! And speak in a nice, loud, slow voice.

⇨   Note to Instructor: Read each poem to the child before asking him to repeat it. If he repeats it accurately, move on to the next poem. If he stumbles, ask him to repeat the line he cannot remember three times, and make a note to review that poem daily until it is mastered. Remind the child that "Anonymous" means we don't know who wrote the poem.

| Lesson | Poem | Author |
|--------|------|--------|
| 2 | "The Caterpillar" | Christina G. Rossetti |
| 15 | "Work" | Anonymous |
| 27 | "Hearts Are Like Doors" | Anonymous |
| 35 | "Days of the Week" | Mother Goose rhyme adapted by Sara Buffington |
| 43 | "The Months" | Mother Goose rhyme |

# Lesson 58

-Pronouns
-Action verbs
-Action poem: "Dancing"
-Copywork: "Dancing"
* The child will need a pencil and paper for this lesson as well as drawing supplies for the enrichment activity.


Instructor: Do you remember the definition of a **noun**? **A noun is the name of a person, place, thing, or idea. A pronoun is a word used in the place of a noun.** Let's say the definition of a **pronoun** together three times.

Together (three times): **A pronoun is a word used in the place of a noun.**

Instructor: Now I'll read you the list of **pronouns** that we talked about earlier. If you can say any of these along with me, jump in and say them! *I, me, my, mine; you, your, yours; he, she, him, her, it, his, hers, its; we, us, our, ours; they, them, their, theirs.*

Instructor: **A verb is a word that does an action, shows a state of being, links two words together, or helps another verb.** Let's repeat the first part of that definition three times.

Together (three times): **A verb is a word that does an action.**

Instructor: Today I'm going to read you a poem that is full of action words. I'm going to read it once for you just to listen. Then I'm going to read it again and you can do the actions while I read.

⇨    Note to Instructor: Read the entire poem aloud while the child listens quietly. Read the poem again slowly, pausing after each action word to give time for the child to act out the motions. Technically, "hop" and "skip" are nouns in this poem, not verbs (and "up" and "down" are prepositions). But as you read, let the child act out any actions he wishes. The goal is for him to recognize action words. Distinctions between verbs and other kinds of words that might express actions will be explained in more detail when the child is older.

Dancing[1]
*Eleanor Farjeon* (FAR-jun)

A hop, a skip, and off you go!
Happy heart and merry toe,
Up and down and in and out,
This way, that way, round about!

Bend like grasses in the breeze,
Wave your arms like wind-blown trees,
Dart like swallows, glide like fish,
Dance like anything you wish.

Soundless as the snowflakes white,
Swift as shooting stars at night,
Nimble as a goblin elf,
Dance, dance, and be yourself.

Stately, sprightly, so and so,
 Quick and slow,
 To and fro,
Kicking high and jumping low,
A skip, a hop, and off you go!

[1]Originally appeared in *Sing for Your Supper* by Eleanor Farjeon.

## Copywork
Ask the child to copy one, two, three, or four lines from the poem,
depending on his ability.

## Enrichment Activity
The child may copy and illustrate any lines from the poem he wishes.

# Lesson 59

-Days of the week
-Action verbs
-Copywork: "Days of the Week"
* Both the instructor and the child will need a pencil and paper.

Instructor: Do you remember the names of the days of the week? I will say them for you: Sunday, Monday, Tuesday, Wednesday, Thursday, Friday, Saturday. Let's say them together.
Together: Sunday, Monday, Tuesday, Wednesday, Thursday, Friday, Saturday.
Instructor: Now I am going to read you a funny poem where members of a family are doing different things on every day of the week. It is called "Monday, Mommy Baked a Cake."

Monday, Mommy Baked A Cake
*Jessie Wise*

Monday, Mommy baked a cake.
Tuesday, Daddy ate a steak.

Wednesday, Brother waved, "Good-bye."
Thursday, Uncle made a pie.

Friday, Sister cooked the meat,
Then we all sat down to eat.

Saturday, we welcomed guests.
Sunday, we all took our rests.

Monday, we began anew—
The days of the week are all too few.

Instructor: Let's name something that we do on each day of the week. What do we usually do on Mondays?
⇨ Note to Instructor: Continue through each day of the week; help the child to identify your family's routine on each day.

**Copywork**

Write "Days of the Week" at the top of the child's paper. Then write out the days of the week on your own paper and ask the child to copy them. If this is too long, finish the copywork in the next lesson.

**Enrichment Activity**

An advanced writer may be able to write the days of the week from memory. Remind him that proper names begin with capital letters.

# Lesson 60

-Introducing initials
-Copywork: "My Initials"
-Oral usage: "Pronouns"
-Poem review: "The Months" (Lesson 43)
* Both the instructor and the child will need a pencil and paper.


⇨ Note to Instructor: Review "The Months" today.

Instructor: You have learned that **proper nouns** begin with capital letters. The first letter of a word is its initial letter. The word "initial" means "first" or "beginning." The initial letter of a **proper noun** begins with a capital letter. What is the first letter of your first name?

*Child: The first letter of my first name is___.*

Instructor: That is the initial letter of your first name. What is the first letter of your middle name?

*Child: The first letter of my middle name is____.*

Instructor: That is an initial letter also. What is the first letter of your last name?

*Child: The first letter of my last name is___.*

Instructor: That is an initial letter too. Now put those three initial letters together. These letters together are called your initials. Sometimes we use initials as a short way to refer to proper names. If I ask you to tell me your full initials, what would you say? Begin your answer with, "My initials are..."

*Child: My initials are __ __ __.*

Instructor: When we write initials, we capitalize each one. We also put a period after each initial.

⇨ Note to Instructor: Write your child's initials for him, putting a period after each initial. Tell him that you place a period after each initial. Show the child how to make a period—just a dot, not huge marks!

Instructor: Now, on paper, I want you to make ten periods in a line.

⇨ Note to Instructor: Ask the child to practice making periods.


## Copywork

Have the child copy his initials and then write them from memory.


## Oral Usage Exercise

⇨ Note to Instructor: Read aloud the first sentence in each pair of sentences below. Then ask the child to substitute a pronoun for the first word (noun) in each sentence. Before beginning, read the list of pronouns to the child: *I, me, my, mine; you, your, yours; he, she, him, her, it, his, hers, its; we, us, our, ours; they, them, their, theirs.*

Instructor: Mary eats cake.

*Child: She eats cake.*

Instructor: Ed is seven years old.

*Child: He is seven years old.*

Instructor: Ducks like to eat crumbs.

*Child: They like to eat crumbs.*

Instructor: The airplane took off with a roar.

*Child: It took off with a roar.*

## Enrichment Activity

Talk about the full names and initials of parents. Ask the child to copy or write these initials.

# Lesson 61

-Initials
-Identifying pronouns in a story
-Oral Usage: "It Is I"
* Both the instructor and the child will need a pencil and paper.

➩ Note to Instructor: Turn back to Lesson 51 and re-read "The Bundle of Sticks" aloud. Ask the child to follow along if he is able. Stop at the end of each sentence and ask the child to identify the pronouns (see "Pronoun Search" at end of story). Use your discretion; it isn't necessary to read the entire story if the child's attention span is short.

Instructor: In the last lesson, we learned that the first letter of a word is its initial letter. The word "initial" means "first" or "beginning." When you write the first letter of your name instead of the whole name, you are writing your initials. Can you tell me the initials of your first, middle, and last name? Begin your sentence, "My initials are…"

*Child: My initials are _____.*

Instructor: Sometimes people use initials for their first and middle names only, and use the full spelling of their last name. If you were to use the initials of your first and middle names along with your full last name, how would you say your name? Begin your sentence, "My name is…"

*Child: My name is [initial] [initial] [last name].*

➩ Note to Instructor: Prompt child, if necessary.

Instructor: Let's talk about the initials of the other members of our family.

➩ Note to Instructor: Talk to the child about the names and initials of members of the family. Let the child see you write the initials and last names for three people in your family. Point out the period after each initial.

## Copywork
Child will copy his own initials, using periods.

## Oral Usage Exercise
➩ Note to Instructor: The subject pronouns "I," "he," and "she" should always be used in the sentence pattern, "It is…" or "This is…." The child should never say, "It is me!" or "It is him!" Read the following dialogue with the child, encouraging him to use the pronouns "I," "he," and "she."

Instructor: I am going to ask you several questions. Answer them using the pronouns I, he, or she. Who is there? Begin your answer

with, "It is…"
*Child: It is I.*
Instructor: Is that your brother?  Begin your answer with, "It is…"
*Child: It is he.*
Instructor: Is that your mother?  Begin your answer with, "It is…"
*Child: It is she.*
Instructor:  Let's pretend that you're knocking on the door.  Go knock on it!  Now I will say, "Who is it?"   What will you answer?
*Child: It is I.*
Instructor:  Now I'll go knock on the door!  Are you going to ask, "Who is it?"
*Child: Who is it?*
Instructor: It is I!

## Enrichment Activity

If child is writing easily, have him copy or write his name using initials and last name. Copy initials and last names for three other people in your family.

# Lesson 62

-Story narration: "The Crow and the Pitcher"
* The child will need a tape recorder, a pencil, and paper for the enrichment activity.

⇨  Note to Instructor: Read aloud the Aesop's fable below. Have the child tell the story back to you; use the suggested questions at the story's end to prompt the child, if necessary.

## The Crow and the Pitcher

A large black crow flew over a long stretch of parched land. He grew thirstier and thirstier! At the edge of a village, he spied a large, deep pitcher at the edge of a patio. He flew down for a drink. To his dismay, there was so little water in the bottom of the pitcher that he could not reach it with his beak.

"I'll push the pitcher over and drink what spills," he thought. But the pitcher was too heavy.

"I'll stretch until I can reach the bottom of the pitcher," he said. But his neck was too short.

"I am too tired to try again," he sighed. So he hopped over into the shade of a tree to think about what else could be done.

As he rested in the cool shade, he noticed a number of large pebbles around the edge of the patio. "I know!" he said to himself. "I can pick up these pebbles one at a time and drop them into the pitcher. As they sink to the bottom, the water will rise above them. Maybe I can collect enough pebbles to make the water rise so that I can reach it."

So he collected the pebbles, one by one, and dropped them into the pitcher. Slowly, pebble by pebble, the water rose. And finally the thirsty crow plunged his beak into the water. He drank and drank until he was full. Refreshed, he spread his wings and flew away.

Moral: Many hard things can be accomplished with patience and perseverance.

⇨  Note to Instructor: Use these question to help the child summarize the story.
Why did the crow fly down to the pitcher? *He was thirsty.*
Why couldn't he take a drink? *His beak couldn't reach the water.*

What did he try to do first? *He tried to push the pitcher over.*

Why didn't that work? *It was too heavy.*

What was the second thing the crow tried to do? *He tried to stretch his neck down to the water.*

Did this work? *No, his neck was too short!*

Where did the tired crow go after that? *He went to rest and think under a tree.*

What did he decide to do? *He decided to drop pebbles into the pitcher.*

What happened to the water when the pebbles were dropped in? *It rose high enough so he could drink it.*

What is the moral of the story? *If you keep trying, you can do many hard things.*

## Enrichment Activity

If your child is writing easily, he could tape-record his retelling and write his summary of the story from the tape recorder.

# Lesson 63

-Days of the week
-Months of the year

Instructor: Do you remember the names of the days of the week? Let me read you the poem you memorized about the days of the week. Then, I'd like you to say it back to me. Note to Instructor: Read the following poem, and then ask the child to repeat it.

Days of the Week
*Mother Goose rhyme*
*Adapted by Sara Buffington*

Monday's child is fair of face,
Tuesday's child is full of grace;
Wednesday's child is ever so sweet,
Thursday's child is tidy and neat;
Friday's child is prone to a giggle,
Saturday's child is easy to tickle;
But the child that is born on restful Sunday
Is happy and cheerful, and loves to play.

Instructor: Good! Now let's say the days of the week together.
Together: Sunday, Monday, Tuesday, Wednesday, Thursday, Friday, Saturday.
Instructor: Can you count them? How many days are in a week?
*Child: Seven.*
Instructor: A week is made up of seven days. Months are made up of thirty days or thirty-one days – and one month only has 28 days. Do you remember which month has 28 days?
*Child: February.*
Instructor: I will read you the poem about the months. Then, I'd like you to say it back to me.

## The Months
*Anonymous*

Thirty days hath September,
April, June, and November;
All the rest have thirty-one,
Except for February alone,
Which has four and twenty-four
Till leap year gives it one day more.

Instructor: Let's say the first three months together, three times. Remember, those months are "January, February, March."
Together (three times): January, February, March.
Instructor: Now let's do the next three: April, May, June.
Together (three times): April, May, June.
Instructor: Now the next three: July, August, September.
Together (three times): July, August, September.
Instructor: And now the last three: October, November, December.
Together (three times): October, November, December.

# Lesson 64

-Introducing seasons
        -Winter
-Copywork: "Winter"
-Oral usage: "It Was I"
* The instructor will need a calendar, a pencil, and paper. The child will need a pencil and paper as well as construction paper and coloring supplies for the enrichment activity.


Instructor: The winter months are December, January, and February. Say the names of the winter months.
*Child: December, January, February*
Instructor: "Winter" is the name of a season. We capitalize the names of the months, but we do not capitalize the names of the seasons.
⇨ Note to Instructor: If your family celebrates any holidays in these three winter months, talk to the child about them. Find the dates on the calendar.
Instructor: How many days does December have?
⇨ Note to Instructor: Help child go through poem "The Months" to find the answer.
*Child: Thirty-one days.*
Instructor: How many days does January have?
*Child: Thirty-one days.*
Instructor: How many days does February have?
*Child: Twenty-eight.*
Instructor: How many days does it have in Leap Year—every four years?
*Child: Twenty-nine.*


## Copywork

Help the child write "Winter" as the title on a sheet of paper. Write the names of these three winter months for the child to copy onto his paper. Then have the child draw or cut out a winter picture or pictures showing the season or a holiday celebrated in these months. If the child asks why you are capitalizing "Winter," explain that titles are always capitalized (this rule will be covered later).

## Oral Usage Exercise

⇨ Note to the Instructor: The subject pronouns "I," "he," and "she" should always be used in the sentence pattern, "It is…" or "This is…." The child should never say, "It is me!" or "It is him!" Read the following dialogue with the child, encouraging him to use the pronouns "I," "he," and "she." This lesson also reviews the following usage rules: "See" is the present tense of "to see." "Saw" is the past tense. "Seen" is also a past form of "to see," but must <u>always</u> be used with the helping verb "has" or "have."

Instructor: Who was that in the snow? Begin your answer with, "It was…"

*Child: It was I.*

Instructor: Who threw the snowball? Was it the boy over there? Begin your answer with, "It was…"

*Child: It was he.*

Instructor: Have you seen snow, before? Begin your answer with "I…"

*Child: I have seen snow before.*

⇨ Note to Instructor: If the child uses "seen" alone, remind him to use "have" along with it.

Instructor: When did you see snow before? Begin your answer with "I…"

*Child: I saw snow last winter.*

⇨ Note to Instructor: If the child uses "seen," remind him that "seen" cannot be used without the word "have," but that "saw" can be used alone.

## Enrichment Activity

You may collect the child's writings and drawings about the seasons and make a booklet entitled, "The Seasons." Today, ask the child to write the words, "The Seasons" on the front cover and decorate it. Save the booklet until all four seasons are studied (Lessons 64, 67, 69, and 70).

# Lesson 65

## -Introducing abbreviations

Instructor: Can you hear the word "brief" in the middle of "abbreviations?" "Brief" means short. Today we will have a short lesson. Right
now the lesson is over!

# Lesson 66

-Initials
-Abbreviations
-Copywork: "Winter Abbreviations"
* The child will need a pencil and paper for this lesson as well as magazines, newspapers, and mail for the enrichment activity.


Instructor: We learned that the first letter of a word is its initial letter. The word "initial" means "first" or "beginning." When you write an initial for a word, instead of writing the whole word, you are abbreviating the word. You are writing it in a brief form. Write your full name for me. Now let's look at the first letters of each word. If you abbreviate this name by writing your initials, what would your initials be?
*Child: My initials are _____.*
Instructor: Remember, initials are always capital letters. Initials should always be followed by a period. When we write the names of the months, we often abbreviate them. But we don't use their initials. We use the first three letters of each month's name, and then place a period after those letters. What are the first three letters of December?
*Child: Dec.*
⇨ Note to Instructor: Write these letters out while the child watches. Place a period after the abbreviation. Follow this procedure for January and February as well.
Instructor: What are the first three letters of January?
*Child: Jan.*
Instructor: What are the first three letters of February?
*Child: Feb.*


## Copywork
Ask the child to copy the abbreviations for December, January, and February. Remind him to put a period after each abbreviation.


## Enrichment Activity
Have the child look at newspapers, magazines, book covers, and mail for people's names written with some of their initials.

# Lesson 67

-Seasons

-Spring

-Noun review

-Copywork: "Spring"

* Both the instructor and the child will need a pencil and paper. The child will also need seed catalogs for the enrichment activity.

Instructor: Let's say the definition of a **noun** together.

Together: **A noun is the name of a person, place, thing, or idea.**

Instructor: Give me the name of a person. Either a **common noun** or a **proper noun** is fine!

*Child: [common noun or proper noun]*

Instructor: Give me the name of a place. Either a **common noun** or a **proper noun** is fine!

*Child: [common noun or proper noun]*

Instructor: Name a thing in this room for me.

*Child: [chair, spoon]*

Instructor: Now, can you think of the name of an idea? Remember, an idea is something you think about in your mind, but cannot see or touch.

*Child: [idea]*

⇨ Note to Instructor: If necessary, prompt the child for feelings such as love, fear, anger, happiness, or for a character quality such as patience, persistence, or obedience.

Instructor: We have talked about December, January, and February—the winter months. Do you know what season comes after winter? Spring comes after winter! The spring months are March, April, and May. Repeat those after me.

*Child: March, April, May.*

Instructor: What are the first three letters of March?

*Child: Mar.*

⇨ Note to Instructor: Write these letters out while the child watches. Place a period after the abbreviation. Follow this procedure for April as well.

Instructor: What are the first three letters of April?

*Child: Apr.*

Instructor: What are the first three letters of May?

*Child: May!*

Instructor: May is only three letters long, so we don't need an abbreviation for it! Remember, abbreviations of months are always capitalized and have a period after them. The names of months are always capitalized when they are written in full, because they are proper names. But "winter" and "spring" are seasons. Their names are not capitalized.

## Copywork

Help the child write "Spring" as the title on a sheet of paper. Write the names of these three spring months for the child to copy onto his paper. Then ask the child draw or cut out a spring picture or pictures showing the season or a holiday celebrated in these months.

## Enrichment Activity

You may plan to collect the child's writing and drawing about the seasons and make a booklet entitled, "The Seasons." For "Spring," the child may use seed catalogs to cut out pictures of spring blooming plants, bulbs, and trees. He may wish to label the pictures to identify the names of the flowers.

# Lesson 68

-Action verbs
-Oral usage: "Was/Were"
* The child will need a pencil and paper for the enrichment activity.

Instructor: **A verb is a word that does an action, shows a state of being, links two words together, or helps another verb.** Let's repeat the first part of that definition three times.
Together (three times): **A verb is a word that does an action.**
Instructor: Now I want you to repeat the second part of the definition one time: **Shows a state of being.** Repeat that for me.
*Child: Shows a state of being.*
Instructor: **Links two words together.**
*Child repeats: Links two words together.*
Instructor: **Or helps another verb.**
*Child repeats: Or helps another verb.*
Instructor: Now, let's see if we can find some action verbs in the story of "The Crow and the Pitcher."
⇨   Note to Instructor: Go back to Lesson 62, "The Crow and the Pitcher," and read it aloud to the child. Help the child to follow along with your finger or a marker. After you and the child read each sentence aloud, stop and help him to find the action verbs. In order of appearance, they are: flew, grew, spied, flew, reach, push, drink, spill, thought, stretch, reach, said, try, sighed, hopped, think, rested, noticed, said, pick, drop, sink, rise, collect, make, rise, reach, collected, dropped, rose, plunged, drank, drank, spread, flew.
Use your discretion: You do not need to read the whole story if his attention span is short.

## Oral Usage Exercise
⇨   Note to Instructor: Use "was" when speaking of one; use "were" when speaking of more than one or when speaking of "you."
Instructor: I am going to read some sentences to you. I want you to tell me which word goes in the blank: was or were? If the sentence speaks of only one person, choose "was." If it speaks of more than one, use "were." Also use "were" along with the word "you."
Instructor: Brenda and Frank _____ playing store.
*Child: Brenda and Frank were playing store.*
Instructor: Carl and Holly_____ in a spelling contest.
*Child: Carl and Holly were in a spelling contest.*
Instructor: Daisy _____ in the swimming pool.

*Child: Daisy was in the swimming pool.*

Instructor: You _____ at home yesterday.

*Child: You were at home yesterday.*

Instructor: Remember, use "were" with the word "you"! The children_____ having a picnic.

*Child: The children were having a picnic.*

Instructor: The mother _____ enjoying the good weather.

*Child: The mother was enjoying the good weather.*

Instructor: The boy and the girl _____ playing soccer.

*Child: The boy and the girl were playing soccer.*

## Enrichment Activity

If the child is writing easily, he may make a list of the verbs in "The Crow and the Pitcher." Title his list, "The Crow's Action Verbs."

# Lesson 69

-Pronouns
-Seasons
    -Summer
-Copywork: "Summer"
\* The instructor will need a pencil, paper, and a calendar. The child will need a pencil, paper, drawing supplies, and magazines for summer pictures.


⇨   Note to Instructor: Read the child the following list of pronouns three times. If the child can chime in with any of the pronouns, encourage him to do so, but he does not need to memorize the list. *I, me, my, mine; you, your, yours; he, she, him, her, it, his, hers, its; we, us, our, ours; they, them, their, theirs.*

Instructor: What two seasons have we learned about?

*Child: Winter and spring.*

Instructor: The winter months are December, January and February. Repeat those months for me.

*Child: December, January, February.*

Instructor: The spring months are March, April, and May. Repeat those months for me.

*Child: March, April, May.*

Instructor: The summer months are June, July, August. Say the names of these summer months with me.

Together: June, July, August.

Instructor: Can you tell me the abbreviations for June and July? Remember, use the first three letters of the month.

⇨   Note to Instructor: Write the abbreviations as the child says them. Point out the period after the abbreviation.

*Child: Jun., Jul.*

Instructor: What are the first three letters of August?

*Child: Aug.*

Instructor: Remember, summer is the name of a season. So we do not capitalize the word "summer."

⇨   Note to Instructor: If your family celebrates any holidays in these three summer months, talk to the child about them. Find the dates on the calendar.


## Copywork

Help the child write "Summer" as the title on a sheet of paper. Write the names of these three summer months for the child to copy onto his paper. Then have the child draw or cut out a summer picture or pictures showing the season, or a holiday celebrated in these months.

## Enrichment Activity
Ask the child to continue illustrating "Summer" with pictures and cutouts for his "Seasons" booklet.

# Lesson 70

-Seasons
　　　-Fall
-Copywork: "Fall"
-Poem review: "The Months" (Lesson 43)
* The instructor will need a pencil, paper, and a calendar. The child will need a pencil and paper as well as drawing supplies, and magazines.

⇨ Note to Instructor: Review "The Months" today.

Instructor: What three seasons have we learned?

*Child: Winter, spring, summer.*

Instructor: I am going to say those months for you. Then we will try to say them together three times. December, January, February, March, April, May, June, July, August.

Together (three times): December, January, February, March, April, May, June, July, August.

Instructor: We have one more season to learn about! The fall months are September, October, and November. Say the names of the fall months with me three times.

Together (three times): September, October, November.

Instructor: Sometimes the season "fall" is also called "autumn." Remember, "fall" and "autumn" are seasons, so we don't capitalize them.

⇨ Note to Instructor: If your family celebrates any holidays in these three fall months, talk to the child about them. Find the dates on the calendar.

Instructor: Now let's write out the abbreviations for September, October, and November. You tell me the first three letters of each word, and I will write them out. I will capitalize each abbreviation and put a period at the end of each one. What are the abbreviations for these months?

*Child: Sep., Oct., Nov.*

Instructor: Sometimes you will also see September abbreviated as "Sept."

## Copywork

Help the child write "Fall" as the title on a sheet of paper. Write the names of these three fall months for the child to copy. Then have the child draw or cut out a fall picture or pictures showing the season or a holiday celebrated in these months.

## Enrichment Activity

Continue to work on the fall section of the child's booklet, "The Seasons."

# Lesson 71

-Seasons

-Holidays

* Both the instructor and the child will need a pencil and paper.


Instructor: Let's try to say the names of all the months together. I'll say them first, and then we'll say them together twice. January, February, March, April, May, June, July, August, September, October, November, December.

Together (twice): January, February, March, April, May, June, July, August, September, October, November, December.

Instructor: The seasons are winter, spring, summer, and fall. Repeat those for me.

Child: *Winter, spring, summer, fall.*

Instructor: When we were talking and writing about the seasons, you drew or cut out pictures about what happens in those months. Most seasons have holidays that families celebrate. When we write, the names of holidays are capitalized. We are going to talk about holidays that we celebrate. I am going to write the name of the holiday, using capital letters. You will copy three of these holidays.

⇨   Note to Instructor: Talk with the child about holidays you celebrate. Write the names of the holidays for the child to copy. Point out that you are beginning the special, proper names of these holidays with capital letters.


## Copywork

Depending on his writing ability, have the child copy the names of three, four, or five holidays your family celebrates.


## Enrichment Activity

Help the child to write the days of week from memory.

# Lesson 72

-Pronouns
     -Capitalization of "I"
-Copywork: "Using 'I'"
-Oral usage: "Sit / Set"
* Both the instructor and the child will need a pencil and paper.

Instructor: Do you remember when we pretended that you were knocking on the door, and I asked, "Who is it?" Let's pretend that again. Go over and knock on the door. "Who is it?" Do you remember the proper answer?
*Child: It is I.*

Instructor: "I" refers to you! "I" is a **pronoun because it stands for a noun**—your name! Whenever you use the **pronoun** "I," it is always capitalized. I will write this sentence out for you, and then I will ask you to copy it.

⇨ Note to Instructor: Write "It is I" on a piece of paper. Show the child the capital "I." Then, ask the child to copy the sentence with proper spacing and capitalization. Remind him to end the sentence with a period.

Instructor: Whenever you are referring to yourself and another person, always use the other person's name first. Let's pretend that you and I are both knocking on the door, and that someone else calls, "Who is it?" You should answer by putting my name before your "I." Answer the question, "Who is it?" for both of us, beginning your sentence with "It is…"
*Child: It is [instructor's name] and I."*

Instructor: I will write that out for you.

⇨ Note to Instructor: Write the sentence for the child, pointing out the capital "I."

## Copywork

Choose one of the following sentences, depending on the child's ability.

It is I.
Emma and I ate lunch.
I have three friends named me, myself, and I.

## Oral Usage Exercise

⇨ Note to Instructor: Use "set" if you are referring to putting or placing an object. Use "sit" if you mean "to sit down" or "to rest."

Instructor: "Sit" and "set" mean two different things. If you need to sit down or rest, use the word "sit." If you have an object that you are putting down or placing somewhere else, use "set." I will read you some sentences. Repeat them back to me by placing "sit" or "set" in the blank.

Instructor: You are tired. Please ___ down.

*Child: You are tired. Please sit down.*

Instructor: Elizabeth, will you ___ the groceries on the table?

*Child: Elizabeth, will you set the groceries on the table?*

Instructor: Go in the bedroom and ___ down.

*Child: Go in the bedroom and sit down.*

Instructor: I was ___ on my chair, thinking.

*Child: I was sitting on my chair, thinking.*

Instructor: Grandmother, please ___ the teakettle on the stove.

*Child: Grandmother, please set the teakettle on the stove.*

Instructor: Be quiet and ___ down, right now!

*Child: Be quiet and sit down, right now!*

# Lesson 73

-Oral composition: "A Story About Me"
* Both the instructor and  the child will need a pencil and paper for this lesson. The child may need drawing supplies for the enrichment activity.

⇨   Note to Instructor: Have the child tell a story about himself. Give him these "story openers" and ask him what happens next. This story can be four sentences long— or as long as you wish! Have the child act out the action verbs of his story when he gets to them. As the child tells the story, write down his sentences. When he is finished, show him all of the capitalized "I" pronouns. Then, ask him to copy out one or more of the sentences that you have written. Remind child that "I" is always capitalized.

Story Starters (choose one if the child needs help beginning his story):
"One day I took my favorite stuffed animals outside for tea."
"I was walking along the road—and I stepped in quicksand!"
"It was the day before my birthday.  When I came into my brother's room, he hid something quickly!"
"I discovered a baby kitten on the sidewalk in front of my house."
"One morning, I woke up and discovered I had turned into a raptor."
"One morning, I woke up and discovered I had turned into a bunny."

**Enrichment Activity**
Ask the child to illustrate his story or to write a sequel.

# Lesson 74

-Story-poem narration: "The Three Little Kittens"
* The child will need a pencil and paper for the enrichment activity.

⇨ Note to Instructor: Read aloud the story below. Have the child tell the story back to you; use the suggested questions at the story's end to prompt the child, if necessary.

The Three Little Kittens
*Traditional*

Three little kittens, they lost their mittens,
And they began to cry.
"Oh, Mommy dear,
We sadly fear,
Our mittens we have lost!"
"What! Lost your mittens,
You naughty kittens,
Then you shall have no pie!"
"Meow, meow, meow, meow,
We shall have no pie."

The three little kittens, they found their mittens,
And they began to cry.
"Oh, Mommy dear,
See here, see here,
Our mittens we have found."
"What! Found your mittens,
You good little kittens,
Then you shall have some pie."
"Purr, purr, purr, purr,
Yes, we shall have some pie!"

The three little kittens put on their mittens,
And soon ate up the pie;
"Oh, Mommy dear,
We greatly fear,
Our mittens we have soiled."
"What! Soiled your mittens,
You naughty kittens!"

Then they began to sigh,
"Meow, meow, meow, meow."
Oh, they began to sigh.

The three little kittens, they washed their mittens,
And hung them up to dry;
"Oh, Mommy dear,
Look here, look here,
Our mittens we have washed."
"What! Washed your mittens,
You darling kittens!
But I smell a rat close by!
Hush! Hush! Hush! Hush!
Yes, I smell a rat close by!"

⇨ Note to Instructor: Use these questions to help the child retell the story.
How many kittens were there? *There were three kittens.*
What did the kittens lose? *They lost their mittens.*
How did their mother react when she heard the kittens lost their mittens? *She was angry and she said they could not have pie.*
Why did the mother change her mind and let the kittens eat pie? *The kittens found their mittens.*
Because they ate the pie with their mittens on, what happened to the mittens? *They got dirty.*
How did their mother react when she heard the mittens were dirty? *She told them that they were naughty.*
Then what did the kittens do to their dirty mittens? *They washed them.*
How did their mother react when she heard the kittens washed their mittens? *She was happy with the kittens.*
What do you think will happen to the rat after the story ends? *The mother might catch the rat!*
⇨ Note to Instructor: Remember to write down the child's summary of the story. Let him look back over your written version of his narration after you have finished.

**Enrichment Activity**
The child may write out his own summary of the story.

# Lesson 75

-Nouns, verbs, and pronouns in "The Three Little Kittens"
-Copywork: "The Kittens"
-Poem review: "The Months" (Lesson 43)
* The child will need a pencil and paper.

⇨ Note to Instructor: Review "The Months" today.

Instructor: Let's say the definition of a **noun** together.

Together: **A noun is the name of a person, place, thing, or idea.**

Instructor: Names of animals are also **nouns**. Let's find the **nouns** in the first part of "The Three Little Kittens."

⇨ Note to Instructor: Read the first stanza to the child while you help him to follow along. He should identify the nouns "kittens," "mittens," "mommy," and "pie."

Instructor: Is the **noun** "kittens" a **common noun** or a **proper noun**?

*Child: The noun "kittens" is a common noun.*

⇨ Note to Instructor: If necessary, remind the child that a proper noun would refer to one particular kitten.

Instructor: How many kittens were there?

*Child: There were three kittens.*

Instructor: Can you give each kitten a proper name?

⇨ Note to Instructor: Help the child find a proper name for each kitten.

Instructor: In the first line of the poem, the kittens did something active. What did they do?

*Child: They lost their mittens.*

Instructor: "Lost" is an **action verb**. Remember: **A verb is a word that does an action**. What action do the kittens do in the second line?

*Child: The kittens cry.*

Instructor: In the last verse of the poem, what did the kittens do with their mittens?

*Child: The kittens washed their mittens.*

Instructor: "Washed" is an action verb. In the first line of the last stanza, can you find a **pronoun** that refers to the kittens? Who washed the mittens?

*Child: They washed their mittens.*

Instructor: It is easier to say, "They washed their mittens" than "The kittens washed the kittens' mittens! When the mother says that she smells a rat, what word does she use to refer to herself?

*Child: She calls herself "I."*

Instructor: The **pronoun** "I" is capitalized. If the kittens have to wear mittens to eat their pie, what season is it—spring, summer, fall, or winter?

*Child: It must be winter!*

Instructor: Yes, because it is cold outside! What months are in the winter season?

*Child: December, January, February.*

## Copywork

Ask the child to copy one of the following sentences:

They began to cry.
Hush. I smell a rat close by.
The three little kittens put on their mittens.

## Enrichment Activity

If your child is writing easily, you may wish to have him copy additional lines from the poem.

# Lesson 76

-Initials
-Months of the year
-Days of the week
-Pronouns
-Copywork: "Days of the Week"
* Both the instructor and the child will need a pencil and paper.


Instructor: Let's review some lessons that we've already learned. The first letter of a name is the initial letter. Let's write out the initials of people that we know. Remember, initials are capitalized and have periods after them.

⇨ Note to Instructor: Supply the child with three names of family members or other people he knows well. Write out the full names. Then ask the child to write the initials for each full name.

Instructor: The period that follows an initial is called a punctuation mark. Remember, periods also follow the abbreviations for the months. Let's say the names of the months together.

Together: January, February, March, April, May, June, July, August, September, October, November, December.

Instructor: Now say the days of the week with me, beginning with Sunday.

Together: Sunday, Monday, Tuesday, Wednesday, Thursday, Friday, Saturday.

Instructor: We've already reviewed the definitions of **nouns** and **verbs**. Now, let's review the definition of a **pronoun**. A pronoun is a word that takes the place of a noun. Let's say that together twice.

Together (twice): **A pronoun is a word that takes the place of a noun.**

Instructor: I will read the list of **pronouns**. Say as many of the **pronouns** as you can along with me. *I, me, my, mine; you, your, yours; he, she, him, her, it, his, hers, its; we, us, our, ours; they, them, their, theirs.*

Instructor: Now, I will read you some sentences. Can you fill in the blank with a **pronoun**? On Monday, Jane rode on a bus. ___went to visit Dad at work.

*Child: She went to visit Dad at work.*

Instructor: On Tuesday, Dad stayed home from work. _____ took Jane to the zoo.

*Child: He took Jane to the zoo.*

Instructor: On Wednesday, Jane went back to the zoo to see the tiger. The zoo was her favorite place. She loved _____.
*Child: She loved it.*
Instructor: On Thursday, Jane and Mommy bought the tiger for a house pet. _____ both love tigers.
*Child: They both love tigers.*
Instructor: On Friday, Jane, Mommy, and Daddy decided the tiger would like to have an adventure. So they went on a boat ride and took the tiger with _____.
*Child: So they went on a boat ride and took the tiger with them.*
Instructor: On Saturday, Jane and Mommy and Daddy fed the tiger everything in the refrigerator and in the freezer. The tiger was still hungry. _____ wanted more.
*Child: It [or he, or she] wanted more.*
Instructor: On Sunday, Jane and Mommy and Daddy took the tiger back to the zoo. The zookeeper said, "Only a silly family would want a tiger for a pet! _____ must be a silly family!"
*Child: You must be a silly family.*

## Copywork

Note to Instructor: Write out the days of the week for the child. Ask him to copy as many as he is able.

## Enrichment Activity

Ask the child to write the days of week in order from memory.

# Lesson 77

-Abbreviations
    -Addresses

\* Both the instructor and the child will need a pencil and paper for the lesson. The child will need a crayon and mail for the enrichment activity.


Instructor: Can you tell me your address?

⇨   Note to Instructor: If necessary, prompt child to give the full address.

Instructor: Today we are going to learn how to abbreviate your address. An abbreviation is a shortened form of a word. It usually ends with a period. Today I am going to show you how to write the abbreviations for street, avenue, and road.

⇨   Note to Instructor: As you explain the abbreviations, write them out for the child to see. Point out the capital letters and periods. You may also explain any other abbreviations in the child's address.

Instructor: We abbreviate the word Street as St. We abbreviate the word Avenue as Ave. We abbreviate the word Road as Rd. Now let's write out your address, using the proper abbreviations.

⇨   Note to Instructor: Write out the child's street address for him to copy. Be sure to use the address abbreviations. Do not write out the city, state, and zip code yet. Ask the child to copy his street address with the proper abbreviations.

Instructor: The post office has special abbreviations for the names of states. They do not have periods like regular abbreviations. Every state abbreviation has two letters, and both letters are capitalized. The abbreviation for our state is _____.

⇨   Note to Instructor: Using the current U.S. Post Office abbreviations, write out the child's city, state, and zip code. Ask the child to copy this line under the first address line.

Instructor: Now you know how to write your address with abbreviations.

⇨   Note to Instructor: Write out the names and addresses of family members or friends. Point out abbreviations and state abbreviations to the child as you write.


## Enrichment Activity

Ask the child to collect addresses from your mail. Have him circle abbreviations on the addresses with a crayon.

# Lesson 78

-Introducing titles of respect
-Copywork: "Titles of Respect"
* Both the instructor and the child will need a pencil and paper.

Instructor: Have you noticed that sometimes people's names start with Mr. or Mrs. or Dr. or Miss? These are called "titles of respect." They show that we respect the position of that person. When these titles are written, they are often abbreviated. Do you remember that an abbreviation is brief—meaning "short"? I am going to show you the abbreviated (short) way to write some common titles of respect.

⇨ Note to Instructor: Write out the following titles of respect with their abbreviations. Point out the capital letters and periods as you do so.

| | | |
|---|---|---|
| Mister | Mr. | This is a title for a man. |
| Mistress | Mrs. | This is a title for a married woman. |
| Doctor | Dr. | This is a title for a physician or for someone with a special degree from a university. |
| Miss | — | This is not an abbreviation, but a title of courtesy for an unmarried girl or woman. |
| * | Ms. | *Ms. is an abbreviation for either Mistress or Miss. You should use it when you do not know whether a woman would prefer to be called Mrs. or Miss. |

⇨ Note to Instructor: Run your finger under the words as you read the following sentences aloud. Ask the child to follow along:

Mr. Smith likes to garden.
Mrs. Smith is a writer.
Dr. Rosenberg works at the hospital.
Ms. Lopez is a nurse.
Miss Collins teaches art.

Instructor: Mr., Mrs., Dr., Ms., and Miss are always written with a capital letter.

## Copywork

Have the child copy as many of the following sentences as seems appropriate.

Mr. stands for Mister.
Dr. stands for Doctor.
Mrs. refers to a married woman.
Miss refers to an unmarried woman.
Ms. can refer to any woman.

## Enrichment Activity

Have the child write several sentences that tell what family members and friends do for a living. Make sure that the child uses the appropriate titles in each sentence.

# Lesson 79

-Titles of respect
-Poem review: "The Caterpillar" (Lesson 2)
* The child will need a pencil and paper.


⇨ Note to Instructor: Review "The Caterpillar" today.

Instructor: What mark of punctuation follows each abbreviation?
*Child: A period.*

Instructor: Which title of respect is not an abbreviation?
*Child: Miss.*

Instructor: Which abbreviation stands for a married woman?
*Child: Mrs.*

Instructor: What is the abbreviation for Doctor?
*Child: Dr.*

Instructor: What title should you use if you don't know whether a woman would like to be called Mrs. or Miss?
*Child: Ms.*

⇨ Note to Instructor: I would not introduce the abbreviation Jr. or Sr. now unless the child notices that a close family member uses it.

Instructor: I am going to say each title of respect. On your paper, write the proper abbreviation for each one.

⇨ Note to Instructor: If the child begins to write a title incorrectly, stop him and show him the correct form of the title.

Instructor: Write abbreviations for the following titles of respect: Mister, Miss, Mistress, Ms., Doctor.

# Lesson 80

-Cumulative poem review

Instructor: Today we are going to review all of the poems you have worked on so far. When we recite a poem, we begin with the title and author. I will read each poem to you, and then I want you to try to say the poem back to me. Remember: Stand up straight! Don't fidget while you're reciting! And speak in a nice, loud, slow voice.

⇨ Note to Instructor: Read each poem to the child before asking him to repeat it. If he repeats it accurately, move on to the next poem. If he stumbles, ask him to repeat the line he cannot remember three times, and make a note to review that poem daily until it is mastered. Remind the child that "Anonymous" means that we do not know who wrote the poem.

| Lesson | Poem | Author |
|--------|------|--------|
| 2 | "The Caterpillar" | Christina G. Rossetti |
| 15 | "Work" | Anonymous |
| 27 | "Hearts Are Like Doors" | Anonymous |
| 35 | "Days of the Week" | Mother Goose rhyme adapted by Sara Buffington |
| 43 | "The Months" | Mother Goose rhyme |

# Lesson 81

Poem memorization: "Mr. Nobody"

⇨ Note to Instructor: For this lesson, read the whole poem aloud. Ask the child: Who do you think Mr. Nobody is?

Mr. Nobody
*Anonymous*

I know a funny little man,
  As quiet as a mouse,
Who does the mischief that is done
  In everybody's house!
There's no one ever sees his face,
  And yet we all agree
That every plate we break was cracked
  By Mr. Nobody.

'Tis he who always tears our books,
  Who leaves the door ajar,
He pulls the buttons from our shirts,
  And scatters pins afar;
That squeaking door will always squeak,
  For, prithee, don't you see,
We leave the oiling to be done
  By Mr. Nobody.

The finger marks upon the door
  By none of us are made;
We never leave the blinds unclosed,
  To let the curtains fade.
The ink we never spill; the boots
  That lying 'round you see
Are not our boots—they all belong
  To Mr. Nobody.

⇨ Note to Instructor: Read the first stanza to the child three times in a row. Encourage the child to chime in with you as he becomes more familiar with the words.

# Lesson 82

-Capitalization in poetry
-Copywork: "Mr. Nobody"
-Poem practice: stanza one of "Mr. Nobody" (Lesson 81)
* The child will need a pencil and paper for this activity as well as drawing supplies for the enrichment activity.

⇨　Note to Instructor: Read all of "Mr. Nobody" to the child. Then read stanza one three times in a row. Encourage the child to begin to say the lines along with you.

Instructor: What is the name of this poem?

*Child: "Mr. Nobody"*

Instructor: The name of the poem is its title. All important words in a poem title should be capitalized. The first word of the title and every other word which is not a little word, like "and" or "the" or "of," should begin with a capital letter. Let's look at the titles of your other poems.

The Caterpillar
Work
Hearts Are Like Doors
Days of the Week
The Months

The first word of every title is capitalized. So are all the other words except for "of" and "the." Look at the poem "Mr. Nobody" again. The first word in every line begins with a capital letter. Let's look down the first words and name the capital letters together.

⇨　Note to Instructor: Move your finger down the left-hand margin of the page next to "Mr. Nobody" and help the child identify the capital letters.

Instructor: Titles of poems and the first word of every line should be capitalized.

## Copywork

Choose one of the following options: Ask the child to copy, from "Mr. Nobody":

1) The title and at least two lines of one stanza
2) The title and four lines of one stanza
3) The title, the "Anonymous" author attribution, and at least one full stanza.

Remind the child that "Mr." is an abbreviation for "Mister." It should have both a capital letter and a period.

## Enrichment Activity
Invite the child to illustrate one or more stanzas of "Mr. Nobody."

# Lesson 83

-Pronouns
-Oral usage: "Is / Are"
-Poem practice: stanza one of "Mr. Nobody" (Lesson 81)

⇨   Note to Instructor: Continue work on stanza one of "Mr. Nobody."
Review helpful poetry memorization techniques from Lesson 2.

Instructor: Let's say the definition of a **pronoun** together.

Together: **A pronoun is a word that takes the place of a noun.**

Instructor: I will read the list of **pronouns**. Say as many of the
**pronouns** as you can along with me. *I, me, my, mine; you, your,*
*yours; he, she, him, her, it, his, hers, its; we, us, our, ours; they, them,*
*their, theirs.* Today we are going to talk about "we, us, our, ours." I am
going to read some sentences and then ask you a question. I want you
to answer using one of the **pronouns** "we, us, our, or ours."

Instructor: We planted sunflower seeds. Who planted sunflower
seeds?

*Child: We planted sunflower seeds.*

Instructor: For whom did the seeds grow?

*Child: The seeds grew for us.*

Instructor: Now, who owns the flowers?

*Child: Now, the flowers are ours.*

Instructor: Are they your flowers?

*Child: They are our flowers.*

## Oral Usage Exercise

Instructor: If you are speaking about one person or thing, use the word
"is." If you are speaking about more than one person or thing, use the
word "are." I will read you several sentences. Choose the correct
word to put in the blank.

Instructor: My pencil ___ in my pocket.

*Child: My pencil is in my pocket.*

Instructor: My pencils ___ all yellow.

*Child: My pencils are all yellow.*

Instructor: Cherries ____ my favorite fruit.

*Child: Cherries are my favorite fruit.*

Instructor: I like cherries because they ___ red.

*Child: I like cherries because they are red.*

Instructor: Mr. Nance and Dr. Alvarez _____ going fishing together.

# Lesson 84

-Oral composition: "Mr. Nobody At Our House"
-Copywork: "Mr. Nobody At Our House"
-Poem practice: "Mr. Nobody"
* Both the instructor and the child will need a pencil and paper.

⇨  Note to Instructor: Read stanza one of "Mr. Nobody" to the child. Ask the child to recite these lines back to you. Then read stanza two out loud to the child three times in a row. Ask the child to join in whenever he is able.
Instructor: Can you tell me some of the things in our house that are done by Mr. Nobody?

⇨  Note to Instructor: Encourage the child to think about the messes that no one admits to! Help him to form these ideas into complete sentences. Write them down in neat handwriting and help him to read the sentences out loud. Write "Mr. Nobody at Our House" at the top of the paper.
Instructor: The title of our own composition is "Mr. Nobody at Our House." Which words are capitalized? Which word is not capitalized?

## Copywork

Ask the child to copy one or more of the sentences you composed for the lesson.

## Enrichment Activity

Ask the child to write a description (either a list or a paragraph) about the things that Mr. Nobody does at your house.

# Lesson 85

-Abbreviations
    -Initials and addresses
-Poem practice: stanzas one and two of "Mr. Nobody" (Lesson 81)
* Both the instructor and the child need a pencil and paper. The child also needs one business size envelope for the lesson and several for the enrichment activity.

⇨ Note to Instructor: Read stanzas one and two of "Mr. Nobody" out loud to the child three times. Then ask the child to begin reciting the poem and to go as far as possible.

⇨ Note to Instructor: Draw light lines on a business size envelope to guide the child in properly addressing a real envelope. On a sheet of paper, write addresses for him to copy. Help the child practice copying his own address in the upper left-hand corner. Then help him copy the name and address of a friend or family member in the proper place on the same envelope. Make sure that you point out the road, street, and avenue abbreviations as well as the state abbreviations. Remind the child that most abbreviations have a capital letter and a period, but that state abbreviations are special. Both letters of a state abbreviation are capitalized, and there is no punctuation mark. When the envelope is completed, ask the child to mail a picture that he has drawn or the description of Mr. Nobody completed in the last lesson to the friend or relative.

## Enrichment Activity

The child will address envelopes to his brothers and sisters, put a picture or message in each, and mail them.

# Lesson 86

-Capitalization and punctuation in poetry
-Copywork: "The Star"
-Poem practice: stanzas one and two of "Mr. Nobody" (Lesson 81)
* The child will need a pencil and paper.

⇨ Note to Instructor: Read stanzas one and two of "Mr. Nobody" out loud to the child twice. Then ask the child to begin reciting the poem and to go as far as possible. Next, read the final stanza of "Mr. Nobody" out loud to the child three times. Ask the child to try to recite the poem from the beginning.

⇨ Note to Instructor: Later in the day, repeat this process.

## Copywork

Read the child the poem "The Star," by Jane Taylor (1783–1824). Ask the child to finish one of the following assignments. Remind him that titles and first words of poem lines should be capitalized.

1. Copy the title, author, and two lines.
2. Copy the title, author, and one stanza.
3. Copy the title, author, and 6–8 lines.

The Star
by Jane Taylor

Twinkle, twinkle, little star,
How I wonder what you are!
Up above the world so high,
Like a diamond in the sky.

When the blazing sun is gone,
When he nothing shines upon,
Then you show your little light,
Twinkle, twinkle, all the night.

Then the traveller in the dark,
Thanks you for your tiny spark.
He could not see which way to go
If you did not twinkle so.

In the dark blue sky you keep
And often through my curtains peep,
For you never shut your eye
Till the sun is in the sky.

As your bright and tiny spark
Lights the traveller in the dark –
Though I know not what you are,
Twinkle, twinkle, little star.

# Lesson 87

-Story narration: "The Boy Who Cried Wolf"
-Poem practice: "Mr. Nobody" (Lesson 81)
* The instructor will need a pencil and paper. The child will need a pencil and paper for the enrichment activity.

⇨ Note to Instructor: Read all three stanzas of "Mr. Nobody" out loud to the child twice. Ask the child to begin reciting and to go as far as possible. For any stanzas that the child cannot remember, repeat them out loud three times.

⇨ Note to Instructor: Read aloud the Aesop's fable below. Have the child tell the story back to you in his own words; use the suggested questions if the child needs prompting. Write the narration down for the child.

## The Boy Who Cried "Wolf"

A young boy kept sheep on a hillside near his home in a village. They were his very own sheep, and when the sheep were sheared, he was allowed to keep the money from the sale of the wool.

While he was on the hillside one warm spring day, he could see the women working in their gardens, and the men working together repairing the thatched roofs. The young shepherd thought that watching the sheep was boring and so he decided to play a trick on the villagers. He ran down the hillside toward the village loudly screaming, "Wolf! Wolf! There is a wolf after my sheep!"

The villagers quickly stopped their work and ran frantically up the hill to rescue the boy's sheep from the wolves. When they arrived where the boy's sheep were quietly grazing, the boy was waiting there. He laughed at them for hurrying so when there was no wolf.

The boy was so amused by the trick he had played on the villagers that he decided to try it again the next week. He ran down the hillside again, loudly screaming, "Wolf! Wolf!"

The kind villagers again quickly stopped their work and ran frantically up the hill to rescue the boy's sheep from the wolves. When they arrived where the boy's sheep were grazing, the boy laughed at them again for hurrying so when there was not a wolf.

The next week a real wolf attacked his flock and started to kill the little lambs. The boy ran down the hillside, loudly screaming, "Wolf! Wolf! There is a wolf after my sheep!"

But the villagers thought he was just playing another trick on them. "Leave us alone!" they snapped at him. "We have work to do! Go back up to your sheep and stop annoying us." And they turned their backs on the boy. No one came to help him—and he lost all of his sheep to the hungry wolf.

Moral: If you tell lies, people will not believe you when you do tell the truth.

⇨ Note to Instructor: Use these questions to help the child summarize the story.

What was the job of the young boy? *He watched a flock of sheep.*
Who did the sheep belong to? *They belonged to the boy.*
When the boy became bored, what did he decide to do? *He decided to play a trick on the villagers.*
What did he tell the villagers? *He said a wolf was eating his sheep.*
How did the villagers respond to the news? *They ran up the hill to help him.*
What did they discover when they ran up the hill? *The boy was lying. There was no wolf.*
Did the boy feel bad about lying? *No, he thought it was funny.*
Because the boy thought the trick was so funny, what did he do the next week? *He played the trick again.*
What happened the week after that? *A wolf really did attack his sheep.*
When the boy told all the villagers about the real wolf, what did they do? *They kept working.*
Why didn't they help the boy? *They thought he was playing another trick.*
What happened to the boy's sheep? *They were killed by the wolf.*
What is the moral of the story? *If you tell lies, no one will believe you when you tell the truth.*

## Enrichment Activity

If the child is writing easily, ask him to write part or all of his own summary after he tells it to you.

# Lesson 88

-Introducing writing dates
-Copywork: "Writing Dates"
-Poem review: "Mr. Nobody" (Lesson 81)
* Both the instructor and the child will need a pencil and paper.


⇨ Note to Instructor: Read all three stanzas of "Mr. Nobody" out loud to the child twice. Ask the child to begin reciting and to go as far as possible. For any stanzas that the child cannot remember, repeat them out loud three times.

Instructor: We have talked about the names of the days of the week. Let's say them together.

Together: Sunday, Monday, Tuesday, Wednesday, Thursday, Friday, Saturday.

Instructor: We have also talked about the names of the months. Let's say those together as well.

Together: January, February, March, April, May, June, July, August, September, October, November, December.

Instructor: Every day of the year has a date. A date is made up of the month of the year, a number telling you what day of the month it is, and a number telling you what year it is. For example, "Thirty days hath September." September has thirty days in it. So the last day of September would be "September 30." Every day of the month has a number. Today is [today's date]. It is the [number] day of the month of [name of month]. Every year also has a number. This year is 20—. Last year was 20—. Next year will be 20—. You were born in ____.

⇨ Note to Instructor: Write out for the child the date on which he was born, and the dates on which any siblings or friends of a similar age were born.

Instructor: When we write a date, we write the month and the day. Then we put a comma between the day and the year.

⇨ Note to Instructor: Show child how to make a comma.

Instructor: I want you to practice making ten neat commas on your own paper.

## Copywork

Ask the child to copy one of the following phrases or sentences. Write the assignment out for the child.

1. [The date on which the child was born, including month, day, and year, with a comma between day and year]
2. I was born on [date].
3. I was born on [date] during the [season – winter, spring, summer or fall].

# Lesson 89

-Dates

-Poem review: "Mr. Nobody" (Lesson 81)

* Both the instructor and the child will need a pencil and paper for this lesson.

⇨ Note to Instructor: Continue to review "Mr. Nobody."

⇨ Note to Instructor: Discuss important dates (days, months, and years) for your family with the child: birthdays of parents and grandparents, holidays the family celebrates, national holidays, or dates of religious significance. Write these dates out. Ask the child to copy four, six, or eight of these dates onto his own paper. Remind him to capitalize the names of months and to place commas between the day and year of each date. You may also use any of the following dates:

| March 15, 44 BC | The Ides of March | Julius Caesar was killed |
| June 15, 1212 | — | King John signed Magna Carta |
| July 4, 1776 | Independence Day | America declared independence |
| July 20, 1969 | — | Neil Armstrong set foot on the moon |
| October 12, 1492 | — | Columbus landed in the New World |
| October 14, 1066 | — | The Battle of Hastings |

## Enrichment Activity

Show the child how to write today's date at the top of a sheet of paper for a friendly letter. Encourage him to write two or three sentences to a friend. Help him to address this letter and mail it.

# Lesson 90

-Seasons
-Use of "I"
-Copywork: "In the Spring I..."
-Poem review: "Mr. Nobody" (Lesson 81)
* Both the instructor and the child will need a pencil and paper.


⇨   Note to Instructor: Continue to review "Mr. Nobody."

Instructor:  Do you remember the four seasons: winter, spring, summer and fall?  What months are the coldest months—the winter months?

*Child:  The winter months are December, January, and February.*

Instructor:  What do you do in winter? Do you celebrate any holidays? How is the weather different from spring and summer?

*Child:  In the winter I...*

⇨   Note to Instructor: Help the child to answer these questions, if necessary.  Remember that answers should be in complete sentences.

Instructor:  After the winter comes spring.  The weather begins to be warmer.  What months are the months of spring? (You may have to start the year for the child, "January, February...")

*Child:  The spring months are March, April, and May.*

Instructor:  What happens to trees and flowers  in spring? What did the trees look like before spring? What flowers do you enjoy looking at? What is spring weather like?

*Child:  In the spring...*

Instructor:  After spring come summer.  What months are the months of summer? (Start naming the months of the year—January, February, March, April, May...)

*Child:  The summer months are June, July, and August.*

Instructor:  What is your favorite thing about summer? Do you have special company?  Do you take a trip? Where do you go to cool off?

⇨   Note to Instructor: If going to the pool, lake, or beach is an activity the child may actually do in summer, suggest that the child use the some of the following list of words to give him ideas: sprinkler, water, pool, lake, boat, fish, beach, shells, sand, ocean.

*Child:  My favorite thing about summer is...*

Instructor:  After winter, spring, and summer comes fall. What are the fall months?

⇨   Note to Instructor: Prompt the child by beginning to name the months of the year, January, February, March, April, May, June, July, August...

*Child:  The fall months are September, October, November.*

Instructor: What do you see happening in fall? Do the leaves on trees change color? Is the weather as hot as it was in summer? What holidays do you celebrate in fall?

*Child: In the fall I...*

⇨ Note to Instructor: Write out one of the "I" statements that the child made in describing the seasons.

## Copywork

Ask the child to copy the "I" statement which you wrote out for him. Remind him that the pronoun "I" is always capitalized.

## Enrichment Activity

Ask the child to write four "I" statements, one about each season. The statements should follow the pattern, "In the [season], I like to..."

# Lesson 91

-Story-poem narration: "Sunflowers"
-Poem review: "Hearts Are Like Doors" (Lesson 27)
* The instructor will need scissors and either a pencil and paper or a photocopy of the poem for the enrichment activity.

⇨ Note to Instructor: Review "Hearts Are Like Doors" today.
⇨ Note to Instructor: Read "Sunflowers" aloud to the child and then have the child tell it back to you. The purpose of this exercise is to retell the sentences in the proper order. As necessary, use the questions following the poem to guide his recall of the sequence.

Sunflowers
*Jessie Wise*

Ben planted sunflower seeds.
The rain fell.
The sun warmed the soil.
Ben waited two weeks.
The seeds sprouted.
One plant grew huge leaves.
A big bud formed on the stem.
A gigantic flower opened.

Who planted? *Ben planted.*
What did he plant? *He planted sunflower seeds.*
What two things were needed before the seeds sprouted? *The seeds needed sunlight and rain to sprout.*
Did they sprout right away? *No, it took awhile for the seeds to sprout.*
How long did Ben have to wait for the seeds to sprout? *Ben waited two weeks.*
After the plant sprouted, tell three things that the plant grew. *The plant grew leaves, a bud, and a flower.*
Which grew first? *The leaves grew first.*
Which grew second? *The bud grew second.*
Which grew third? *The flower opened third.*

## Enrichment Activity

Photocopy or write out the sentences. Cut them apart and have the child put them back into order again.

# Lesson 92

-Introducing sentences
-Copywork: "Practice Makes Perfect"
-Poem review: "Mr. Nobody" (Lesson 81)
* The child will need a pencil and paper.


⇨ Note to Instructor: Continue to review "Mr. Nobody."

Instructor: Today we are going to begin to learn about **sentences**. I will say the definition of a sentence for you three times. **A sentence is a group of words that expresses a complete thought.**

⇨ Note to Instructor: Repeat three times.

Instructor: Now let's say that definition together three times.

Together (three times): **A sentence is a group of words that expresses a complete thought.**

Instructor: A **sentence** begins with a capital letter and ends with a punctuation mark. Let's look at the **sentences** from the last lesson. Can you show me the capital letter at the beginning of each **sentence**? Can you show me the punctuation mark at the end of each **sentence**?


Ben planted sunflower seeds.
The rain fell.
The sun warmed the soil.
Ben waited two weeks.
The seeds sprouted.
One plant grew huge leaves.
A big bud formed  on the stem.
A gigantic flower opened.


Instructor: **A sentence is a group of words that expresses a complete thought.** Listen to the difference between these two groups of words.

Ben planted sunflower seeds.
Sunflower seeds.

Which group of words expresses a complete thought? The first one. The second group of words is a "**fragment,**" not a **sentence**! **A fragment means a piece of something.** I will read you several groups of words. Listen to each, and tell me which group of words is a **sentence** and which is not.

One plant grew huge leaves.  (sentence)
Grew huge leaves.  (fragment)

The dinosaurs roamed over the land.  (sentence)
The dinosaurs.  (fragment)

Children on the soccer field.  (fragment)
Children on the soccer field whooped for joy.  (sentence)

Chocolate candy is the.  (fragment)
Chocolate candy is the best dessert of all.  (sentence)

## Copywork

Choose one of the following sentences for the child to copy. After he
has finished, ask him to show you the capital letter and the ending
punctuation mark.

1. Practice makes perfect.
2. Do to others as you would have them do to you.
3. Never leave for tomorrow what you can do today.

# Lesson 93

-Introducing sentence type 1: statements

* The child will need a pencil and paper for the enrichment activity.

Instructor:  Listen to the definition of a **sentence.  A sentence is a group of words that expresses a complete thought.** Let's say that together three times.

Together (three times): **A sentence is a group of words that expresses a complete thought.**

Instructor:  All **sentences** begin with a capital letter and end with a punctuation mark. There are four different types of sentences. Today, we are going to talk about first type of sentence — **statements**. Statements tell you something. **Statements give information.** They end with a period.   Here are several statements that tell you something and give you information.

The wind blows.

The girl skates.

The dogs run.

Trees have green leaves.

Cement is hard.

Now let's look back at the sentences in "Sunflowers" (Lesson 91) Each one of these sentences is a statement.  Each statement tells us something about Ben or about the sunflowers.  Point to the capital letter at the beginning of each statement.  Now show me the period at the end.

⇨  Note to Instructor: Ask the child to make five statements about people or objects he can see in the room where he is sitting.  Make sure that these are complete sentences that give information.

## Enrichment Activity

Ask the child to make a statement giving information about a member of your family. He will begin the statement with the person's name. Then ask him to make a statement about himself, beginning with "I." He may write these statements, remembering to begin each statement with a capital letter and to end each statement with a period.

# Lesson 94

-Introducing sentence type 2: commands
-Copywork: "Fried Octopus"
-Poem review: "Days of the Week" (Lesson 35)
* The child will need a pencil and paper.

⇨ Note to Instructor: Review "Days of the Week" today.

Instructor: Now let's say the definition of a **sentence** together.

Together: **A sentence is a group of words that expresses a complete thought.**

Instructor: All **sentences** begin with a capital letter and end with a punctuation mark. Let's say that together three times.

Together (three times): All sentences begin with a capital letter and end with a punctuation mark.

Instructor: Last lesson we talked about the first type of sentence: the **statement. Statements give information.** Let's repeat that together three times: **Statements give information.**

Together (three times): **Statements give information.**

Instructor: Can you make a **statement** about yourself? Begin with "I am…"

*Child: I am… [a boy, a girl, hungry, thirsty, etc.]*

Instructor: There are four types of **sentences**. Today I am going to tell you about the second type of **sentence**: The **command. Commands give an order or make a request.** Let's say that together three times.

Together (three times): **Commands give an order or make a request.**

Instructor: Commands usually end with a period. I am going to give you some commands or requests:

Pick up your book.
Stand up.
Come here.

Other commands or requests you have heard are:

Come to breakfast.
Eat your supper.
Put your books away.
Pick up your toys.

Now it is your turn to give me some commands!

⇨ Note to Instructor: Allow the child to give you reasonable commands. You may want to lay some ground rules first!

Instructor: Now we have learned about two types of sentences. Statements give information. Commands give an order or make a request.

## Copywork

According to the child's ability, choose one to three of these commands and have the child copy them. Remind the child that sentences begin with capital letters and that commands usually end with a period.

1. Eat neatly.
2. Do not eat with your toes.
3. Wipe your mouth after eating the fried octopus.

## Enrichment Activity

Make a game of having the child give requests and commands to different members of the family. Silly, fun requests and commands are allowed if they are possible. If the child is writing easily, have him list these on paper. He may title the paper "Requests and Commands."

# Lesson 95

-Introducing sentence type 3: questions
-Copywork: "Smaller Than an Elephant"
\* Both the instructor and the child will need a pencil and paper. Also, in preparation for the lesson, consult your penmanship curriculum for the style of the question mark, which can differ from program to program.

Instructor: Let's say the definition of a **sentence** together.

Together: **A sentence is a group of words that expresses a complete thought.**

Instructor: All sentences begin with a capital letter and end with a punctuation mark. Now let's say that together.

Together: All sentences begin with a capital letter and end with a punctuation mark.

Instructor: We have talked about **sentences** that are **statements** and **sentences** that are **commands**. Which type of **sentence** gives information?

*Child: A statement gives information.*

Instructor: Which type of **sentence** gives an order or makes a request?

*Child: A command gives an order or makes a request.*

Instructor: Today we are going to talk about a third type of **sentence**. **A sentence that asks something is called a question.** It ends with a question mark. Now I am going to ask you some questions. I'll ask the **question** and you answer the **question** in a complete **sentence**.

Instructor: What is your name?

*Child: My name is _____.*

Instructor: You just answered my **question** with a **statement**. You gave me information. Now I will ask you another **question**. What is your favorite food?

*Child: My favorite food is _____.*

Instructor: What type of **sentence** did you just use?

*Child: I just used a statement.*

Instructor: Now you may ask me a **question**.

⇨ Note to Instructor: Answer in a complete sentence! Point out that you have used a statement to answer a question.

Instructor: What type of **sentence** is this? "Tell me your birthday."

*Child. That is a command.*

163

Instructor: What type of **sentence** is, "When is your birthday?"
*Child: That is a question.*
Instructor: Now you know three different types of **sentences. A statement gives information. A command gives an order or makes a request. And a question asks something.** The answers to **questions** are usually **statements.** What punctuation mark comes at the end of a **statement** or **command**?
*Child: Statements and commands end with periods.*
Instructor: What punctuation mark comes at the end of a **question**?
*Child: A question mark comes at the end of a question.*
Instructor: I will show you how to make a question mark. Then I want you to practice making five question marks on your own paper.

## Copywork
Instructor: According to the child's ability, choose one to three of the following questions.

1. How much do you weigh?
2. Are you bigger than a kangaroo?
3. Are you bigger than a dog and smaller than an elephant?

## Enrichment Activity
Play the commands and questions game, "May I?" The instructor gives a command such as, "Stand up." Then follow with possible commands such as: "Pick up your pencil," "Come here," Turn around," "Pick up one foot," "Put your foot down," etc. Before the student obeys the command, he must say, "May I?" If he fails to ask "May I?" he must sit down where he is until told to stand up again.

# Lesson 96

-Introducing sentence type 4: exclamations

-Copywork: "The Pig Is Radiant!"

* Both the instructor and the child will need a pencil and paper.


Instructor: Now, we have talked about three types of **sentences**. **Statements give us information. Commands give an order or make a request. Questions ask something.** What does a **question** do?

*Child: A question asks something.*

Instructor:  What does a **command** do?

*Child:  A command gives an order or makes a request.*

Instructor: What does a **statement** do?

*Child: A statement gives information.*

Instructor.  The fourth type of **sentence** is called an **exclamation**. **An exclamation shows sudden or strong feeling.** It ends with an exclamation point.  Some sudden or strong feelings are excitement, surprise, fear, and anger. Here are some **exclamations** that show strong feeling and end with exclamation points.

⇨    Note to Instructor:  When reading exclamatory sentences, speak louder and use lots of expression!

Instructor:

I won!

Ouch, I touched that hot stove!

Help, I can't swim!

The sink is running over!

Watch out for the giant pink alien!

There is a twelve-legged spider on your head!

Instructor:  I am going to make a **statement**.  "A pig with wings just flew by the window."  Can you make that into a **question**?

*Child: Did a pig with wings just fly by the window?*

Instructor:  Now can you make that into an **exclamation**?

*Child: A pig with wings just flew by the window!*

Instructor:  Look at the pig with wings.  What type of sentence is that?

Child: That is a **command**.

Instructor: I am going to make an exclamation point for you.  Then, you make a line of ten neat exclamation points on your own paper.

## Copywork

Ask the child to copy one to three of the following sentences. Remind him to begin each sentence with a capital letter and end it with an exclamation point.

1.  The pig is radiant!
2.  The radiant pig is doing a backflip!
3.  That spider just wove words into her web!

## Enrichment Activity

Let the child read the exclamatory sentences above, speaking loudly and using lots of expression!

# Lesson 97

-Four types of sentences

\* The child may need a pencil and paper for the enrichment activity.

Instructor: Remember, all **sentences** begin with capital letters and end with punctuation marks. As we read the **sentences** below about a sunflower garden, I want you to point to the capital letter at the beginning of each **sentence** and say, "All sentences begin with a capital letter." We will read the sentences together. When we have finished reading the **sentence**, tell me what mark of punctuation is at the end of each, and what type of **sentence** it is.

⇨ Note to Instructor: If the child cannot yet read these sentences, read them aloud while moving your finger beneath the words. When necessary, guide the child by asking questions.

*Child (reads):* Ben planted sunflower seeds.

Instructor: What kind of letter begins all **sentences**?

*Child (Pointing to beginning of sentence): All sentences begin with a capital letter.*

Instructor: What type of **sentence** is this?

*Child: This sentence is a statement.*

Instructor: A **statement** ends with what kind of punctuation mark?

*Child (Pointing to end of sentence): A statement ends with a period.*

*Child (reads):* Do not step where I planted seeds.

Instructor: What kind of letter begins all **sentences**?

*Child: (Pointing to beginning of sentence) All sentences begin with a capital letter.*

Instructor: This **sentence** isn't a **statement**. What does this **sentence** do?

*Child: This sentence gives an order or a makes a request.*

Instructor: This **sentence** is a **command**. With what kind of punctuation mark does a **command** or a request usually end?

*Child: A command or a request usually ends with a period.*

167

*Child (reads):* When will the sunflowers ever come up?

Instructor: What kind of letter begins all **sentences**?

*Child (pointing to beginning of sentence): All sentences begin with a capital letter.*

Instructor: What type of **sentence** is this?

*Child: This sentence is a question.*

Instructor: With what kind of punctuation mark does a **question** end?

*Child: A question ends with a question mark.*

*Child (reads):* Wow! My sunflower is huge!

Instructor: What kind of letter begins all **sentences**?

*Child: (Pointing to beginning of sentence) All sentences begin with a capital letter.*

Instructor: What type of **sentence** is this?

*Child: This sentence is an exclamation.*

Instructor: What does an **exclamation** do?

*Child: An exclamation shows sudden or strong feeling.*

Instructor: With what punctuation mark does an **exclamation** end?

*Child: An exclamation ends with an exclamation point.*

## Enrichment Activity

Have the child make up one of each type of sentence. If he is writing easily, he should write the sentence with correct capitalization and punctuation.

# Lesson 98

-Nouns
-Types of sentences
-Verbs

Instructor: Let's say the definition of a **noun** together.
Together: **A noun is the name of a person, place, thing, or idea.**
Instructor: Can you make a **statement** about a person in this room?
*Child: [statement]*
Instructor: Can you ask a **question** about a place you would like to visit?
*Child: [question]*
Instructor: Can you give me a **command**? Tell me what to do with a thing in this room.
*Child : [command]*
Instructor: Finally, make a strong **exclamation** about an idea—a feeling such as joy, surprise, happiness, or fear.
*Child: [exclamation]*
Instructor: I am going to say the definition of a **verb** three times for you.
Instructor (repeat three times): **A verb is a word that does an action, shows a state of being, links two words together, or helps another verb.**
Instructor: Now I want you to repeat parts of this definition after me: **A verb is a word that does an action.**
*Child: A verb is a word that does an action*
Instructor: Now listen to the second part of the definition: **Shows a state of being.** Repeat that for me.
*Child: Shows a state of being.*
Instructor: **Links two words together.**
*Child repeats: Links two words together.*
Instructor: **Or helps another verb.**
*Child repeats: Or helps another verb.*
Instructor: Now you have learned all about **nouns** and **verbs**—and about the four types of **sentences** that use them! I think that you should run around and do some **action verbs** instead of doing copywork today!

# Lesson 99

-Cumulative poem review

Instructor: Today we are going to review all of the poems you have worked on so far. When we recite a poem, we begin with the title and author. I will read each poem to you, and then I want you to try to say the poem back to me. Remember: Stand up straight! Don't fidget while you're reciting! And speak in a nice, loud, slow voice.

⇨ Note to Instructor: Read each poem to the child before asking him to repeat it. If he repeats it accurately, move on to the next poem. If he stumbles, ask him to repeat the line he cannot remember three times, and make a note to review that poem daily until it is mastered. Remind the child that "Anonymous" means we don't know who wrote the poem.

| Lesson | Poem | Author |
|---|---|---|
| 2 | "The Caterpillar" | Christina G. Rossetti |
| 15 | "Work" | Anonymous |
| 27 | "Hearts Are Like Doors" | Anonymous |
| 35 | "Days of the Week" | Mother Goose rhyme adapted by Sara Buffington |
| 43 | "The Months" | Mother Goose rhyme |
| 81 | "Mr. Nobody" | Anonymous |

## Lesson 100
-Identifying sentences in "The Goops"

Instructor: For this lesson, I am going to read you a poem about the Goops. Can you find an **exclamation** in this poem? Can you find a **question**? Can you find a **statement**?

⇨ Note to Instructor: Because this is cast into poetic form, you should consider each line to be a separate sentence, with the exception of the last two lines; "And that is why I'm glad that I am not a Goop," is one sentence, while "Are you?" is a separate sentence. "Oh, they lead disgusting lives!" is an exclamation. "Are you?" is a question. The other lines in the poem are statements.

"The Goops"
*By Gelett Burgess*

The Goops they lick their fingers,
And the Goops they lick their knives,
They spill their broth on the tablecloth-
Oh, they lead disgusting lives!

The Goops they talk while eating,
And loud and fast they chew,
And that is why I'm glad that I
Am not a Goop - are you?

# The End of First Grade

⇨ Note to Instructor: Reread page 17 in the introduction for instructions on how to proceed from one year to the next.

# Second Grade

⇨ Note to Instructor: Assume that lessons 101-200 all require that both the instructor and the child have a pencil and paper. Additional supplies will be listed at the beginning of each lesson. If you wish to gather all your supplies in advance, you will need colored pencils, crayons, markers, construction paper, a folder, a highlighter marker, glue, scissors, two or more business size envelopes, first class letter stamps, five or more postcards, first class postcard stamps, a pack of index cards, a place setting (fork, knife, spoon, plate, glass, napkin), and a tape recorder. You will also need a dictionary and a thesaurus. My favorites for this age are *Merriam-Webster's Elementary Dictionary* (2000) and *Roget's Children's Thesaurus* (Scott Foresman-Addison Wesley, 1994).

⇨ Note to Instructor on Oral Usage: Because the second half of the book gives priority to writing exercises, oral usage exercises are no longer included. For additional practice in proper speech, use *Oral Language Exercise, Grades One Through Six* by William A. Kappele (Pensacola, FL: A Beka Book Publication, 1982). This book can be ordered from A Beka Book at www.abeka.com or 1-877-223-5226.

# Lesson 101

-Noun review

Instructor: **A noun is the name of a person, place, thing, or idea.** Repeat that definition with me.

Together: **A noun is the name of a person, place, thing, or idea.**

Instructor: **A common noun is the name of any person, place, thing, or idea.** Can you tell me what a **proper noun** is?

*Child: A proper noun is the special, particular name of a person, place, thing, or idea.*

⇨ Note to Instructor: Help child with this definition, if necessary. "Proper noun" and "proper name" both have the same meaning.

Instructor: Is "boy" a **proper or common noun?**

*Child: "Boy" is a common noun.*

⇨ Note to Instructor: Remember to encourage child to answer in complete sentences.

Instructor: Can you give me a **proper noun** that names a particular boy?

*Child: [name]*

Instructor: Is "girl" a **proper or common noun?**

*Child: "Girl" is a common noun.*

Instructor: Can you give me a **proper noun** that names a particular girl?

*Child: [name]*

Instructor: Can you tell me some **common nouns** that name places?

*Child: [city, park, store, library, room, yard, etc.]*

Instructor: Now, can you think of a **proper name** for one of these places?

*Child: [Child names familiar proper name for a place]*

⇨ Note to Instructor: Help child think of a proper name for a store, restaurant, or other familiar landmark.

Instructor: There are lots and lots of common things in the world. I will name some of them, and I want you to give me **proper names** for them. The first is "toy." There are many, many toys. What is the **proper name** of one of your toys?

*Child: [Gives proper brand name of a toy—Legos™, Hot Wheels™]*

Instructor: **Nouns are names of persons, places, and things. Nouns also name ideas.** Remember, an idea is something that you can think about or feel, but not touch or see. Happiness, joy, freedom, sadness, and excitement are all **nouns**. They are names of ideas. Here are some sentences that use "idea" **nouns**.

⇨ Note to Instructor: Emphasize the names of ideas in the following sentences.

*Happiness* can be shared.

She was filled with *joy* when her kitty was rescued.

A caged bird has no *freedom*.

*Excitement* filled the room during the birthday party.

*Sadness* makes me want to cry.

I was filled with *fear* when I was lost.

Instructor: Can you make up a sentence about an idea?

⇨ Note to Instructor: Help the child say out loud complete sentences that have "idea" nouns in them.

# Lesson 102

-Poem memorization: "The Goops" (Lesson 100)
-Copywork: "The Goops"
-Poem review: "Mr. Nobody" (Lesson 81)
* You will need a pencil and paper for this lesson as well as drawing supplies for the enrichment activity.

⇨    Note to Instructor: Review "Mr. Nobody" today.

Instructor: We have learned that the name of a poem—its title—and the first word in every line of poetry should be capitalized. Let's look back at the poem "The Goops" together. How many words does the title have in it?

*Child: The title has two words in it.*

Instructor: Both words are capitalized. "The" is capitalized because it is the first word of the title. "Goops" is capitalized because it is an important word in the title. Now run your finger down the left-hand side of the poem. There is a capital letter at the beginning of each line. The first word of every line of a poem should be capitalized. Now we will work on memorizing this poem. I will read it out loud to you three times.

⇨    Note to Instructor: Read the poem out loud three times. Later in the day, read it again three times. See Lesson 2 for memorization techniques.

## Copywork:

Choose one of the following copywork assignments, depending on the child's ability. You may want to copy the assignment in the style of print that the child is using in his handwriting lessons.

1. The Goops
   Gelett Burgess
2. They spill their broth on the tablecloth.
3. They spill their broth on the tablecloth.
   Oh, they lead disgusting lives!

## Enrichment Activity

The child can copy the poem "The Goops" and illustrate it.

# Lesson 103

-Verbs

      -Action verbs

-Capitalizing "I"

-Copywork: "The Baby and I"

-Poem practice: "The Goops" (Lesson 100)

⇨   Note to Instructor: Read "The Goops" three times.  Encourage the child to chime in as he is able.

Instructor: Let's review the definition of a **verb. A verb is a word that does an action, shows a state of being, links two words together, or helps another verb.**

Instructor: Now I want you to repeat parts of this definition after me: **A verb is a word that does an action.**

*Child: A verb is a word that does an action.*

Instructor: Now listen to the second part of the definition: **Shows a state of being.**  Repeat that for me.

*Child: Shows a state of being.*

Instructor: **Links two words together.**

*Child repeats: Links two words together.*

Instructor: **Or helps another verb.**

*Child repeats: Or helps another verb.*

Instructor:  **A verb is a word that does an action.**  Let's think of some **action verbs** together.

⇨   Note to Instructor: Help child to think of action verbs such as: walk, stoop, run, laugh, write, erase, cry, skip, throw, catch, dance, eat, skip, roll, fall, jump, eat, sing, sleep, jump, skate, talk, read, kick, hit, crawl, hop, bark, dance, play, look, paint, climb, swing, float, fly, open, close, move, race, smell, shout, yell, laugh, clean, bark, squeak, mew, roar, growl.

Instructor: If you were doing these **verbs**, you would use the word "I" to tell me about it.  You would say, "I run," or "I crawl," or "I smell," or "I laugh."  You use the word "I" instead of saying your own name. Do you remember what we call a word that takes the place of a noun?

*Child: A pronoun is a word that takes the place of a noun.*

⇨   Note to Instructor: Prompt child for this definition, if necessary.

Instructor:  The **pronoun** "I" is always capitalized.  I will write "I run" out for you so that you see the capital "I."

⇨   Note to Instructor: Write "I run" and several other "I" sentences, using action verbs, while the child watches.  Point out the capital I in each sentence.

## Copywork

Note to Instructor: Choose one of the following sentences.

1. The baby and I crawl.
2. The baby and I crawl and wallow together.
3. The baby and I crawl, wallow, and giggle together.

# Lesson 104

-Pronouns
-Copywork: "Emily Sang"
-Poem review: "The Goops" (Lesson 100)

⇨ Note to Instructor: Review "The Goops" today. Encourage the child to say the poem alone.

Instructor: **A pronoun is a word used in the place of a noun.** Let's say that definition together three times.

Together (three times): **A pronoun is a word used in the place of a noun.**

Instructor: You use the **pronouns** "I, me, my, mine" when you talk about yourself. Let's repeat those together three times.

Together (three times): I, me, my, mine.

Instructor: Can you use the **pronoun** "mine" in a sentence?

*Child: [gives sentence]*

⇨ Note to Instructor: Prompt child, if necessary, to use the pronoun correctly.

Instructor: The **pronouns** "you, your, yours" can take the place of the person to whom you are speaking. Let's say those together three times.

Together (three times): *You, your, yours.*

Instructor: Use the **pronoun** "you" in a sentence for me.

*Child: [gives sentence]*

Instructor: Now say the **pronouns** "he, she, him, her, it, his, hers, its" together three times.

Together (three times): He, she, him, her, it, his, hers, its.

Instructor: Use the **pronoun** "she" in a sentence for me.

*Child: [gives sentence]*

Instructor: The **pronouns** "we, us, our, ours" mean more than one person. Let's say them together three times.

Together (three times): We, us, our, ours.

Instructor: Now make up a sentence about you and me. Use the **pronoun** "we."

*Child:* [gives sentence]

Instructor: The **pronouns** "'They, them, their, and theirs" are also used in place of **nouns** that mean more than one person. You use them when you are talking about a group of people that does not include you! Let's say "They, them, their, theirs" together three times.

Together (three times): They, them , their, theirs.

Instructor: Make up a sentence using the **pronoun** "they."

*Child: [gives sentence].*

Instructor: Now I will say the whole list of **pronouns** for you! *I, me, my, mine; you, your, yours; he, she, him, her, it, his, hers, its; we, us, our, ours; they, them, their, theirs.*

## Copywork

Choose one of the following copy assignments.

1. Emily sang.  She sang well.
2. Don't look, or you will be scared!
3. Kim and Alex had ice cream.  They ate too much!

## Enrichment Activity

Have the child write other sentences that use pronouns and action verbs.

# Lesson 105

-Introducing state of being verbs
-Copywork: "State of Being Verbs"
-Poem review: "The Goops"

⇨ Note to Instructor: Review "The Goops" today.

Instructor: **A verb is a word that does an action, shows a state of being, links two words together, or helps another verb.** We have been practicing **verbs** that do actions. But did you hear in the definition that some **verbs "show state of being"**? Let's say, **"A verb is a word that does an action or shows a state of being"** together three times.

Together (three times): **A verb is a word that does an action or shows a state of being.**

Instructor: Let's talk about what that means! Some **verbs** are words that you can do. But some **verbs** show that you just are! Sit perfectly still for me. You are not jumping, running, crawling, wallowing, or giggling. But you are still here! You just are. **Verbs** which tell us that something "just is" are called **"state of being" verbs**. **"State of being"** means that you are in a state of just being or existing. The **"state of being" verbs** are: am, is, are, was, were, be, being, been." I am going to say this list of **state of being verbs** five times.

Instructor (five times): (Do this in the form of a chant.)

Am [clap]
Is [clap]
Are, was, were. [clap]
Be [clap]
Being [clap]
Been. [clap] [clap]

Instructor: Now you say them with me five more times.

Together: (Repeat chant five times, with clapping.)

Instructor: I am going to put some of these **state of being verbs** in very short sentences that just tell that someone or something exists. These sentences don't tell anything about the person, and they don't tell an action that the person does. These short sentences only say that a person exists. The boy is. The girl is. The man was. The woman was. The people were. Now I will say those sentences to you again. Can you tell me the **state of being verb** in each sentences.

182

Instructor: The boy is.

*Child: Is*

⇨ Note to Instructor: If the child answers "the" or "boy," say the list of state of being verbs again and ask, "Is 'the' in the list?" (etc.) Do not require the child to use a complete sentence— your goal is to have him name the verb only.

Instructor: The girl is.

*Child: Is*

Instructor: The man was.

*Child: Was*

Instructor: The woman was.

*Child: Was*

Instructor: The people were.

*Child: Were*

Instructor: Now let's chant our list five more times.

⇨ Note to Instructor: Chant the list with the child five additional times.

## Copywork

Note to Instructor: Write the following chart onto a sheet of paper. Have the child copy it onto his own paper.

State of Being Verbs

Am
Is
Are, was, were.
Be
Being
Been

# Lesson 106

-State of being verbs

Instructor: **A verb is a word that does an action, shows a state of being, links two words together, or helps another verb.** Let's say, **"A verb is a word that does an action or shows a state of being"** together three times.

Together (three times): **A verb is a word that does an action or shows a state of being.**

Instructor: Can you name an **action verb** for me?

*Child: [names an action verb]*

Instructor: You can do an **action verb**. But a **state of being verb** just shows that you exist. Let's chant our **state of being verbs** together five times.

Together (five times):

Am [clap]

Is [clap]

Are, was, were. [clap]

Be [clap]

Being [clap]

Been. [clap] [clap]

Instructor: We can combine those **state of being verbs** with **pronouns**. Listen: I am. He is. She is. It is. We are. You are. They are. I was. He was. She was. It was. You were. They were. Did you hear any action in what I read?

*Child: No*

Instructor: All of those sentences used **pronouns** and **state of being verbs**. Now I am going say some questions and answers for you. These will show you how **state of being verbs** can be used without showing action.

⇨   Note to Instructor: Read both the question and the answer, using different voices to pretend that one person asks a question and another answers.

Instructor:

Are you in this room? I am.

Is he in the room with you? He is.

Is your baby sister in bed? She is.

Is your book on the table? It is.

Who is in this room? We are.

Who is with me? You are.

Are there other people here? They are.
Who was at lunch? You were.
Who else was at lunch? She was.
Is the delicious sandwich all gone? It is.

Instructor: I just used the **state of being verbs** "am, is, are, was," and "were." The **state of being verbs** "be, being, and been" have to have another **verb** to help them. We will talk about **helping verbs** later. Let's say the **state of being verbs** together one more time. Together: Am, is, are, was, were, be, being, been.

⇨   Note to Instructor: Identifying state of being verbs is difficult for many children. This is due to the fact that the verbs *am, is, are, was, were, be, being,* and *been* can function as either state of being verbs or, more commonly, as linking verbs. Introduce the concept, but don't worry if the child cannot fully understand it. Distinguishing between linking verbs and state of being verbs is covered in more advanced grammar.

## Enrichment Activity
Have the child make up his own questions and answers. He may ask them to you or to another family member. Remind him that the answers should use pronouns and state of being verbs.

# Lesson 107

-Introducing linking verbs
-Poem review: "The Goops" (Lesson 100)
* The instructor will need three light colors of construction paper, glue or tape, and a marker for the enrichment activity. This enrichment activity is strongly recommended to reinforce the lesson on linking verbs.


⇨ Note to Instructor: Review "The Goops" today.

⇨ Note to the Instructor: Today, you will introduce the child to the concept of linking verbs. Linking verbs can connect a pronoun and a noun ("I am a woman"), two nouns ("The woman is President"), a pronoun and an adjective ("I am hungry"), and a noun and an adjective ("The woman is kind"). In the oral exercises that follow, allow the child to select a noun or an adjective to follow the linking verbs. At this point, do not sidetrack him from understanding linking verbs by focusing on the words that follow the linking verb!

Instructor: Last lesson we talked about **state of being verbs**: Am, is, are, was, were, be, being, been. Say those **state of being verbs** with me three times.

Together (three times): Am, is, are, was, were, be, being, been.

Instructor: Listen to the definition of a **verb**: **A verb is a word that does an action, shows a state of being, links two words together, or helps another verb.** Today we're going to talk about the third part of that definition: **"Links two words together."** Let's say the **verb** definition together as far as **"links two words together."** I will say it first: **"A verb is a word that does an action, shows a state of being, or links two words together."** Let's say that together three times.

Together (three times): **A verb is a word that does an action, shows a state of being, or links two words together.**

Instructor: We have talked about **action verbs**. Can you give me an **action verb**?

*Child: [gives action verb].*

Instructor: We have also talked about **state of being verbs**. **State of being verbs** just tell us that something exists! In the last lesson, I read you some questions and answers that used **state of being verbs**. I will repeat some of them for you.

⇨ Note to Instructor: Read these again, using different voices for the question and the answers.

Are you in this room? I am.

Is he in the room with you? He is.

Is your baby sister in bed? She is.

Is your book on the table? It is.

Who is in this room? We are.

Who is with me? You are.

Are there other people here? They are.

Who was at lunch? You were.

Who else was at lunch? She was.

Is the delicious sandwich all gone? It is.

Instructor: The answers to these questions are very short in order to help you identify **state of being verbs**. In this lesson you will learn about another type of verb: **linking verbs**. Most **linking verbs** are easy to recognize because they are the same verbs as the **state of being verbs**: am, is, are, was, were, be, being, been. A **linking verb** links two words together. Do you know how to link hands with someone else? Let's link hands. We are joining hands. Now we are connected together? Do you know what we call the parts of a chain that are joined together?

⇨  Note to Instructor: Wait for response if it is forthcoming, but continue without much delay if the child does not know what to call the parts of a chain.

Instructor: We call the parts of a chain "links." If a lot of people hold hands, we sometimes say we "link" hands. A "link" is something that connects or joins things. **Linking verbs** can link or connect words together to make interesting sentences. Am, is, are, was, and were are most often used as **linking verbs**. I will read you a **noun** and a **linking verb** and let you complete the sentence. Then the **linking verb** will connect the **noun** that I use, with the interesting words that you choose to tell me more about the **noun**! Here is the first sentence: "The toad was..." Can you tell me what color the toad was?

*Child: The toad was green [or brown].*

Instructor: The **linking verb** "was" connects "toad" with its color! Can you tell me something about a freight train if I say, "The freight train is _____."

*Child: The freight train is long [or another appropriate word].*

Instructor: The **linking verb** "is" connects the freight train with the word _____. Now finish this sentence: "Chocolate is..."

*Child: Chocolate is good!*

Instructor: The **linking verb** "is" connects "chocolate" with "good!" Now can you tell me something about yourself? Begin your sentence

187

with "I am..."

*Child: I am [appropriate noun or adjective].*

Instructor: The **linking verb** "am" connects the word "I" with a word that tells me more about you! Now finish this sentence: "Dogs are..." What can you tell me about dogs?

*Child: Dogs are [noun or adjective].*

Instructor: The **linking verb** "are" connects "dogs" with the word that explains more about dogs! Now finish one more sentence for me: "In long ago times, knights in armor were..."

*Child: Knights in armor were [appropriate phrase].*

Instructor: Good job! Now you have used the **linking verbs** "am, is, are, was, were" to tell me more about the **nouns** and **pronouns** I gave you.

Instructor: Now let's say the state of being verbs we learned last lesson.

Together: Am, is, are, was, were, be, being, been.

Instructor: Now let's say the linking verbs we learned this lesson. These are the same verbs we just said together!

Together: Am, is, are, was, were, be, being, been.

⇨ Note to Instructor: Verbs which can serve as either linking or action verbs are: Taste, feel, smell, sound, look, appear, become, seem, grow, remain, stay. However, this concept is too advanced for second grade; it will be taught in a later year. (Most grammar books introduce these verbs in late third or early fourth grade.)

## Enrichment Activity

Help the child make a three-link paper chain from three different colors of construction paper that are light enough for the child to clearly see writing on them. The middle link should be yellow or white. While the links are flat, before putting the chain together: 1. Write a linking verb on the yellow or white link. 2. Write a noun or pronoun on another color link. 3. Write an adjective on the third color link. Glue or tape the chain together, showing that the yellow (or white) linking verb "links" the noun or pronoun with the adjective to make a sentence. You could repeat this project writing a noun instead of an adjective for number three. If possible, look at a real chain and talk about how the links connect or join parts of the chain.

# Lesson 108

-Linking verbs

-Poem review: "The Caterpillar" (Lesson 2)

\* The instructor will need twenty-five index cards and a pen or marker for this lesson. The child will need additional index cards for the enrichment activity.

⇨ Note to Instructor: Review "The Caterpillar" today.

⇨ Note to Instructor: For today's lesson, you will need twenty-five index cards. On the first five, write the linking verbs (one on each card): Am, is, are, was, were. On eight more cards, write the following eight words and phrases (one on each card):

Dinosaurs

The beach

Goldilocks

Baby kittens

High speed trains

Candy

Mommy

Caterpillars

On the last twelve cards, write the following words and phrases (one on each card):

ferocious

delicious

cuddly

sandy

fuzzy

cute

thunderously loud

hungry

dangerous

cheerful

purple

tiny

Help the child to combine the "subject cards" (nouns) with the "descriptive cards" (adjectives) using the linking verb cards to connect them. As you form each sentence, point out the linking verb to the child, and remind the child that the linking verb is connecting the two parts of the sentence together.

## Enrichment Activity
The child can make up his own nouns and adjectives to assemble into sentences.

# Lesson 109
-Story narration: "The Camel's Nose"

⇨ Note to Instructor: Read aloud the Aesop's fable below. Have the child tell the story back to you; use the suggested questions at the story's end to prompt the child, if necessary. Write down the child's narration and read it back to him.

## The Camel's Nose

A man who lived in the desert bought a favorite pet camel. The camel carried spices, wood, and tents from place to place for the man. Sometimes the man rode on the camel. They made many journeys together.

Every night, the man cooked his supper over a fire, and then set up his tent nearby. The tent was warm—and the desert nights were very cold. One night, the camel stuck just his nose in the opening of the tent. "Master," said the camel, "my nose is a little bit cold. If I could put just my nose inside your tent, I would sleep better."
"Yes," said the man, "the tent is large enough for your nose. You may put your nose into the tent." So the camel stuck his nose under the front flap of the tent.

Not long after, the camel said, "Good master, thank you for letting me put my nose into the tent. My nose is beautifully warm! But the rest of my head would like to be near you, too."
The man thought, "My camel is too large to come into this tent. But his head is small! He can put his head into my tent." So he said, "Of course. You may put your whole head into my tent."
The camel wriggled his head into the tent. But, very soon, the camel said, " Kind Master, I may catch cold if my head is warm and my body is cold. May I please put my neck inside, too?"
The camel's request seemed reasonable, so the man said, "You may put your neck in the tent, too."

After a little while, the camel said, "Generous master, I am tired of standing here. May I kneel with my front legs in the tent?" The master did not want his animal exhausted in the morning, so he moved over and allowed the camel to put his nose, his head, his neck, and his front legs inside the tent.

The man was beginning to fall asleep when he heard, "Wonderful master, I do not want you to be uncomfortable in the night and I worry that when I kneel this way, half-in and half-out of the tent, cold air rushes into your tent. Perhaps I should come all the way in, so that you can close the flaps behind me."

The man agreed, and he opened the tent flaps for the camel to come inside. But when the camel was in the tent all the way, the camel said, "We have a problem. The tent is too small for us both to lie down and sleep. I think it would be better if you went outside to sleep." And with that, the camel pushed his master out of the tent and would not let him back in.

While shivering outside in the cold, the man thought to himself, "I should never have let the camel put his nose into the tent! I didn't think his nose was a bad thing—but if I had stopped his nose from coming in, the rest of him would not have followed! And I would still be in my warm bed."

⇨ Note to Instructor: Ask the child to tell you the story back in his own words. If the child has trouble remembering, use these questions:
Why did the camel want to put his nose into the tent? *The camel's nose was cold.*
What did the camel want to do after his nose was inside the tent? *He wanted to put his head into the tent.*
What did the camel want to do next? *He wanted to put his neck inside the tent.*
Why did the man let the whole camel inside the tent? *The man wanted to close the tent flaps to keep out the cold air.*
Once the camel was inside, what did he tell the man to do? *He told the man to go outside the tent so that he would have room to sleep.*

⇨ Note to Instructor: Use the following information as a guide for discussion if you wish.

Bad habits are things that should be stopped before they get started and crowd out good habits. What are some bad habits that it would be good to stop before they are too hard to break? Bad friends are another thing that should be stopped before they get started. Little by little, bad company can crowd out good companions. What can you do to prevent bad companions from taking over your time?

## Enrichment Activity
Have the child write down his own narration of the story.

# Lesson 110

-Linking verbs
-Poem review: "Mr. Nobody" (Lesson 81)
* The child will need thirteen index cards for the enrichment activity.

⇨ Note to Instructor: Review "Mr. Nobody" today.

Instructor: I will say the definition of a **verb** for you: **A verb is a word that does an action, shows a state of being, links two words together, or helps another verb.** We have learned about **action verbs**, **state of being verbs**, and **linking verbs**. Let's say the first three parts of the definition together three times. I will say it first: **A verb is a word that does an action, shows a state of being, or links two words together.**

Together: **A verb is a word that does an action, shows a state of being, or links two words together.**

Instructor: Listen to the following sentences from "The Camel's Nose." Each sentence has a **linking verb** in it.

The tent was warm.

The desert nights were very cold.

My nose is a little bit cold.

The tent is large enough for your nose.

My nose is beautifully warm!

My camel is too large to come into this tent.

But his head is small!

The tent is too small for us both.

Now I will read you each sentence again. Can you find the linking verb in each sentence?

⇨ Note to Instructor: Help the child identify the verbs am, is, are, was, and were in each sentence.

Instructor: Now let's find the words that the **verbs** link together. In "The tent was warm," what was warm?

*Child: The tent was warm.*

Instructor: "Was" links "tent" and "warm" together. Now you know more about the tent. What were the desert nights like?

*Child: The desert nights were very cold.*

Instructor: The linking verb "were" links "the desert nights" together with "very cold." In the sentence, "The tent is large enough for your nose," what word links "The tent" with the description "large enough for your nose"?

194

*Child: The word "is."*
Instructor: "Is" is a **linking verb**. The next sentence is, "My nose is beautifully warm!" What does "beautifully warm" describe?
*Child: "Beautifully warm" describes "my nose."*
Instructor: What word links "my nose" to "beautifully warm?"
*Child: The word "is" links "my nose" to "beautifully warm."*
Instructor: Can you use a **linking verb** to connect these two phrases? "The tent" and "too small for us both."
*Child: The tent is too small for us both.*

## Enrichment Activity

Ask the student to write the following words and phrases on separate index cards (you can help with the longer phrases). When the cards are finished, ask the student to assemble the sentences properly.
The tent
was
warm
My nose
is
a little bit cold
large enough for your nose
beautifully warm
My camel
too large to come into this tent
But his head
small
too small for us both.

# Lesson 111

-Beginning poem booklet
-Copywork: "The Year"
-Poem review: "The Goops" (Lesson 100)
\* The child will need art supplies and either two pieces of construction paper or a folder.

➪   Note to Instructor: Review "The Goops" today.
➪   Note to Instructor: Over the course of the next twenty lessons, the child will make pages for a booklet entitled "The Year." He will need thirteen sheets of lined paper for this project, as well as construction paper or a folder to use for a cover.

Instructor: Today we are going to read a poem about the twelve months of the year. The poem begins with January, the first month of the year. January is a winter month. The season of winter officially begins on December 21, but January 1 is considered the first day of the year. I will read the poem to you. Follow along as I move my finger beneath the words.

The Year
*Sara Coleridge, adapted by Sara Buffington*

January brings the snow,
Helps the skis and sleds to go.

February brings the rain,
Thaws the frozen lake again.

March brings breezes loud and shrill,
Stirs the dancing daffodil.

April brings the primrose sweet,
Scatters daisies at our feet.

May brings sunshine full and bright,
Sends the busy bees to flight.

June brings tulips, lilies, roses,
Fills the children's hands with posies.

Hot July brings stormy showers,
Lemonade, and lazy hours.

August brings the warmest air,
Sandy feet and sea-wet hair.

September brings the fruit so sweet,
Apples ripe from summer heat.

October brings the colored trees,
Scampering squirrels and cooling breeze.

Dull November brings the blast,
Then the leaves are whirling fast.

Chill December brings the sleet,
Blazing fire, and Christmas treat.[1]

[1] An alternate last line: "Blazing fire, and winter treat."

⇨   Note to Instructor: On one sheet of lined paper, have the child copy the title of the poem "The Year." Help him center the title (this will serve as his title page). Remind him that each word in the title begins with a capital letter. Have him illustrate a folder or piece of construction paper to serve as the booklet's cover. You will assemble the booklet when he has copied all twelve verses.

⇨   Note to Instructor: If you live in a location where the seasons are so different that the poem has little meaning for the child, you do not have to use this poem. Instead, substitute a sentence you write for the child (poetry is not necessary!) describing something that happens each month of the year in your area. The child will copy your sentence each day in his "The Year" book.

## Enrichment Activity

Make two-line rhyming couplets about one or more months and substitute these couplets for the suggested poem. Have a family or group poetry composing session in which everyone contributes ideas.

# Lesson 112

-Four types of sentences
-Seasons
-Copywork: "January"
* The child will need art supplies.


Instructor: In the poem we read last lesson, we read **statements** about the months. We read that "February brings the rain," and that "April brings the primrose sweet." Those are **sentences. A sentence is a group of words that expresses a complete thought.** Let's say that definition together three times.

Together (three times): **A sentence is a group of words that expresses a complete thought.**

Instructor: A sentence begins with a capital letter and ends with a punctuation mark. Let's say that together three times.

Together (three times): A sentence begins with a capital letter and ends with a punctuation mark.

Instructor: There are four different types of sentences. **A statement gives information.** Repeat that definition for me.

*Child: A statement gives information.*

Instructor: Here are some **statements**. December, January, and February are winter months. March, April, and May are spring months. Both of those sentences give you information. The second type of sentence is a **command. A command gives an order or makes a request.** Let's say that together three times.

Together (three times): **A command gives an order or makes a request.**

Instructor: Suppose it were August. August is a summer month. I might command you, "Go play in the snow!" Would you be able to do it?

*Child: No!*

Instructor: What if I made the command a request? Please, go get me an icicle! Could you do it then?

*Child: No!*

Instructor: It is too hot for snow and icicles during June, July, and August. They are all summer months. The third type of sentence is a **"question." A question asks something.** Is September a fall month?

*Child: Yes.*

Instructor: Did I just ask you a **question**?
*Child: Yes.*
Instructor: Did you answer yes? I keep asking you **questions**! I am asking you for information. You can make a **statement** in answer to my question. You can say, "September is a fall month." There is one more type of **sentence** left—an **exclamation**. If I were to say, "The fall colors are spectacular!" with sudden, strong emotion, that would be an **exclamation**. **An exclamation shows sudden or strong feeling.** It ends with an exclamation point. Say that with me: **An exclamation shows sudden or strong feeling.**
Together: **An exclamation shows sudden or strong feeling.**
Instructor: Now we have reviewed the four types of **sentences**. They are: **Statement, command, question, exclamation.** Say that with me twice.
Together (twice): **Statement, command, question, exclamation.**

## Copywork
Have the child copy the "January" couplet from the poem "The Year" onto a blank sheet of lined paper. If the child has great difficulty copying both lines of the couplet, have him copy one line and you write the second line for him. He can illustrate the paper by drawing a picture of a January activity (sledding, building a snowman). If he prefers, he can cut pictures from a magazine and paste them onto the page.

## Enrichment Activity
Have the child come up with his own statements, questions, commands, and exclamations. He can write these down, or simply say them orally.

# Lesson 113

-Commas
   -Dates
   -Addresses
-Copywork: "February"
-Poem review: "Days of the Week" (Lesson 35)
* The child will need art supplies.


⇨   Note to Instructor: Review "Days of the Week" today.

Instructor: The poem that you are working on lists the proper names of all of the months. In which month were you born? Write that month on your paper.

⇨   Note to Instructor: Help the child to spell his birthday month correctly. Remind him that it should begin with a capital letter.

Instructor: On what day of that month were you born? Write that day now. In what year were you born? Write that year next. This is the date of your birthday. Remember, when we write a date, we put a comma between the day of the month and the year.

⇨   Note to Instructor: Help the child to write the date of his birthday correctly.

Instructor: Let's practice writing another date correctly. We will write today's date: the month, the day, a comma, and then the year.

⇨   Note to Instructor: Help the child write today's date correctly.

Instructor: We use a comma whenever we need to separate two words or numbers. The comma that separates the day from the year helps you to keep those two numbers apart. Otherwise, you might think they were all one long number! We also use a comma to separate the name of a city from the name of a state. Otherwise, you might think that they were one long name! I will write out the name of our city and state for you.

⇨   Note to Instructor: Write the name of your city and state for the child. Point out the comma that separates them.

Instructor: Your city and state are part of your address. I will write the rest of your address for you now. Then you will copy it, putting commas where they belong.

⇨   Note to Instructor: Write the child's address neatly. Ask him to copy it. Point out any commas in the address.

Instructor: Your birthday is the special day on which you were born, and your address is the special place where you live! Both of these have commas in them.

## Copywork

Have the child copy the "February" couplet from the poem "The Year" onto a blank sheet of lined paper. If the child has great difficulty copying both lines of the couplet, have him copy one line and you write the second line. He can illustrate the paper by drawing a picture of a February activity (perhaps one that has to do with a holiday: President's Day, Valentine's Day). If he prefers, he can cut pictures from a magazine and paste them onto the page.

# Lesson 114

-Commas in a series
-Copywork: "Snuggles, Wiggles, Grins, and Giggles"
-Poem review: "The Goops" (Lesson 100)

⇨ Note to Instructor: Review "The Goops" today.

Instructor: We put a comma between a city and a state. We also put one between the day and the year in a date. Commas separate words! You can also separate words by using "and." If I were to give you a cookie, I could also give you milk to go with it. I could say, "I will give you a cookie and milk." The "and" comes between the cookie and the milk. But if I were also to give you an apple and a napkin, the list of things I am giving you is beginning to get long! I would have to say, "I will give you a cookie and milk and an apple and a napkin." Instead of putting "and" between each one of those items, I can just put a comma between them! I will put a comma after every item I am giving you—except for the last one at the end of the sentence. It has a period after it! Now I can say, "I will give you a cookie, COMMA, milk, COMMA, an apple, COMMA, and a napkin. PERIOD."

⇨ Note to Instructor: Read these sentences to the child just as written. Then, show the child the written sentences below.

I will give you a cookie and milk and an apple and a napkin.
I will give you a cookie, milk, an apple, and a napkin.

Instructor: Whenever you separate items in a series by putting a comma after each one, you should keep the very last "and." "Series" is another word for "list." Listen to me read these series and follow along as I move my finger under the words.

⇨ Note to Instructor: Pause as you come to each comma.

I am going to play baseball. I need a ball, a bat, a glove, and a helmet.
I am going to make cookies. I will use flour, sugar, butter, vanilla, and eggs.
I went to the zoo. I saw tigers, elephants, lions, monkeys, and snakes.

Instructor: These lists have commas after each item. In each list, the word *and* comes before the last item. Read the following sentences to me.

⇨ Note to Instructor: Have the child read the following pairs of sentences from the book.

Tables are set with plates and bowls and glasses and cups.
Tables are set with plates, bowls, glasses, and cups.

My art work is done with pencils and crayons and paints.
My art work is done with pencils, crayons, and paints.

Parts of my body are hands and arms and legs.
Parts of my body are hands, arms, and legs.

Instructor:  Items in a list should be separated by commas.

## Copywork

Choose one of the following copy exercises:

1.  A baby can yell, smile, and sleep.
2.  My pet can run, growl, play, escape, and bite!
3.  My little sister snuggles, wiggles, grins, and giggles.

## Enrichment Activity

Ask the child to write original sentences that contain three or more items in a series.

# Lesson 115

-Introducing helping verbs
-Copywork: "March"
-Poem review: "Work" (Lesson 15)
* The child will need art supplies.

⇨ Note to Instructor: Review "Work" today.

Instructor: **A verb is a word that does an action, shows a state of being, links two words together, or helps another verb.** Let's say, **"A verb is a word that does an action, shows a state of being, links two words together, or helps another verb"** three times.

Together (three times): **A verb is a word that does an action, shows a state of being, links two words together, or helps another verb.**

Instructor: Can you name an **action verb** for me?

*Child: [names an action verb]*

Instructor: You can do an **action verb**. But a **state of being verb** just shows that you exist. Let's chant our **state of being verbs** together five times.

Together (five times):
Am [clap]
Is [clap]
Are, was, were. [clap]
Be [clap]
Being [clap]
Been. [clap] [clap]

Instructor: These **verbs** can also function as **linking verbs**. These **linking verbs** link two words together: "She is happy," or "The mother was glad to see her little boy!" Now it's time for us to talk about that last part of the **verb** definition: **A verb can help another verb**. Say that with me three times:

Together (three times): **A verb can help another verb.**

Instructor: Listen to this sentence: The camel was pushing his way into the tent. The camel was doing something active. What was he doing?

*Child: He was pushing.*

Instructor: But if I just said, "The camel pushing his way into the tent," that would sound odd! "Pushing" needs another **verb** to help it. The **verb** "was" is helping the **verb** "pushing." Together, they make

204

sense. "The camel was pushing his way into the tent." Do you recognize the **verb** "was?" You have learned that it can act as either a **state of being verb** or a **linking verb**. The verbs am, is, are, was, were, be, being, and been can help **action verbs** to get their job done. Let's repeat those **verbs.**

Together: Am, is, are, was, were, be, being, been.

Instructor: Now I am also going to add some other **helping verbs**:

Have, has, had [clap]

Do, does, did [clap]

Shall, will, should, would, may, might, must [clap] [clap]

Can, could!

That is a very long list, but you have already found out that you can learn lots of long things if you just say them enough times. So that is what we will do today and for other days to come.

⇨ Note to Instructor: Repeat the whole chant for the child three times.

Am [clap]

Is [clap]

Are, was, were. [clap]

Be [clap]

Being [clap]

Been. [clap] [clap]

Have, has, had [clap]

Do, does, did [clap]

Shall, will, should, would, may, might, must [clap] [clap]

Can, could!

Instructor: Listen to this sentence: A man who was living in the desert bought a pet camel. Repeat that sentence for me.

*Child: A man who was living in the desert bought a pet camel.*

Instructor: Now listen: A man who living in the desert bought a pet camel. I left a word out. Do you know what word I left out?

⇨ Note to Instructor: Repeat both versions of the sentence until the child can identify the missing "was."

Instructor: "Was" is a **helping verb**. The **verb** "living" has to have the **helping verb** "was" with it, or else it doesn't make sense! What **action verb** comes after the **helping verb** was?

*Child: Living.*

Instructor: "Was" and "living" are both **verbs**. "Living" is the **action verb** and "was" is the **helping verb**. There is another action word in this sentence, too. What action had the man done to get a camel?

*Child: The man "bought" a camel.*

Instructor: "Bought" is a **verb** that shows action. But the **action verb** "bought" doesn't need a **helping verb** with it. Listen to the next sentence: The camel carried spices and wood for the man. What is the **action verb** in this sentence?

*Child: Carried.*

⇨ Note to Instructor: Give the child any necessary help to identify the action verb.

Instructor: "Carried" doesn't need a **helping verb** either. But listen to this next sentence: Sometimes the man would ride on the camel. Listen to it again: Sometimes the man would ride on the camel. Now listen one more time: Sometimes the man ride on the camel. What word did I leave out?

*Child: Would.*

Instructor: The **action verb** "ride" needs the helping verb "would" in this sentence. Without the **helping verb**, it doesn't sound right!

Now I will say the whole list of **helping verbs** for you again. Listen carefully:

Am [clap]
Is [clap]
Are, was, were. [clap]
Be [clap]
Being [clap]
Been. [clap] [clap]
Have, has, had [clap]
Do, does, did [clap]
Shall, will, should, would, may, might, must [clap] [clap]
Can, could!

⇨ Note to Instructor: Repeat this list for the child three more times.

## Copywork

Note to Instructor: Have the child copy the "March" couplet from the poem "The Year" onto a blank sheet of lined paper. If the child has great difficulty copying both lines of the couplet, have him copy one line and you write the second line. He can illustrate the paper by drawing a picture of a March activity (perhaps one involving wind or kites—see "Enrichment Activity" on the next page). If he prefers, he can cut a from a magazine and paste them onto the page.

**Enrichment Activity**

Read, illustrate, or memorize the following poem about wind.

The Wind
*Robert Louis Stevenson*

I saw you toss the kites on high
And blow the birds about the sky;
And all around I heard you pass,
Like ladies' skirts across the grass—
    O wind, a-blowing all day long,
    O wind, that sings so loud a song!

I saw the different things you did,
But always you yourself you hid.
I felt you push, I heard you call,
I could not see yourself at all—
    O wind, a-blowing all day long,
    O wind, that sings so loud a song!

O you, that are so strong and cold,
O blower, are you young or old?
Are you a beast of field and tree,
Or just a stronger child than me?
    O wind, a-blowing all day long,
    O wind, that sings so loud a song!

# Lesson 116

-Noun review
-Verb review
-Copywork: "April"
-Poem review: "Hearts Are Like Doors" (Lesson 27)
* The child will need art supplies.

⇨ Note to Instructor: Review "Hearts Are Like Doors" today.

Instructor: Let's review what a **noun** is. Say after me: **A noun is the name of a person, place, thing, or idea.**

*Child: A noun is the name of a person, place, thing, or idea.*

Instructor: I am going to give as an example the common name of a person, place, or thing, and I want you to give me a special, **proper name** for each. Here is a kind of person: Girl. Now, can you give me the special, **proper name** of a girl.

*Child: [the proper name of a real girl]*

Instructor: "State." That is a **common noun** that names a place—there are many states. Can you give me the **proper name** of our state?

*Child: [name of state]*

Instructor: Cereal is a **common noun**. Can you think of the **proper name** of a cereal that you like?

*Child: [Cheerios™ or some other cereal name]*

Instructor: We will talk only about **common nouns** for ideas. Remember that an idea is something you can think about in your mind, but can't see or touch. I'll tell you one idea and you try to remember others we have talked about. I'm thinking about the idea **noun** "excitement." Can you think of another **noun** that names an idea?

*Child: [possible answers: happiness, joy, freedom, sadness, fear, etc.]*

Instructor: Remember, **proper nouns** always begin with capital letters. Your name is a **proper noun**, because there is only one you! Write your full **proper name** on your paper now.

⇨ Note to Instructor: As the child writes, remind him to begin his names with capital letters. Help him to write his first, middle, and last name.

Instructor: **Nouns** are one kind of word. **Verbs** are a different kind of word. I will say the definition of a **verb** for you: **A verb is a word that does an action, shows a state of being, links two words together, or helps another verb.** Let's say, "A verb is a word that does an action, shows a state of being, links two words together, or helps another verb" three times.

Together (three times): A verb is a word that does an action, shows a state of being, links two words together, or helps another verb.

Instructor: We have learned about **action verbs**, **state of being verbs**, **linking verbs**, and **helping verbs**. We learned a whole list of **helping verbs**. I will say them for you now:

Am [clap]

Is [clap]

Are, was, were. [clap]

Be [clap]

Being [clap]

Been. [clap] [clap]

Have, has, had [clap]

Do, does, did [clap]

Shall, will, should, would, may, might, must [clap] [clap]

Can, could!

Let's recite that list together three times.

Together (three times):

Am [clap]

Is [clap]

Are, was, were. [clap]

Be [clap]

Being [clap]

Been. [clap] [clap]

Have, has, had [clap]

Do, does, did [clap]

Shall, will, should, would, may, might, must [clap] [clap]

Can, could!

Instructor: I will read you some sentences where some **nouns** are doing some **action verbs**! Each **action verb** has a **helping verb** with it. We will find the **action verb** and then talk about which word helps it.

Instructor: The bullfrog was leaping from lily pad to lily pad. Who or what was leaping?

*Child: The bullfrog was leaping.*

Instructor: Bullfrog is the name of an animal. It is a noun. What was the bullfrog doing?

*Child: The bullfrog was leaping.*

Instructor: If I say, "The bullfrog leaping," that doesn't make sense! What word did I leave out? I left out the word "was." "Was" is a **helping verb** that helps the **verb** "leap." Now I will read you another sentence. The pigs were wallowing in a huge puddle of gooey mud. Who or what was wallowing?

*Child: The pigs were wallowing.*

Instructor: "Pigs" is a **noun**. What were the pigs doing?

*Child: The pigs were wallowing.*

Instructor: Does it sound right if I just say, "The pigs wallowing in a huge puddle of gooey mud?

*Child: No.*

Instructor: What word helps the **verb** "wallowing?"

*Child: "Were"*

Instructor: The garbage truck is rattling down the street. Who or what is rattling?

*Child: The garbage truck.*

Instructor: "Truck" is a **noun**. It is the name of a thing. What is the truck doing?

*Child: The garbage truck is rattling down the street.*

Instructor: What **helping verb** goes along with the **verb** "rattling"?

*Child: "Is."*

Instructor: Good! I will say the list of **helping verbs** to you one more time. Am, is, are, was, were. Be, being, been. Have, has, had, do, does, did. Shall, will, should, would, may, might, must, can, could.

## Copywork

Have the child copy the "April" couplet from the poem "The Year" onto a blank sheet of lined paper. If the child has great difficulty copying both lines of the couplet, have him copy one line and you write the second line. He can illustrate the paper by drawing a picture of something he would observe or celebrate in April (flowers, a religious holiday). If he prefers, he can cut this picture from a magazine and paste them onto the page.

## Enrichment Activity

Help the child to make up sentences that use helping verbs to help out action verbs. The child can write these sentences down, or dictate them as you write.

# Lesson 117

-Capitalization
     -Proper names
     -Initials
     -Titles of respect
     -Addresses
     -Poems
* The instructor will need five index cards for the enrichment activity.

⇨   Note to Instructor: Chant the helping verb list three times: *Am, is, are, was, were. Be, being, been. Have, has, had, do, does, did. Shall, will, should, would, may, might, must, can, could.*

Instructor: Today we are going to review capital letters. What is your full name?

*Child: (gives full name)*

Instructor: Each of your names begins with a capital letter because your names are your special, **proper names**. And you have learned that **proper nouns** begin with capital letters. Let's say that I want to put your name on something that belongs to you — maybe a ball you take to the playground, or a toy you take to the beach, or a coat that looks just like your friend's coat. But I don't want to write out all of your names. Do you know how I could do that? I could write just the first letter of each of your names. Remember, we call the first letter of a proper name its "initial." The word 'initial" means "first" or "beginning." The initial letter of a proper noun begins with a capital letter. What is the first letter of your first name?

*Child: (initial letter of first name)*

Instructor: What is the first letter of your middle name?

*Child: (initial letter of middle name)*

Instructor: What is the initial letter of your last name?

*Child: (initial letter of last name)*

Instructor: Now, I want you to write your initials. When we write initials, we capitalize each one. We also put a period after each initial.

*Child: (Writes initials)*

⇨   Note to Instructor: Assist as necessary.

Instructor: Initials are a short way to write a word. Remember, there are other kinds of words that we also write in a short way. Instead of writing the whole word, we only write two or three letters of the word. We call this "abbreviating" or "shortening" a word. Titles of respect, like Mr., Mrs., Miss., and Dr. show we respect the position of a person.

When these titles are written, they are often abbreviated. I am going to review with you the abbreviated (short) way to write some common titles of respect.

⇨ Note to Instructor: Have the child watch you write—one at a time— the following abbreviations for titles of respect and the titles for which the abbreviations stand. As you write each one, say the word aloud and show the child that each starts with a capital letter and ends with a period (except for "Miss"). As you write, form lists in two columns so you can alternate covering the columns for a practice exercise.

| | |
|---|---|
| Mr. | Mister |
| Dr. | Doctor |
| Mrs. | married woman |
| Miss | unmarried woman |
| Ms. | can refer to any woman |

Instructor: I want you to copy each of these abbreviations and say the word for which it stands. Notice that "Miss" is written with no period after it.

*Child: (copies each abbreviation and pronounces the word for which it stands)*

Instructor: Other abbreviations we have studied are for street, avenue and road.

⇨ Note to Instructor: Have the child watch you write —one at a time— the following abbreviations and the words for which they stand. If your address contains any abbreviation other than those below, include it in the list. Copy the following abbreviations and the words for which they stand in two columns so you can alternate covering the columns for a practice exercise .

Instructor: I want you to copy these words and their abbreviations.

*Child: (Copies the lists)*

| | |
|---|---|
| St. | street |
| Rd. | road |
| Ave. | avenue |

Instructor: All of the abbreviations we have written today begin with a capital letter because they stand for the special, proper name of a person or a place. Remember, the names of states are abbreviated in a special way. Each state has a two-letter abbreviation. Both letters are capitalized, and there is no period after them.  State abbreviations break all the rules!  The post office wants everyone to write their state abbreviation in the same way so that the machines that sort the mail can read the addresses easily.  Here is the abbreviation for our state.

⇨   Note to Instructor: Write out the full name of your state and its postal abbreviation. Ask the child to copy both the name and the abbreviation.

Instructor: Before we finish today's lesson, I want to review one more rule about capital letters.  Capitalize titles and the beginning of every line in poetry.  Let's look back at the poem "The Wind" in Lesson 115.  Both words in the title are capitalized.   Can you point to the capital letter that begins each line?

Instructor: Now I would like you to repeat each one of these capitalization rules after me.  **Proper names** begin with capital letters.

*Child: Proper names begin with capital letters.*

Instructor: When we write initials, we capitalize each one.

*Child: When we write initials, we capitalize each one.*

Instructor: Initials are followed by periods.

*Child: Initials are followed by periods.*

Instructor: Abbreviated titles of respect are capitalized and followed by periods.

*Child: Abbreviated titles of respect are capitalized and followed by periods.*

Instructor: Remember, we don't put a period after the title "Miss." Capitalize titles and the beginning of every line in poetry.

*Child: Capitalize titles and the beginning of every line in poetry.*

## Enrichment Activity
On five cards, copy the titles of respect on one side and the words for which they stand on the other side. The child may use these to practice saying and writing titles of respect in proper form.  This same activity may be used for other abbreviations.

# Lesson 118
-Picture narration: "Summer Picnic"

How many people are in this picture? There are five people in this picture. They are the Garcia family. The father's name is Mr. Garcia. The mother's name is Mrs. Garcia. The name of the daughter flying the kite is Sara. The son's name is Emilio. The younger daughter's name is Isabel. The people in the Garcia family are Mr. Garcia, Mrs. Garcia, Sara, Emilio, and Isabel. I will write that sentence down for you and point out the commas.

⇨ Note to Instructor: Copy the sentence above that starts with "The people…" for the child to see. Point out the commas, explaining that they separate people or items in a series.

Let's look back at the picture. What is the Garcia family doing? They are having a picnic. It is a summertime picnic. What months are in the season of summer? June, July, and August are the summer months.

The family is about to have lunch. Look at all the food they brought with them! Can you find three things that the Garcias will have for lunch? As you say them, I will write them down for you.

⇨ Note to Instructor: Write down the items that the child lists in a column entitled "What the Garcia family will eat." If the child has trouble finding items, prompt him by asking questions like "What is in the bowl?" and "What is Emilio eating?" and "What is the father lifting onto the plate?"

The Garcias had to take more than just food to the park. Can you find three things on the table that the Garcias cannot eat? As you say them, I will write them down for you.

⇨ Note to Instructor: Write down the non-food items in a separate column entitled "What the Garcia family also brought." If the child has problems finding the items, prompt him with questions like "What is stacked next to the salad bowl?" and "What is next to the soda bottle?" and "What is resting under Emilio's elbow?"

Let's look at the picture again. Who is already eating? Emilio is eating a peanut butter and jelly sandwich. He is very hungry, and peanut butter and jelly sandwiches are his favorite food. Who do you think will be the next to eat? I think it will be Isabel. Look at her face. What is she looking at? She is staring at the cheeseburger. She looks like she can't wait to take a bite! Now look at Sara. Does she look hungry? What do you think she wants to do? Maybe she wants to keep on flying her kite. (See page following picture.)

⇨ Note to Instructor: After you have finished looking at the picture, look back at the paper on which you have been writing. Show the child the first sentence that you wrote about the Garcia family. Point out the commas again, explaining that they separate items in a list. Now, have the child orally compose sentences using the items in the first column. You may have to prompt him with the starter "The Garcia family will eat...." Once the child has composed a sentence orally, help him write it down with correct comma use (or write it down for him, depending on his level of writing ability). Remind the child that commas separate items in a list. Do the same for column two, prompting the child, if necessary, with "The Garcia family also brought...."

## Enrichment Activity

Have the child point out more items in the picture. You may choose headings like "What the Garcia family is wearing." Or add items to "The things the Garcia family also brought." After the child has written at least three items in a column, help him compose and write a sentence using correct comma placement. Remind the child that commas separate items in a list.

# Lesson 119

-Contractions

* The child will need a highlighter marker.

⇨ Note to Instructor: Chant the helping verb list three times:
Am [clap]
Is [clap]
Are, was, were. [clap]
Be [clap]
Being [clap]
Been. [clap] [clap]
Have, has, had [clap]
Do, does, did [clap]
Shall, will, should, would, may, might, must [clap] [clap]
Can, could!

Instructor: We have already studied initials and abbreviations. Using initials and abbreviations are two ways to shorten a word. Today we will talk about another way to shorten words—contractions. A contraction is made up of two words, put together into one word, with some letters left out. A punctuation mark called an apostrophe is put in the place of the missing letters.

⇨ Note to Instructor: Write the contractions "I'm" and "you're," showing the child how to make an apostrophe. Continue to write as directed in the dialogue below.

Instructor: The contraction "I'm" is a short way of saying "I am." Instead of saying, "I am hungry," you might say, "I'm hungry." First, I will write "I am" for you. Then, I will write them together: "Iam." That looks funny, doesn't it? When we put the words "I" and "am" together, we leave out the "a" and put an apostrophe in its place to show that a letter has been left out. Now I will write the contraction properly: "I'm." Repeat this sentence after me: "I am learning to speak properly."

*Child: I am learning to speak properly.*

Instructor: Now use the contraction "I'm" instead of "I am."

*Child: I'm learning to speak properly.*

Instructor: "You are" can be contracted into "You're." I will write both of those out for you. Can you show me which letter has been left out?

⇨ Note to Instructor: Write "You are" on the paper, and then write "You're" directly underneath it.

*Child: The letter "a."*

Instructor: The apostrophe takes the place of the "a."

⇨ Note to Instructor: Repeat for the following set of contractions, writing each contraction directly underneath the full form the word so that the child can see which letter or letters has been replaced by the apostrophe.

| He is | She is | It is | We will | You are |
|-------|--------|-------|---------|---------|
| He's | She's | It's | We'll | You're |

| I cannot | She will not | He does not | They were not |
|----------|--------------|-------------|---------------|
| I can't | She won't | He doesn't | They weren't |

## Copywork

Title a paper "Contractions." Have the child copy the following list:

| He is | She is | It is | We will | You are |
|-------|--------|-------|---------|---------|
| He's | She's | It's | We'll | You're |

With a colored marker, have the child highlight letters in the first row that were left out in the second. Save this sheet and add to it in the next lesson.

# Lesson 120

-Contractions
-Copywork: "Contractions"
* The child will need a highlighter marker.


Instructor: A contraction is made up of two words put together into one word with some letters left out. A punctuation mark called an apostrophe is put in the place of the missing letters. Today I will say some sentences that do not use contractions. I want you to try to say the sentence back to me, using the correct contraction. For example, I will say, "I cannot wait until lunch!" And you will say back to me, "I can't wait for lunch!" "Can't" is the contraction for "cannot."

⇨    Note to Instructor: Prompt the child if he cannot identify the correct contraction.

Instructor: He is going to ride the subway home.

*Child: He's going to ride the subway home.*

Instructor: She is hoping to find a quarter under one of the seats.

*Child: She's hoping to find a quarter under one of the seats.*

Instructor: It is hidden down beneath the cushion.

*Child: It's hidden down beneath the cushion.*

Instructor: They will buy a piece of candy if they find the quarter.

*Child: They'll buy a piece of candy if they find the quarter.*

Instructor: She said, "I cannot find the quarter!"

*Child: She said, "I can't find the quarter!"*

Instructor: He said, "I will try!"

*Child: He said, "I'll try."*

Instructor: And then they found the quarter and bought candy with it. There aren't any contractions in that sentence! But I just used one—"aren't." What do you think "aren't" is short for?

⇨    Note to Instructor: Help the child identify "aren't" as a contraction for "are not."

Instructor: We use contractions when we speak and when we write stories and friendly letters. But usually, contractions are not used in formal writing like compositions and business letters.

## Copywork

Have the child copy the following list onto the "Contractions" page begun in the last lesson:

| I cannot | She will not | He does not | They were not |
|----------|--------------|-------------|---------------|
| I can't  | She won't    | He doesn't  | They weren't  |

With a highlighter marker, have the child highlight letters in the first row that were left out in the second.

## Enrichment Activity

Cover the contractions row and try writing each contraction from memory by looking at the two words from which the contraction is made.

# Lesson 121

-Contractions using "not"
-Copywork: "May"
-Poem review: "Mr. Nobody" (Lesson 81)
* The child will need art supplies as well as construction paper for the enrichment activity.

⇨   Note to Instructor: Review "Mr. Nobody" today.

Instructor: A contraction is made up of two words put together into one word with some letters left out. I am going to show you a list of today's contractions. They all end with the same letters.

⇨   Note to Instructor: Show the child the following list

aren't
weren't
hasn't
haven't
doesn't
didn't
shouldn't
couldn't
wouldn't
don't
can't
isn't

Instructor: If we wrote out the words that make up these contractions, you would see that the same word would end every phrase. Can you tell what it would be?

*Child: They all end with the word "not."*

Instructor: When you write a contraction with "not," you put the words together with no space or punctuation mark between them. Then you put an apostrophe in the place of the "o" in "not."

⇨   Note to Instructor: Write "would not" on your paper. Then write "wouldnot." Then, erase the "o" in "not" and substitute an apostrophe. Do the same for "did not" and "were not."

Instructor: In some of these contractions, other letters disappear too! "Will not" is written "won't." What letters have disappeared? One letter has changed! Can you tell which one?

⇨ Note to Instructor: Write "will not" and then write "won't" beneath it. Point out that the "i" has changed to an "o" and that each "l" has disappeared, as well as the "o" in "not"!

Instructor: You don't have to memorize any rules about these contractions. You probably already know these words! I will say the full forms of the words, and you can tell me whether you know the contraction that goes with them.

⇨ Note to Instructor: Read the following list to the child. Wait for the child to respond with the appropriate contraction. Prompt him if he is unable to think of it.

| | |
|---|---|
| Are not | aren't |
| Were not | weren't |
| Has not | hasn't |
| Have not | haven't |
| Does not | doesn't |
| Did not | didn't |
| Should not | shouldn't |
| Could not | couldn't |
| Would not | wouldn't |
| Do not | don't |
| Cannot | can't |
| Is not | isn't |

## Copywork

Have the child copy the "May" couplet from the poem "The Year" onto a blank sheet of lined paper. If the child has great difficulty copying both lines of the couplet, have him copy one line and you write the second line. He can illustrate the paper by drawing a picture of something he would observe or celebrate in May (birds, spring picnics, Memorial Day, Mother's Day, or another holiday that your family celebrates). If he prefers, he can cut pictures from a magazine and paste them onto the page.

## Enrichment Activity

Make a Mother's Day card. Even if it isn't Mother's Day, Mother will appreciate the card!

# Lesson 122

-Introducing dictation: "March"
-Poem review: "The Caterpillar" (Lesson 2)

⇨ Note to Instructor: Review "The Caterpillar" today.

⇨ Note to Instructor: Now that the child has practiced copying, it is time to move on to dictation. Copying teaches the child the conventions of written language. Now you will begin to use dictation as a teaching tool. You will read a sentence aloud to the child and ask him to write it down without looking at a written model. Through this process, the child will learn to picture a properly written sentence in his head before setting it down on paper. Dictation must come before original writing! Through dictation, the child learns how to formulate words into grammatical, properly punctuated sentences, without the additional strain of coming up with his own original words. Dictation is necessary preparation for original writing and should be practiced before a child is asked to write his own compositions.

To do dictation, explain to the child that he will write down the words that you are going to read, but that he will not be able to look at them. Read the selection aloud, slowly, once. Then say to the child, "Now I will read the sentence again, and then you will write it." Read it the second time and encourage the child to write without a further repetition. You are training the child not only to write correctly, but also to *hear* correctly. If he has not been used to doing this, it will take some practice on his part to listen actively. You should feel free to prompt him a third time. By the end of second grade, the child should be able to hear a sentence once and write it.

Begin dictation with sentences of two or three words. The goal is to gradually lengthen the amount that the child is required to "hold in his mind" and then write down. Helpful techniques for beginners:

Step 1. After you read a selection, ask the child to visualize the beginning capital letter and the end punctuation mark.

Step 2. Repeat the sentence once more.

Step 3. Have the child repeat what you just read.

Step 4. Have him write what he just said if it is accurate. (If it is not accurate, repeat steps 1 & 2.)

The first dictation exercise (below) is scripted for you; after this, dictation will appear at the end of lessons. Follow the same pattern given in the script. Be patient! Don't be surprised if the child appears to have forgotten all of his spelling and punctuation rules the first time he writes from dictation; this is a new skill and will take some time to master. Don't give up if the child complains; just shorten the amount done at one sitting, and keep practicing and gradually lengthening the amount included in one dictation. Most lessons will have a choice of options of length for dictations: 2–3 words, 5–6 words, or 7–10 words.

If you are teaching one child, watch the child as he writes. If he begins to make a mistake, stop him and have him correct the mistake immediately. If you are giving the dictation to more than one child, have the children make corrections at the end of the dictation by comparing it with the written model.

Instructor: You have learned how to copy sentences. When you copy, you can look at the sentence and see that it begins with a capital letter. You can copy the punctuation mark at the end. You can copy the spelling of words and the spaces between them. Today, we are going to do something a little different. I am going to give you a sentence to write, but I am going to say it, rather than show it to you. I will say the sentence now. Listen very carefully to what I am about to read:
March is a windy month.
What kind of letter does a sentence begin with?
*Child: A sentence begins with a capital letter.*
Instructor: What type of sentence is "March is a windy month"? Does it ask a question? Does it give a command? Does it show sudden, strong emotion? Does it give information?
*Child: The sentence gives information.*
Instructor: This sentence is a **statement.** What kind of punctuation mark goes at the end of a sentence?
*Child: A statement ends with a period.*
Instructor: Now I will read the sentence to you one more time. Repeat it back to me.
March is a windy month.
*Child: March is a windy month.*
Instructor: Now write that sentence on your own paper.
Note to Instructor: Help the child sound out each word. Remind him as he writes to leave spaces between the words. Do not allow him to become frustrated with spelling— it is acceptable to tell him that the "e" sound at the end of "windy" is spelled with a "y." When he is finished writing from dictation, show him the original sentence in the book. Point out the capital letter, the period at the end, and the spacing between the words. Make corrections and praise him for doing a good job!

# Lesson 123

-Introducing adjectives
-Copywork: "June"
-Poem review: "Days of the Week" (Lesson 35)
* The child will need art supplies or magazines for summer pictures.

⇨   Note to Instructor: Review "Days of the Week" today.

Instructor: Repeat with me the definition of a **noun**.

Together: **A noun is the name of a person, place, thing, or idea.**

Instructor:  A **noun** names, but it doesn't give any description of the person, place, or thing it names.   If I say "flower" to you, you don't know whether it is blue or red, tall or tiny, wild, or in a pot.  You can't make a picture of it in your mind.  If I want to tell you more about the flower, I have to use other words to describe this naming word.  I have to use **adjectives. An adjective is a word that describes a noun.**  Let's say that together three times: **An adjective is a word that describes a noun**.

Together (three times): **An adjective is a word that describes a noun**.

Instructor: I am going to read to you some words that describe naming words.  I want you to follow along as I read these **adjectives**—these describing words.  When I say one of these **adjectives**, I want you to name a **noun** that it could describe!

⇨   Note to Instructor: Show the following list to the child as you read. With your finger, point to each adjective as you read it.  Then ask the child to name a person, place, or thing it could describe. (For example, point to "cold" and the child responds, "ice."  When you point and say, "hot," the child might respond "chocolate.")

**Lists of adjectives:**  cold, hot, round, square, sad, happy, funny, new, old,  blue, red, tall, short, little, small, sticky, hungry, soft, furry, white, curly, sour, sweet, tasty, crunchy, cloudy, soft, hard, fuzzy, huge, heavy, loud, seven, fifteen.

Instructor:  Now, I want you to describe a **noun**.  Think of every **adjective** that can possibly tell me more about this **noun**.

⇨   Note to Instructor:  Choose something in the room (a person or thing). Point to it.  Help the child find adjectives to describe it.  Ask him to tell you about its color, shape, and size.  Encourage him to put his description into the form of a complete sentence, such as "The sofa is soft, green, and large."

Instructor:  Let's repeat the definition of an **adjective** together three more times. **An adjective is a word that describes a noun**. Together (three times): **An adjective is a word that describes a noun**.

### Copywork

Have the child copy the "June" couplet from the poem "The Year" onto a blank sheet of lined paper. If the child has great difficulty copying both lines of the couplet, have him copy one line and you write the second line. He can illustrate the paper by drawing a picture of a June activity (swimming, picnics, vacation, Flag Day, Father's Day). If he prefers, he can cut pictures from a magazine and paste them onto the page.

# Lesson 124

-Adjectives
-Introducing predicate adjectives
-Copywork: "July"
-Poem review: "Work" (Lesson 15)
\* The child will need art supplies or old magazines for summer pictures.


⇨ Note to Instructor: Review "Work" today.

⇨ Note to Instructor: The term "predicate adjective" is for the instructor only. The child will learn that adjectives are sometimes written next to the noun, but can also be written after a linking verb.

Instructor: We have learned that **an adjective is a word that describes a noun**. Let's repeat that definition together three times.

Together (three times): **An adjective is a word that describes a noun**.

Instructor: Today, let's practice using **adjectives**. First, let's think about words that describe how something tastes. What kind of **adjectives** tell us how a cookie tastes? How about a pickle? A potato chip? A piece of cake? An apple? A lemon? A taco?

⇨ Note to Instructor: Encourage the child to use adjectives such as sweet, sour, delicious, cold, warm, hot, spicy, juicy, etc.

Instructor: Now let's think about **adjectives** that describes how something feels when you touch it. What if you were to touch the stove? How would it feel to touch an ice cube? How about a kitten? A patch of glue? Tree bark? Glass?

⇨ Note to Instructor: Encourage the child to use adjectives such as hot, cold, sticky, soft, hard, fuzzy, furry, rough, smooth, etc.

Instructor: Sometimes **adjectives** come right next to the **noun** they describe. If I say, "The happy baby giggled," what word describes baby?

*Child: Happy describes baby.*

Instructor: If I say, "The baby is happy," does the word "happy" still describe the baby?

*Child: Yes, happy still describes the baby.*

Instructor: Sometimes **adjectives** come later in the sentence, after a **linking verb**. Do you remember your **linking verbs**? I will say them for you: "Am, is, are, was, were, be, being, been." Let's say that together three times.

Together (three times): Am, is, are, was, were, be, being, been.

Instructor: If I say, "I am hungry," can you find the **linking verb** in that sentence?

⇨ Note to Instructor: Emphasize the word *am* slightly if the child is unable to identify the verb.

*Child: "Am" is the linking verb.*

Instructor: In the sentence "I am hungry," which word describes me?

*Child: Hungry.*

Instructor: "Hungry" is an **adjective**. Now I would like to write that sentence on your paper. Listen to me repeat it once more: "I am hungry." Repeat it back to me.

*Child: I am hungry.*

Instructor: Now write that sentence on your paper. Remember that the **pronoun** "I" is always capitalized!

## Copywork

Read the "July" couplet from the poem "The Year" to the child. Point out the three adjectives in the couplet: "hot" describes "July," "stormy" describes "showers," and "lazy" describes "hours." Have the child copy the couplet onto a blank sheet of lined paper. If the child has great difficulty copying both lines, have him copy one line and you write the second line. He can illustrate the paper by drawing a picture of a July activity (swimming, Fourth of July, a beach trip). If he prefers, he can cut pictures from a magazine and paste them onto the page.

## Enrichment Activity

Tell the child to use adjectives that describe the weather on a stormy day. After the child tells you as many as he can think of, give him these ideas: windy, cloudy, rainy, snowy, blustery, hot, warm, cold, cool, sunny. If you wish, he may write a short description of his stormy day and draw a picture showing his adjectives.

# Lesson 125

-Nouns
-Pronouns
-Verbs
-Adjectives
* The child will need art supplies or old magazines for summer pictures.


Instructor: We have learned about four different kinds of words: **Nouns, pronouns, verbs**, and **adjectives**. Let's review what each kind of word does. **A noun is the name of a person, place, thing, or idea.** Let's repeat that together three times.

Together (three times): **A noun is the name of a person, place, thing, or idea.**

Instructor: Can you name a person for me? A place? A thing? An idea? All of those words are nouns.

⇨  Note to Instructor: Give the child as much help as necessary to come up with these four nouns. You may have to remind him that an idea is something you think about in your mind, but cannot see or touch.

Instructor: **A pronoun is a word used in the place of a noun.** Let's say that together three times.

Together (three times): **A pronoun is a word used in the place of a noun.**

Instructor: Instead of saying to you, "Christina is coming to play today," I could say "*She* is coming to play today." Repeat those two sentences for me.

*Child: "Christina is coming to play today." "She is coming to play today."*

Instructor: The **pronoun** "she" is used in place of the noun "Christina." Now let's review our third kind of word: **Verbs. A verb is a word that does an action, shows a state of being, links two words together, or helps another verb.** Let's say that together three times.

Together (three times): **A verb is a word that does an action, shows a state of being, links two words together, or helps another verb.**

Instructor: Can you finish these sentences for me, using **action verbs**? "The baby…"

*Child: The baby [laughed, drooled, crawled, giggled].*

⇨  Note to Instructor: If necessary, prompt the child for the appropriate action verb.

Instructor: The new puppy...
*Child: The new puppy [barked, played, slept].*
Instructor. These are **verbs** that do actions. **Verbs** also show "state of being." The **state of being verbs** are: Am, is, are, was, were, be, being, been. Let's repeat those together three times.
Together: (three times)
Am [clap]
Is [clap]
Are, was, were. [clap]
Be [clap]
Being [clap]
Been. [clap] [clap]
Instructor: Some **verbs** help other **verbs**. The "**helping verbs**" are: Have, has, had, do does, did, shall, will, should, would, may, might, must, can, could. Let's repeat those together three times.
Together: (three times)
Have, has, had [clap]
Do, does, did [clap]
Shall, will, should, would, may, might, must [clap] [clap]
Can, could!
Instructor: Sometimes a **verb** links two words together. If I say, "You are smart!" I am using a **pronoun** in the place of a **noun**—your name. I am linking the **pronoun** "you" to a word that describes what you are— smart! The **verb** "are" links "you" with "smart." It is a **linking verb**. "Smart" is an **adjective**. It describes you! Let's review the definition of an **adjective**: **An adjective is a word that describes a noun**. Let's repeat that definition together three times.
Together (three times): **An adjective is a word that describes a noun**.
Instructor: I will give you some sentences with **nouns** and **linking verbs**. I want you to add an **adjective** to each sentence that describes the **noun**.
Note to Instructor: If necessary, prompt the child to complete each sentence by asking questions such as "What color is the dress?" or "What size is the horse?"
Instructor: The wall is...
*Child: The wall is [white].*
Instructor: The dress is...
*Child: The dress is [pretty, blue].*

Instructor: The horse is...
*Child: The horse is [big].*
Instructor: My room is...
*Child: My room is [neat, messy].*

## Copywork

Look at the couplet "August" from "The Year" together. Help the child identify the nouns, verbs, and adjectives. See key below:

noun    action verb    adjective    noun
August brings the warmest air,

adjective noun    adjective    noun
Sandy feet and sea-wet hair.

Have the child copy the "August" couplet from the poem "The Year" onto a blank sheet of lined paper. If the child has great difficulty copying both lines of the couplet, have him copy one line and you write the second line. He can illustrate the paper by drawing a picture of an August activity (eating ice-cream, family birthdays, religious holidays). If he prefers, he can cut pictures from a magazine and paste them onto the page.

# Lesson 126

-Helping verbs
-Dictation exercise: "God Made Them So"
-Copywork: "September"
-Poem review: "Hearts Are Like Doors" (Lesson 27)
* The child will need art supplies or old magazines for fall pictures.

⇨ Note to Instructor: Review "Hearts Are Like Doors" today.
⇨ Note to Instructor: Review the "Helping Verb" chant today:
Am [clap]
Is [clap]
Are, was, were. [clap]
Be [clap]
Being [clap]
Been. [clap] [clap]
Have, has, had [clap]
Do, does, did [clap]
Shall, will, should, would, may, might, must [clap] [clap]
Can, could!

Instructor: Today I am going to give you some sentences in which the **action verb** needs another **verb** to help it. I will emphasize the **verbs** as I read. I want you to tell me which **verb** is the **action verb**, and which **verb** is the **helping verb**.

⇨ Note to Instructor: Emphasize the italicized words in the following sentences. Give the child any necessary help. If the child cannot identify the helping verb, read the sentence without it and ask which word has disappeared.

Instructor: "I'm glad the sky *is painted* blue." Which verb is the **action verb**? Which is the **helping verb**?

*Child: "Painted" is an action verb. "Is" is a helping verb.*

Instructor: "And the earth is painted green."

*Child: "Painted" is an action verb. "Is" is a helping verb.*

Instructor: Those sentences are the beginning of a poem. I am going to read the poem aloud while you follow along with me.

I'm glad the sky is painted blue,
And the earth is painted green,
With such a lot of nice fresh air
All sandwiched in between.

Instructor: Which helping verb do you see in line one?

*Child: Is.*
Instructor: Which helping verb do you see in line two?
*Child: Is.*
Instructor: This poem is an anonymous poem – we don't know who wrote it. Here is another line from a poem, called "Let Dogs Delight to Bark and Bite." It was written by Isaac Watts.

Let dogs delight to bark and bite,
For God <u>has</u> <u>made</u> them so.

The verbs in the last line are "has made." Which **verb** is the **action verb**? Which is the **helping verb**?
*Child: "Made" is an action verb. "Has" is a helping verb.*
Instructor: I will read you the whole poem now:

Let dogs delight to bark and bite,
For God has made them so.
Let bears and lions growl and fight,
For it is their nature too.
But children, you should never let
Such angry passions rise;
Your little hands were never made
To tear each other's eyes.

Instructor: Listen to the **verbs** in this line: "But children, you *should* never *let* / Such angry passions rise." The **verbs** are "should" and "let." "Let" is the **action verb**. What is the **helping verb**?
*Child: "Should" is the helping verb.*
Instructor: "Should" helps the verb "let." Listen to this line:

Your little hands <u>were</u> never <u>made</u>
To tear each other's eyes.

Can you hear the **verbs** "were made?" "Were" is the **helping verb**. What is the **action verb**?
*Child: "Made" is the action verb.*
Instructor: Now I would like you to write this sentence on your paper: "God has made them so." Listen to me as I say it again: "God has made them so." Can you repeat that sentence back to me?
*Child: "God has made them so."*

Instructor: Write that sentence on your own paper. Remember that the first letter should be capitalized. What punctuation mark should come at the end of the sentence?

*Child: A period should come at the end of the sentence.*

⇨ Note to Instructor: Repeat the dictation sentence once more, if necessary.

## Copywork

Have the child copy the "September" couplet from the poem "The Year" onto a blank sheet of lined paper. If the child has great difficulty copying both lines of the couplet, have him copy one line and you write the second line. He can illustrate the paper by drawing a picture of a September activity (fall leaves, books and pencils for "back to school," religious or family holidays). If he prefers, he can cut pictures from a magazine and paste them onto the page.

# Lesson 127

## -Story narration: "The Quarrel"

⇨   Note to Instructor: Read aloud the old fable below. Have the child tell the story back to you; use the suggested questions at the story's end to prompt the child, if necessary. When the child has completed his oral narration, repeat the first sentence of his narration back to him as a dictation exercise. Then, complete the narration yourself by writing the child's remaining sentences.

### The Quarrel

Once upon a time, all of the different parts of the body started to quarrel with each other. "We do all of the work around here!" the legs complained. "We take the rest of you where you need to go. Our muscles work and work—and the rest of you don't do anything to help us out."

"You think you work hard?" groaned the feet. "What about us? We carry everyone else's weight! And we're stuck in these hot, dark shoes all day long. We can't even see where we're going! We work much harder than the legs!"

The hands snapped, "Stop whining. If we didn't open doors, you'd be stuck in one place. We do all of the work—carrying toys, holding pencils for writing, patting dirty dogs. And we're always being washed with nasty soap! Even when the feet and legs are relaxing, we're still at work—feeding the mouth, or turning pages of books. We have the most difficult time of all."

"What are you complaining about?" asked the mouth. "You may put the food into me—but I have to chew it! I chew and chew, and chew—and you're not even grateful! You get all the nutrition from the food I swallow. I'm not going to feed you any more!"

"You're all wrong," grumbled the eyes. "We work all day long. We're open from dawn to dusk. We have to keep on watching even when the rest of you are doing nothing. If we weren't looking out for you, the legs and feet would be running into walls all of the time, and the hands wouldn't be able to find toys or food. What ingratitude! We're not going to look out for you any more."

"Fine!" said the legs. "We quit!"

"So do we!" squeaked the feet. "No more walking!"

The legs, the feet, the hands, the eyes, and the mouth all sulked.

They refused to do anything. The body didn't get fed. It didn't get any exercise. It couldn't even watch TV! It got thinner and weaker and more and more bored.

Finally the parts of the body held a meeting. "I haven't eaten for days," the mouth groaned. "I've almost forgotten how."

"We have nothing to do!" moaned the hands.

"We are weak and helpless without food and exercise!" agreed the legs and the feet.

"Let's all agree to work together," suggested the eyes. "None of us can work unless the others do their jobs. Instead of complaining about who does the most, let's each do our own tasks. We'll go back to looking out for the rest of you. The legs and feet can carry us around. The mouth can feed us, and the hands can work for us. Then the body will be healthy again."

So the parts of the body agreed to help each other, rather than quarrelling about who worked the hardest. Soon the body was strong and healthy again—and the legs, feet, hands, mouth, and eyes were happy once more.

⇨ Note to Instructor: Ask the child to tell you the story back in his own words. If the child has trouble remembering, use these questions:

Why did the legs complain? *The legs said that they worked harder than anyone else.*

What did the shoes complain about? *They were stuck in hot shoes and worked harder than the legs.*

What sorts of things did the hands do for the body? *The hands carried toys, held pencils, patted dogs, fed the mouth, turned pages of books.*

What did the parts of the body decide to do? *Each part decided to refuse to do its work.*

What happened to the body? *It got weak, thin, and bored.*

What did the parts of the body decide to do then? *They decided to help each other again.*

# Lesson 128

-Contractions
-Copywork: "October"
-Poem review: "The Goops" (Lesson 100)
* The child will need art supplies or October pictures to cut and paste.


Note to Instructor: Review "The Goops" today.

Instructor: We have learned that a contraction is made up of two words, put together into one word, with some letters left out. A punctuation mark called an apostrophe is put in the place of the missing letters. Let's read back through "The Quarrel" together and find all of the contractions. When we find each contraction, we will decide for which two words it stands. I will write those words out for you next to each contraction.

⇨ Note to Instructor: As you find each contraction, write it on your paper. Across from it, write the full form of the word. Use the key below:

| | | |
|---|---|---|
| Paragraph 1: | don't | do not |
| Paragraph 2: | we're | we are |
| | can't | can not |
| | we're | we are |
| Paragraph 3: | didn't | did not |
| | you'd | you would |
| | we're | we are |
| Paragraph 4: | didn't | did not |
| | you'd | you would |
| | we're | we are |
| | we're | we are |
| Paragraph 5: | you're | you are |
| | I'm | I am |
| Paragraph 6: | you're | you are |
| | we're | we are |
| | weren't | were not |
| | wouldn't | would not |
| | we're | we are |
| Paragraph 7: | none | |
| Paragraph 8: | none | |
| Paragraph 9: | didn't | did not |
| | didn't | did not |
| | couldn't | could not |
| Paragraph 10: | haven't | have not |
| | I've | I have |
| Paragraph 11: | none | |

Paragraph 12:   none
Paragraph 13:   let's           let us
                let's           let us
                we'll           we will
Paragraph 14:   none

## Copywork

Have the child copy the "October" couplet from the poem "The Year"
onto a blank sheet of lined paper.  If the child has great difficulty
copying both lines of the couplet, have him copy one line and you
write the second line.  He can illustrate the paper by drawing a picture
of an October activity (frost, pumpkins, fall leaves, holidays). If he
prefers, he can cut pictures from a magazine and paste them onto the
page.

# Lesson 129

-Four kinds of verbs review
-Copywork: "November"
* The child will need art supplies or November pictures to cut and paste.


Instructor: **A verb is a word that does an action, shows a state of being, links two words together, or helps another verb.** Let's say the definition of a verb together.

Together: **A verb is a word that does an action, shows a state of being, links two words together, or helps another verb.**

Instructor: This tells us that there are four kinds of **verbs**: **action verbs**, **state of being verbs**, **linking verbs**, and **helping verbs**. **Action verbs** tell about something you can do. I will say some **action verbs**, and I want you to act them out. Wiggle, hop, crawl, stand, smile, giggle. Now I want you to stand perfectly still and just *be*. **State of being verbs** tell us that something exists. The **state of being verbs** are: Am, is, are, was, were, be, being, been. Let's repeat those together.

Together:

Am [clap]

Is [clap]

Are, was, were. [clap]

Be [clap]

Being [clap]

Been. [clap] [clap]

Instructor: **Some verbs help other verbs**. The "**helping verbs**" are the verbs we just said as well as: Have, has, had, do does, did, shall, will, should, would, may, might, must, can, could. Let's repeat those additional **helping verbs** together.

Together:

Have, has, had [clap]

Do, does, did [clap]

Shall, will, should, would, may, might, must [clap] [clap]

Can, could!

Instructor: **Linking verbs connect two words together.** If I say, "The mouth was upset, and the eyes were annoyed," I am linking "mouth" with "upset" by using the **linking verb** "was." I am linking "eyes" with "annoyed" by using the linking verb "were." Now we are going to look at a poem together. This poem has both **action verbs**

and **helping verbs** in it. We will try to find all of the **action verbs** and all of the **helping verbs**. First I will read the poem "How Creatures Move," and then we will look for helping verbs and action verbs. Note to Instructor: Read the poem all the way through as the child listens. Then, read the poem again. Use your finger to help the child follow along as you read, stopping as necessary to identify the helping verbs and action verbs. The helping verbs and action verbs are as follows:
walks (action), leaps (action), can (helping), crawl (action), can (helping), dive (action), swim (action), wiggles (action), swings (action), may (helping), hop (action), spread (action), sail (action), have (This is an action verb. But since "have" can be used in both ways, don't correct him if he names it as a helping verb.), leap (action), dance (action), walk (action), run (action).

How Creatures Move
*Anonymous*


The lion walks on padded paws,
The squirrel leaps from limb to limb,
While flies can crawl straight up a wall,
And seals can dive and swim.
The worm, he wiggles all around,
The monkey swings by his tail,
And birds may hop upon the ground,
Or spread their wings and sail.
But boys and girls have much more fun;
They leap and dance
And walk and run.

**Copywork**
Have the child copy the "November" couplet from the poem "The Year" onto a blank sheet of lined paper. If the child has great difficulty copying both lines of the couplet, have him copy one line and you write the second line. He can illustrate the paper by drawing a picture of a November activity (religious holidays, Thanksgiving). If he prefers, he can paste pictures onto the page.

# Lesson 130

-Adjectives
-Copywork: "December"
\* The child will need art supplies or December pictures to cut and paste.

Instructor: In the poem about "How Creatures Move," the lion "walks on padded paws." "Padded" is a word that describes "paws." It tells you more about the paws. "Padded" is an adjective that describes the noun "paws." **An adjective is a word that describes a noun.** Let's repeat that definition together three times.

Together (three times): **An adjective is a word that describes a noun.**

Instructor: Let's practice making up some sentences that use **adjectives**. I will suggest the names of people, places, and things. You will tell me some adjectives that describe them, and I will write those adjectives down. Then I will help you to put your adjectives into complete sentences.

⇨ Note to Instructor: List the names of three people, places, or things that the child can look at – either in the room, or in a magazine or book. It is important for the child to have an actual, concrete image to describe. Write the adjectives down as the child says them. You can help the child by prompting him with these questions: "What color is it? What size is it? Is it young or old? How many? How does it feel? How does it smell? How does it taste? What shape is it?" After you have written down a list of adjectives for each noun, help the child form the description into a complete sentence, such as: "The little brown dog is fluffy and cute," or "The chair is big, blue, and soft." Choose one of these sentences and repeat it back to the child several times. Then ask the child to write the sentence from dictation. If the sentence has more than two adjectives in a row (for example, "My book is thick, brown, and square"), you may need to review commas in a series (Lesson 114).

## Copywork

Have the child copy the "December" couplet from the poem "The Year" onto a blank sheet of lined paper. If the child has great difficulty copying both lines of the couplet, have him copy one line and you write the second line. He can illustrate the paper by drawing a picture of a December activity (snow, ice, religious holidays). If he prefers, he can paste pictures onto the page.

# Lesson 131

- Poem memorization: "The Year"

⇨ Note to Instructor: Read this poem out loud three times. Later in the day, read it again three times. See Lesson 2 for memorization techniques.

The Year
*By Sara Coleridge, adapted by Sara Buffington*

January brings the snow,
Helps the skis and sleds to go.

February brings the rain,
Thaws the frozen lake again.

March brings breezes loud and shrill,
Stirs the dancing daffodil.

April brings the primrose sweet,
Scatters daisies at our feet.

May brings sunshine full and bright,
Sends the busy bees to flight.

June brings tulips, lilies, roses,
Fills the children's hands with posies.

Hot July brings stormy showers,
Lemonade, and lazy hours.

August brings the warmest air,
Sandy feet and sea-wet hair.

September brings the fruit so sweet,
Apples ripe from summer heat.

October brings the colored trees,
Scampering squirrels and cooling breeze.

Dull November brings the blast,
Then the leaves are whirling fast.

Chill December brings the sleet,
Blazing fire, and Christmas treat.[1]

[1] Alternate last line: "Blazing fire, and winter treat."

# Lesson 132

-Introducing interjections
-Four types of sentences
-Copywork: "Ouch!"
-Poem review: "The Year" (Lesson 131)

⇨ Note to Instructor: Read the poem "The Year" out loud three times.

Instructor: A few lessons ago (Lesson 127), we read a story about a quarrel between the parts of the body. The story was interesting to read because it contained so many different types of **sentences**. It didn't just state facts. Sometimes the parts of the body made **statements**, sometimes they gave **commands**, sometimes they asked **questions**, and sometimes they used **exclamations**! We are going to read some of those **sentences** again today. But first we are going to review the definition of a **sentence**. **A sentence is a group of words that expresses a complete thought.** Let's say that definition together three times.

Together (three times): **A sentence is a group of words that expresses a complete thought.**

Instructor: A **sentence** begins with a capital letter and ends with a punctuation mark. Let's say that together three times.

Together (three times): A **sentence** begins with a capital letter and ends with a punctuation mark.

Instructor: Remember the four different types of sentences? They are: **statements, commands, questions**, and **exclamations**. Repeat with me three times: **statements, commands, questions, and exclamations.**

Together (three times): **Statements, commands, questions, and exclamations.**

Instructor: **A statement gives information.** Repeat that definition for me: **A statement gives information**.

*Child: A statement gives information.*

Instructor: Here is a **statement** from the story "The Quarrel." "Once upon a time, all of the different parts of the body started to quarrel with each other." Here is another **statement**: "The legs, the feet, the hands, the eyes, and the mouth all sulked." Both of those sentences give you information. They are **statements**. The second type of **sentence** is a **command**. **A command gives an order or makes a request.** Let's say that together twice: **A command**

244

**gives an order or makes a request.**

Together (twice): **A command gives an order or makes a request.**

Instructor: In the story, when the hands became irritated because the feet and legs were complaining, the hands snapped, "Stop whining." The hands gave an order or made a request that the feet and legs stop whining. "Stop whining" is a **command**. The third type of sentence is a **question**. **A question asks something.** It ends with an **question mark**. Let's say the definition of a **question** together three times: **A question asks something.** It ends with a question mark.

Together (three times): **A question asks something.** It ends with a question mark.

Instructor: In the story, the feet asked the legs, "You think you work hard?" "What about us?" Those are **questions**. The feet asked the legs for information! The fourth type of sentence is an **exclamation**. **An exclamation shows sudden or strong feeling.** It ends with an exclamation point. Say that with me three times: **An exclamation shows sudden or strong feeling.** It ends with an exclamation point.

Together (three times): **An exclamation shows sudden or strong feeling.** It ends with an exclamation point.

Instructor: The story of the quarrel was full of sudden and strong feelings. The parts of the body were showing lots of strong feelings when they were quarrelling. Do you ever quarrel or fuss with anyone? Do you have sudden and strong feelings when you quarrel and fuss? But there are other times when we show sudden or strong feelings, but we aren't quarrelling. Other sudden or strong feelings can be excitement: "We're going to see a baby panda!" Or surprise: "Thank you for this present!" Or happiness: "Spring always makes me feel happy!" You might have sudden or strong feeling of fear and concern if you think someone is going to get hurt. At a time like that, you might yell, "That's hot!" because the baby is about to touch a hot stove.

We have learned about the ways that different kinds of words work together these sentences. We have learned about **nouns, pronouns, verbs** and **adjectives. A noun names a person, place, thing, or idea. A pronoun is a word used in the place of a noun. A verb does an action, shows a state of being, links two words together, or helps another verb. An adjective is a word that describes a noun.** Today we are going to talk about another kind of word called an "interjection." When we say just one word suddenly with sudden or strong feeling, we call that word an **interjection**. **Interjections** are followed by exclamation marks. Say the definition of an **interjection** with me three times: **An interjection is a word that expresses sudden or strong feeling.** Together (three times): **An interjection is a word that expresses sudden or strong feeling.**

Instructor: I am going to tell you something imaginary that happened, and I want you to tell me a word that you might say. That word is an **interjection**! Running across the yard, you stepped on something sharp and cut your foot. What would you say?

*Child: [Ouch!]*

Instructor: [Ouch] is an **interjection**. Now imagine that your baby sister is about to run into the street. What would you say?

*Child: [Stop!]*

Instructor: [Stop] is an **interjection**. Now imagine that you're at the grocery store. You are walking slo-o-wly! But your mother wants to move fast and finish the shopping. What word might your mother interject into her conversation to get you to speed up?

*Child: [Hurry!]*

Instructor: [Hurry] is an **interjection**. When we write an **interjection**, we put an exclamation point after the **interjection**. When an **interjection** is all alone with an exclamation point after it, it should begin with a capital letter.

## Copywork

Have the child copy one of these sentences of appropriate length for his ability. Remind him that the interjection begins with a capital letter and ends with an exclamation point. If necessary, remind him that the sentence following the exclamation begins with a capital letter and ends with a period.

Ouch! I just cut my foot.
Stop! Don't run into the street.
Hurry! If we don't finish shopping, we won't get home on time.

## Enrichment Activity

Write one or more of the above sentences as dictation.

# Lesson 133

-Adjectives
-Commas in a series
-Dictation exercise: "The Brown Bird"
-Poem review: "The Year" (Lesson 131)

⇨ Note to Instructor: Review "The Year" today.

Instructor: Last lesson, we learned about **interjections**. **An interjection is a word that expresses sudden or strong feeling**. Let's repeat that together three times.

Together: **An interjection is a word that expresses sudden or strong feeling**.

Instructor: Let's imagine that I walked into a room, saw something sitting on a table, and said, "Wow!" That's an **interjection**. Then I added two more **interjections**: "Fantastic! Delicious! Yummy!" What do you think that I just saw!

*Child: Something to eat!*

Instructor: Let's think about words that describe delicious, yummy, fantastic foods. Let's start with *cake*. The word "cake" is a **noun**, because *cake* is a thing. Do you remember what words describe **nouns**?

*Child: An adjective is a word that describes a noun.*

Instructor: Any words that you use to describe the **noun** "cake" will be **adjectives**. Let's think of some **adjectives** that describe "cake," and I will write them down.

⇨ Note to Instructor: If necessary, prompt the child with the following list: chocolate, strawberry, vanilla, caramel, lemon, layer, round, square, birthday, gooey, delicious, scrumptious, frosted, glazed, decorated. Write down adjectives as the child gives them.

Instructor: Now put four of those **adjectives** into a sentence that begins, "The cake was..." Say that sentence to me, and I will write it down.

*Child: The cake was [chocolate, round, frosted, and gooey].*

Note to Instructor: Write the sentence down for the child. Put a comma after each item in the list; use the word "and" before the last item, as illustrated above. Point to each comma.

Instructor: Look at this sentence with me. What punctuation mark separates the adjectives in the list?

*Child: A comma.*

Instructor: Words in a list should be separated by commas. We could put an "and" between each one of these **adjectives**: The cake was [chocolate and round and frosted and gooey]. But that would sound awkward. So we just put a comma between each adjective instead. Let's make another "food list." Tell me a food that you enjoy, and then we will think of **adjectives** to describe it.

⇨ Note to Instructor: Help the child think of a food noun and of at least four adjectives that describe it. Ask the child to put the noun and adjectives into a sentence following the format above: "The [food] is [adjective], [adjective], [adjective], and [adjective]." Write the sentence down. Remind the child that these describing words are adjectives. Point to each comma, and then remind the child that words in a list should be separated by commas.

## Dictation Exercise

Choose an appropriate sentence from the list below and dictate to the child. Repeat the sentence twice and then ask the child to repeat it back to you before he begins to write. Remind him that commas follow items in a list. Tell him that when you are reading aloud, you will pause whenever a comma comes in the sentence; as you read, pause for a few moments at each comma. Remember to watch the child and correct any mistakes as he writes.

The bird was brown.
The robin hops, sings, and pecks.
The robin pulls, tugs, and eats worms from the ground.

# Lesson 134

-Introducing conjunctions
-Dictation exercise: "I Was Tired"
-Poem review: "The Year" (Lesson 131)

⇨ Note to Instructor: Review "The Year" today.

Instructor: In a car, all the parts of the motor have to do their jobs properly to make a car run. All the parts of a washing machine have to work together properly to make a washing machine work. Have you wondered why we are learning about these **nouns, pronouns, verbs, adjectives**, and **interjections**? It is because they are called "**parts of speech**." The **parts of speech** make a sentence work properly—just like the parts of a motor make a car work properly. If you wanted to build a car motor, you would need to know all of the different parts. And if you want to make a good sentence, you need to know all of the sentence parts! So far, we have learned about **nouns, pronouns, verbs, adjectives**, and **interjections**. I am going to review them with you. After I tell you what the **part of speech** does in a sentence, repeat the definition with me.

Instructor: **A noun names a person, place, thing, or idea.**

Together: **A noun names a person, place, thing, or idea.**

Instructor: **A pronoun is a word used in the place of a noun.**

Together: **A pronoun is a word used in the place of a noun.**

Instructor: **A verb does an action, shows a state of being, links two words together, or helps another verb.**

Together: **A verb does an action, shows a state of being, links two words together, or helps another verb.**

Instructor: **An adjective is a word that describes a noun.**

Together: **An adjective is a word that describes a noun.**

Instructor: **An interjection is a word that expresses sudden or strong feeling.**

Together: **An interjection is a word that expresses sudden or strong feeling.**

Instructor: Now we are going to learn about another little part of speech. It is called a **conjunction**. Sometimes, when you are in the car on the highway, you might see a sign that says "Junction." A "junction" sign means that two roads are joining together. "Junction" means "joining." **A conjunction is a word that joins words or groups of words together.** I am going to say the definition of a

**conjunction** for you slowly, then you join with me as we say it three times more. **A conjunction joins words or groups of words together.**

Together (three times): **A conjunction joins words or groups of words together.**

Instructor: The **conjunctions** you will use most often are: *and, but, or.* If you were going to tell me that two kinds of pets— rabbits and hamsters—both eat lettuce you would say, "Rabbits and hamsters eat lettuce." The conjunction "and" joins the words "rabbits" and "hamsters." Can you tell me a sentence about two things that can fly?

*Child: [Birds and butterflies] fly.*

Instructor: Now, tell me a sentence about two things that can swim.

*Child: [Fish and tadpoles] swim.*

Instructor: In both of these sentences you used "and" to join the names of two things. Now, let's make some sentences that use "and" to join two action words. I can walk *and* write. The dog barks *and* chases. Now tell me two actions you can do.

*Child: [I can run and jump.]*

Instructor: The conjunction "and" usually connects two words together. The **conjunction** "or" usually means that you will have to choose between the two words that are joined! If I say, "Play a game, or go to bed," that joins together two actions—but you can't do both. You will have to choose one or the other! If I say, "You can wear your blue sweater or your red sweatshirt," you can pick one or the other—but you can't wear both! Think about two things that I could do. Now, make a sentence that gives me permission to do one thing or the other.

*Child: [You can go swimming or you can use the computer.]*

Instructor: The last **conjunction** is "but." If I say, "I started to read my book, but I fell asleep," I am joining together two groups of words. "I started to read my book" is joined to "I fell asleep." Now I will give you two groups of words. I want you to join them together with the **conjunction** "but." "I want to go outside." "I cannot find my coat." Join those together with the **conjunction** "but."

*Child: I want to go outside, but I cannot find my coat.*

Instructor: Let's repeat that definition three more times: **A conjunction joins words or groups of words together.**

Together (three times): **A conjunction joins words or groups of words together.**

250

## Dictation Exercise

Choose one or more of the following sentences. Remind the child that you will pause wherever a comma should go.

I was tired, and I slept.

I want to go outside, but I can't find my coat.

You can go swimming, or you can use the computer.

# Lesson 135

-Interjections
-Conjunctions
-Dictation exercise: "The Zoo"
-Poem review: "The Goops" (Lesson 100)
* The child may need art supplies for the enrichment activity.


⇨  Note to Instructor: Review "The Goops" today.

Instructor: Let's review some of the definitions we've learned.  Repeat this with me three times: **An interjection is a word that expresses sudden or strong feeling.**

Together (three times): **An interjection is a word that expresses sudden or strong feeling**.

Instructor (with feeling!): Oh!  Fantastic!  Wonderful!  Great!

⇨  Note to Instructor: Pause for a moment to see whether the child recognizes your use of interjections.  If not, point out that you have just expressed strong feeling with the words above.

Instructor: If I say, "Wonderful!  You are using your brain *and* getting your work done," I am joining together two groups of words.  I am joining "You are using your brain" to "getting your work done" with the **conjunction** *and*.  Remember: **A conjunction joins words or groups of words together.**   Let's repeat that together three times.

Together (three times): **A conjunction joins words or groups of words together.**

Instructor: The **conjunctions** you will use most often are: "and," "but," "or."  Say these sentences after me:  "I would eat my spinach, *but* I am not hungry."

*Child: I would eat my spinach, but I am not hungry.*

Instructor: "You may eat your spinach, or you may choose Brussels sprouts instead."

*Child: You may eat your spinach, or you may choose Brussels sprouts instead.*

Instructor: Both sentences used a **conjunction** to join groups of words.  What **conjunction** does the first sentence use?  Listen to it again: "I would eat my spinach, *but* I am not hungry."

*Child: The sentence uses the conjunction **but**.*

Instructor: What **conjunction** does the second sentence use?  Listen to it again: "You may eat your spinach, or you may choose Brussels sprouts instead."

*Child: The sentence uses the conjunction **or**.*

Instructor: Now I will use the **conjunction** "and" to join words together. "I went to the zoo and saw a monkey and a lion and a zebra and a giraffe." I will write that sentence down for you.

⇨ Note to Instructor: Write the above sentence on your paper.

Instructor: In Lesson 114 we talked about using commas to separate items in a series—a list of items. When you have more than two items in your list, you use commas instead of **conjunctions**. I will write this sentence again, using commas to separate the list of animals that you saw at the zoo. "I went to the zoo and saw a monkey, a lion, a zebra, and a giraffe."

⇨ Note to Instructor: Write the above sentence on your paper. Point out the commas. Remind the child that the last "and" should remain in the list.

Instructor: Items in a series should be separated by commas. Items in a series can be **nouns**—like the names of the animals. Commas are also used in a sentences to separate **adjectives** that describe things. If I write "The zoo is hot and interesting and noisy and crowded," I am listing **adjectives** that describe the zoo. I am joining those adjectives with the conjunction "and."

⇨ Note to Instructor: Write the sentence above on your paper. Point out the adjectives and the conjunctions.

Instructor: But it would be easier to use commas to separate those **adjectives**. Now I will write, "The zoo is hot, interesting, noisy, and crowded." Commas will replace all of the "ands"—except for the very last one.

⇨ Note to Instructor: Write the above sentence on your paper. Point out the commas. Remind the child that the last "and" should remain in the list.

Instructor: If I write, "I walked and laughed and pointed and saw animals at the zoo," I am listing four actions that you can do. Those actions are also items in a series. I am joining them together with the **conjunction** *and*.

⇨ Note to Instructor: Write the sentence above on your paper. Point out the adjectives and the conjunctions.

Instructor: It would be better to use commas to separate those actions. I will write, "I walked, laughed, pointed, and saw animals at the zoo." Now commas separate those items in a series.

⇨ Note to Instructor: Write the above sentence on your paper. Point out the commas. Remind the child that the last "and" should remain in the list.

## Dictation Exercise

Choose one or more of the following sentences. Remind the child that you will pause wherever a comma should go. Remember to pause at each comma!

The baby is sweet, fat, and damp.
The zoo is hot, interesting, noisy, and crowded
The legs, the feet, the hands, the eyes, and the mouth all sulked.

## Enrichment Activity

Help the child make up sentences that have items in a list. Ask the child for a series of adjectives that describe a favorite activity, a list of activities that he enjoys, and a list of things in his room. Help him to write the sentences out, using commas properly. He may illustrate the lists. Title the paper "Items in a Series."

# Lesson 136

-Introducing letter-writing
  -Writing a thank-you note
-Poem review: "The Year" (Lesson 131)


⇨  Note to Instructor: Review "The Year" today.

⇨  Note to Instructor: Today you will begin to help the child write a thank-you note to an adult using a title of respect. Even if the adult is a close relative, practice using a title of respect. Using the form on the following page as a model for a friendly letter, *you will write for the child a rough draft* of a real thank-you note to a real person, thanking them for a real gift. Use the suggestions in the model to help the child compose the letter's content. Then, write your rough draft in proper form, so that the child can copy directly from it.

You will address an envelope and mail the letter in the next lesson. If the child mails this note to a relative, you put a note in the envelope explaining that the child is practicing writing titles of respect.

**Date** (Today's date, written on the right-hand side of the paper)

**Greeting** (Dear _____,)
(Remember that a comma comes after the greeting. Remind the child that a title of respect which is abbreviated begins with a capital letter and has a period following it).

**Body of the Letter** (Thank you for the _____. Here, name the gift. Help the child tell something he liked about the gift, choosing an appropriate adjective to describe it (pretty, big, little, cute, special, bright, good, delicious, funny, interesting). Then ask him to describe how he will use the gift. If he is writing a thank-you note for a trip or for some other favor, have him describe his favorite part of the trip or favor. The body of the letter should be one brief paragraph. Remember to indent the first line of this paragraph.)

**Closing** (You may use "Love," "Sincerely," or "Yours truly." Remember that a comma comes after the closing. The closing should be in line with the date above.)

**Writer's Name** (Child signs his own name.)

➪    Note to Instructor: Now ask the child to copy the letter neatly onto his own paper. Supervise as the child copies the letter, reminding him of needed corrections as necessary. In the next lesson he will address an envelope and mail the letter.

# Lesson 137

-Addressing an envelope
-Poem review: "Mr. Nobody" (Lesson 81)
* Both the instructor and the child will need a business size envelope.

⇨ Note to Instructor: Review "Mr. Nobody" today.

⇨ Note to Instructor: Today the child will address a real envelope for the thank-you note he wrote last lesson. (Using a business size envelope will give a young child more room to write!). You will address a model envelope for him. Write his name and address on the top left-hand corner of the envelope. As you are writing, remind him to abbreviate street names properly, to capitalize names of cities, etc., to use the proper postal code for his state, and to use his zip code. Write the recipient's name and address in the center of the envelope. As you are writing, remind him to use a period after titles of respect and other appropriate abbreviations. After you finish writing the model envelope, draw light lines on a second envelope as below:

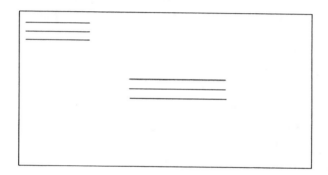

Most young children need lines to guide them as they write. Help the child to copy the names and addresses onto his own envelope, to fold the letter neatly and put it in the envelope, and to mail it. Remember that letters should be folded into thirds: First, fold up the bottom third, and then fold down the top third.

# Lesson 138

-Introducing direct quotations
-Copywork: "The Little Bird"

⇨ Note to Instructor: Chant the helping verb list three times:
Am [clap]
Is [clap]
Are, was, were. [clap]
Be [clap]
Being [clap]
Been. [clap] [clap]
Have, has, had [clap]
Do, does, did [clap]
Shall, will, should, would, may, might, must [clap] [clap]
Can, could!
Instructor: I am going to read a poem called "The Little Bird" to you. Listen as I read.
⇨ Note to Instructor: Read the following poem without showing it to the child. Make a distinct voice for the quotation (the bold print).

The Little Bird
*Mother Goose rhyme*

Once I saw a little bird
Come hop, hop, hop;
So I cried, **"Little bird,**
**Will you stop, stop, stop?"**
And was going to the window
To say **"How do you do?"**
But he shook his little tail,
And far away he flew.

Instructor: Now I will show you the poem and read it again. Follow along with your eyes as I read. This time, I want you to read the words that the child says in the poem.
⇨ Note to Instructor: Read the poem below, running your finger under the words you are saying as the child follows along. When you get to the direct quotations, pause and let the child read the bold print.
Instructor: The words that you read are called "direct quotations." Direct quotations are the exact words that someone says. Look back at the exact words that the child says in the poem when she sees the bird.

258

There are special punctuation marks on either side of those exact words. We call these "quotation marks." Quotation marks are two apostrophes, put together. You learned how to make apostrophes when we learned about contractions (Lesson 119).

⇨ Note to Instructor: Write out the contraction "can't" on your paper, and show the child the apostrophe

Instructor: Now, I will make quotation marks for you on my paper, and then you will practice making quotation marks as well.

⇨ Note to Instructor: Make several sets of quotation marks for the child to copy. Consult your handwriting program for the style of quotation marks.

## Copywork

Choose one or more of the sentences below for the child to copy.

"How do you do?"
"Little bird, will you stop, stop, stop?"
So I cried, "Little bird, will you stop, stop, stop?"

# Lesson 139

-Poem memorization: "The Little Bird"

⇨ Note to Instructor: Read this poem out loud three times. Later in the day, read it again three times. See Lesson 2 for memorization techniques. Because this is such a short poem, the child may be able to memorize it in a brief time. Encourage him to use a special voice for the quotations in the poem.

The Little Bird
*Mother Goose rhyme*

Once I saw a little bird
Come hop, hop, hop;
So I cried, "Little bird,
Will you stop, stop, stop?"
And was going to the window
To say "How do you do?"
But he shook his little tail,
And far away he flew.

# Lesson 140

-Story narration: "The Little Red Hen"
-Copywork: "The Little Red Hen"
-Poem review: "The Little Bird" (Lesson 139)
* The child will need a tape recorder for the enrichment activity.
* In Lesson 149, the child will need five or six first class postcard stamps and postcards to address to relatives. Plan now to have these on hand.

⇨ Note to Instructor: Review "The Little Bird" today.

⇨ Note to Instructor: Read aloud the folk tale below. Have the child tell the story back to you; use the suggested questions at the story's end to prompt the child, if necessary. When the child has completed his oral narration, write the narration out for the child. Do not have him write it himself, since he will have copy work to do at the end of this lesson.

The Little Red Hen

The Little Red Hen was walking along the road with the dog, the cat, and the duck when she found some wheat that had been dropped by a farmer when he harvested his field.

"Who will help me plant this wheat?" said the Little Red Hen.

"Not I," said the dog.

"Not I," said the cat.

"Not I," said the duck.

"Then I will plant the wheat," said the Little Red Hen.

So the Little Red Hen called her little chicks to help her. Together, they scratched out a little place in the garden and planted the wheat.

A rain shower watered the wheat seeds, and the sun warmed the soil. By and by, tiny green shoots of wheat began to come up. But grass seeds and weed seeds, sown by the wind, also began to come up. The weeds began to crowd out the tiny little wheat shoots.

"Who will help pull the grass and weeds out of the garden of wheat?" said the Little Red Hen.

"Not I," said the dog.

"Not I," said the cat.

"Not I," said the duck.

"Then my chicks and I will keep the grass and weeds from crowding out the tiny, little wheat plants," said the Little Red Hen. She called her chicks, and they ran happily to help her. They tended the little garden of wheat for many weeks, pulling weeds and grass. Often she asked, "Who will help pull the grass and weeds out of the garden of wheat?" But the cat, the dog, and the duck lay outside the garden, resting and watching while the hen and her chicks worked.

The wheat grew tall, and soon was ready to harvest. "Who will help me harvest the wheat?" said the Little Red Hen.

"Not I," said the dog.

"Not I," said the cat.

"Not I," said the duck.

"Then my chicks and I will harvest it," said the Little Red Hen. She cut down the stalks of wheat with her sharp bill, so that they lay on the ground. Then she called her chicks. "Now we must take the wheat to the thresher," she said, "so that he can separate the grains of wheat from the stalks! Who will help us carry the wheat down the road to the thresher?

"Not I," said the dog.

"Not I," said the cat.

"Not I," said the duck.

"Then we will do it alone," said the Little Red Hen. Her little chicks ran back and forth, helping her take the wheat to the thresher, one stalk at a time. He separated the wheat from the stalks, so that the hen and her chicks had a big bag of grain.

"Who will help me take the bag of wheat to the miller, so that he can grind it into flour?" said the Little Red Hen.

"Not I," said the dog.

"Not I," said the cat.

"Not I," said the duck.

"Then we will," said the Little Red Hen. So she and the chicks dragged the bag of wheat all the way to the miller. After the miller ground the wheat into a fine flour, the Little Red Hen said, "Who will help me bake some bread?"

"Not I," said the dog.

"Not I," said the cat.

"Not I," said the duck.

"Then we will bake the bread," said the Little Red Hen and her chicks. Her little chicks loved to help their mother in the kitchen. They mixed and kneaded and shaped the bread into loaves and let it rise. Then they stoked the fire and put the bread into the oven to bake. The smell of the bread floated out into the yard. The dog, the cat, and the duck smelled the bread. They wandered lazily over to the kitchen. There, they found the Little Red Hen, just taking the warm fragrant bread out of the oven. The little chicks all crowded around, ready to eat.

"Who will eat this loaf?" asked the Little Red Hen.

"I will!" said the dog.

"I will!" said the cat.

"I will!" said the duck.

"No, you won't!" said the Little Red Hen. "You would not help plant the grain, nor weed the garden, nor take the wheat to the thresher and miller. You would not help make the bread. So now you will not eat any bread! My chicks and I will eat it together."

So the Little Red Hen together with her helpful chicks enjoyed their delicious warm bread, fresh from the oven.

⇨ Note to Instructor: Ask the child to tell you back the story in his own words. If the child has trouble remembering, use these questions:

What did the Little Red Hen find that had been dropped by the farmer? *The Little Red Hen found some wheat.*

Who would not help her plant the wheat? *The dog, cat, and duck would not help.*

After the hen planted her wheat, what else grew in the garden? *Weeds and grass crowded the little wheat sprouts.*

Did anyone help the hen and her chicks pull the weeds? *No, no one helped them.*

Name two other things that needed to be done to the wheat before it could be eaten. *The wheat needed to be harvested, taken to the thresher to be separated, taken to the miller to be ground into flour, and the bread needed to be made.*

Why do you think the hen did not give any bread to the dog, the cat, or the duck? *They did not help do any of the work.*

Who did get to eat the bread? *The hen and her chicks.*

Why did the chicks get to share the bread? *The chicks helped the hen with the work.*

## Copywork

Have the child copy some part of the following section of the Little Red Hen's story, depending on his ability. Good writers could copy the entire section. Remind the child how to make quotation marks. Help him place punctuation properly, inside the quotation marks (you need not explain the rule that governs this at this point).

"Who will help pull the grass and weeds out of the garden of wheat?" said the Little Red Hen.

"Not I," said the dog.

"Not I," said the cat.

"Not I," said the duck.

**Enrichment Activity**
Have the child title a sheet of notebook paper "The Little Red Hen." Have him tape record his answers to the questions at the end of the story. He will then play back the recording and take dictation from himself.

# Lesson 141

-Introducing indirect quotations
-Copywork: "Not I"
-Poem review: "The Little Bird" (Lesson 139)

⇨ Note to Instructor: Review "The Little Bird" today.

⇨ Note to Instructor: Reread the story of the Little Red Hen while the child follows along. Ask the child to read each direct quotation. Encourage him to use different voices. Give him all necessary help with unfamiliar words (this is not primarily a reading exercise, so don't frustrate him by having him sound out difficult words). This exercise will reinforce the rule that direct quotations are enclosed in quotation marks.

Instructor: In the story, the Little Red Hen said, "Who will help me take the bag of wheat to the miller, so that he can grind it into flour?" That is a direct quotation. Those are the actual words said by the Little Red Hen. But if I said, "The Little Red Hen wanted to know who would help her take the bag of wheat to the miller," I am changing the Little Red Hen's actual words into my own words. That is no longer a direct quotation. A direct quotation is the actual words that a person says. An indirect quotation tells you what a person says, without using his or her actual words. Read this direct quotation from the Little Red Hen with me: "Who will help me plant this wheat?"

⇨ Note to the Instructor: Show the child this quotation and point out the quotation marks around it. Go back to the story and show the child this quotation in the second paragraph. Point out that these are the Little Red Hen's actual words.

Instructor: Now I will tell you what the Little Red Hen said by using an indirect quotation. The Little Red Hen asked someone to help her plant wheat.

⇨ Note to Instructor: Show the child the sentence above. Point out that there are no quotation marks around the words.

Instructor: This is the same information, but not the actual words of the Little Red Hen, so we do not put quotation marks around these words. Now I want you to read me some direct quotations. I will turn them into indirect quotations. Follow along with me as we read together.

⇨ Note to Instructor: Allow the child to read the following script along with you. Use your finger to help him follow.

*Child reads:* "Who will help pull the grass and weeds out of the garden of wheat?"

Instructor: The Little Red Hen wanted to know who would help her weed the garden.

*Child reads:* "Not I," said the dog.
Instructor: The dog said that he would not help.

*Child reads:* "Who will help me harvest the wheat?"
Instructor: The Little Red Hen asked for help harvesting the wheat.

*Child reads:* "Not I," said the cat.
Instructor: The cat said that he would not help either.

*Child reads:* "Who will help me bake some bread?"
Instructor: The Little Red Hen wondered if anyone would help her bake bread.

*Child reads:* "Not I," said the duck.
Instructor: The duck also said that he would not help.

Instructor: Remember, a direct quotation has quotation marks around it to show the actual words that a person (or a duck) says. An indirect quotation does not use a person's actual words. Indirect quotations have no quotation marks.

**Copywork**
Choose one of the sentence sets below. Point out that the first sentence is a direct quotation, and the second is an indirect quotation.

"Not I."
The dog said that he wouldn't help.

"Who will help me bake some bread?"
The Little Red Hen wanted help baking her bread.

"Who will help pull the grass and weeds out of the garden of wheat?"
The Little Red Hen wanted to know who would help her weed the garden.

266

# Lesson 142

-Titles of respect
-Adjectives
-Quotation marks
-Dictation exercise: "Bag of Wheat"
-Poem review: "Work" (Lesson 15)

⇨  Note to Instructor: Review "Work" today.

Instructor: Let's review one of the lessons we've already learned. Do you remember what a "title of respect" is? It is a word, like "Mr.," "Mrs.," "Dr.," or "Miss," that goes in front of a person's name. We usually abbreviate these titles of respect. Let's look together at these titles and their abbreviations.

⇨  Note to Instructor: Show the child the following chart of titles and abbreviations. Read through it as the child follows along.

| | | |
|---|---|---|
| Mister | Mr. | This is a title for a man. |
| Mistress | Mrs. | This is a title for a married woman. |
| Doctor | Dr. | This is a title for a physician or for someone with a special degree from a university. |
| Miss | — | This is not an abbreviation, but a title of courtesy for an unmarried girl or woman. |
| * | Ms. | *Ms. is an abbreviation for either Mistress or Miss. You should use it when you do not know whether a woman would prefer to be called Mrs. or Miss. |

Instructor: Abbreviated titles of respect begin with capital letters and end periods. Copy the abbreviations "Mr.," "Mrs.," "Dr.," and "Ms." onto your paper now.

⇨  Note to Instructor: Allow the child to look at the book while he copies. Remind him that Miss does not have a period because it is not actually an abbreviation.

Instructor: Now let's review another lesson. Do you remember the definition of an **adjective**?

⇨  Note to Instructor: Give the child a chance to remember the definition. Praise him if he can remember it! If he cannot, remind him: **An adjective is a word that describes a noun**.

Instructor: Let's repeat the definition of an **adjective** together twice.

Together (two times): **An adjective is a word that describes a**

**noun**.

Instructor: Can you think of five **adjectives** that tell what color something is?

⇨ Note to Instructor: Prompt child, if necessary: Yellow, blue, red, green, white, black, brown, orange, maroon, purple, violet, tan, pink.

Instructor: Now, can you think of five **adjectives** that tell what size something is?

⇨ Note to Instructor: Prompt child, if necessary: Big, small, short, tall, wide, narrow, huge, little, tiny, enormous, fat, thin.

Instructor: Now, can you think of four **adjectives** to describe something in this room? I will write the **adjectives** down while you say them.

⇨ Note to Instructor: Help the child think of descriptive words for an object in the room. Write the adjectives down. Then help him to form them into a sentence: "The [object] is [adjective], [adjective], [adjective], and [adjective]." Write the sentence down and point out the commas that separate the adjectives. These adjectives are items in a series.

Instructor: For the last part of your lesson today, we will review quotation marks. Remember, a *direct* quotation has quotation marks around it to show the actual words that a person says. An *indirect* quotation does not use a person's actual words. Indirect quotations have no quotation marks. Here is a direct quotation:

"Who will eat this loaf?" asked the Little Red Hen.

Here is an indirect quotation:

The Little Red Hen wanted to know who would eat the loaf.

⇨ Note to Instructor: Show the child the sentences above. Point out the quotation marks around the direct quotation. Point out that the indirect quotation has no quotation marks.

Instructor: Now you read the direct quotations below, and I will read the indirect quotations. Follow along with me as we read.


*Child reads:* "I will!" said the dog.

Instructor: The dog said that he would eat some bread.


*Child reads:* "No, you won't!" said the Little Red Hen.

Instructor: The Little Red Hen said that the dog could not eat the bread.


*Child reads:* "My chicks and I will eat it together."

Instructor: The Little Red Hen said that she and the chicks would eat the bread.


268

## Dictation Exercise

Tell the child that you will dictate a direct quotation. Remind the child that quotation marks should go on either side of the direct quotation. Choose one of the direct quotes below. If you choose the last sentence, remind the child that you will pause at the comma.

"Who will help me eat this loaf?"

"Who will help me take the bag of wheat to the miller?"

"You would not help us make the bread, so you cannot help us eat the bread."

## Enrichment Activity

Help the child to write a dialogue between the dog and the cat, who are deciding that they <u>will</u> help the Little Red Hen the next time she asks. Assist the child in placing quotation marks correctly.

# Lesson 143

-Four types of sentences
-Dictation exercise: "The Dump Truck"
-Poem review: "The Little Bird" (Lesson 139)

⇨ Note to Instructor: Review "The Little Bird" today.

Instructor: Let's review the definition of a **sentence**. Listen first, and then repeat with me: **A sentence is a group of words that expresses a complete thought.**

Together: **A sentence is a group of words that expresses a complete thought.**

Instructor: Repeat with me: All sentences begin with a capital letter and end with a punctuation mark.

Together: All sentences begin with a capital letter and end with a punctuation mark.

Instructor: There are four types of sentences. Can you remember what they are?

⇨ Note to Instructor: Give the child time to think and remember before reminding him.

Instructor: The four types of sentence are: **Statement, command, question,** and **exclamation**. Let's review those definitions. Repeat with me: **Statements give information.**

Together: **Statements give information.**

Instructor: Can you make a **statement** that gives me information about something in this room?

⇨ Note to Instructor: If necessary, prompt the child with a question: "Can you tell me where the book is? The book is on the table. That is a statement."

Instructor: Let's say the definition of a **command** together: **A command gives an order or makes a request.**

Together: **A command gives an order or makes a request.**

Instructor: Can you give me a **command**?

⇨ Note to Instructor: If the command is reasonable, act out the command after the child gives it.

Instructor: When you write **statements** and **commands, statements** always end with a period. **Commands** usually end with a period. Now let's repeat the definition of the third type of sentence: **A question asks something.** Let's say that together.

Together: **A question asks something.**

Instructor: A question ends with a question mark. Ask me a **question,**

270

and I will write it down on my paper.

⇨ Note to Instructor: Write the child's question on your paper. Make a question mark at the end, and point out the question mark.

Instructor: Now let's repeat the last definition: **An exclamation shows sudden or strong feeling.** Say that with me.

Together: **An exclamation shows sudden or strong feeling.**

Instructor: Do you remember what punctuation mark comes at the end of an **exclamation**? An exclamation point. I will ask you a **question**, and I want you to answer it with an **exclamation**. Do you <u>love</u> your birthday?

*Child: I <u>love</u> my birthday!*

⇨ Note to Instructor: Remind the child to say this with strong feeling. Write the exclamation down on your paper, and show the child the exclamation point.

Instructor: Let's pretend that we are on a car trip together—a very long car trip. You are the parent, driving the car, and I am the little child in the back seat. I am very tired of riding! I am going to read you some things I might say on this very long, long trip. You follow along. I want you to tell me for each sentence if it is a statement, a question, a command, or an exclamation.

⇨ Note to Instructor: To help the child keep his place, move your finger along above each sentence (or place a paper marker under each line). Laugh and have fun with this lesson.


Are we there yet?
Can we stop for a hamburger?
Give me an apple, please.
Are we there yet?
My brother is touching me!
How much farther is it?
Can we get some ice cream?
I see an enormous truck with cars on it!
Give me the water, please.
I have to go to the bathroom.
Are we there yet?
I'm tired of wearing my seat belt.
It's hot back here.
Now it's cold back here.
How much farther is it?
Are we there yet?

## Dictation Exercise

Choose one or more of the following sentences to dictate to the child. Remind him of the proper punctuation mark for each.

Stop.
Is a car is coming?
It isn't a car.  It is a dump truck.
The dump truck is full of rocks, and they are falling out!

## Enrichment Activity

The instructor should pretend to be a four-year-old.  Have fun with it; talk in a little child's voice. Have the child talk in a "big grown-up's voice." Answers in brackets are only suggestions.  Accept any reasonable answer.  If the child answers in a fragment, rephrase the information to form a complete sentence and have the child repeat the correct form back to you.  For example, if the child answers the first question with just "No," you give the complete sentence, "No, we are not there yet."  Then have the child repeat the complete sentence after you.

Instructor (pretending to be the child): Are we there yet?
*Child (pretending to be parent): [No, we are not there yet.]*
Instructor (pretending to be the child): May we get some ice cream?
*Child (pretending to be the parent): [Yes, we will get some soon.]*
Instructor (pretending to be the child):  Are we there yet?
*Child (pretending to be the instructor):  [No, it will be awhile.]*

Instructor (in regular voice): Pretending to be a child, I will give a command or request.  Pretending to be the parent, you tell whether or not you will do it.

Instructor (pretending to be the child):  Read me a story.
*Child (pretending to be the parent):  [No, I am driving.]*
Instructor (pretending to be the child):  Stop at a playground, please.
*Child (pretending to be the parent):  [Yes, I will as soon as I can.]*
Instructor (pretending to be the child):  Look at those huge mountains!
*Child (pretending to be the parent):  [Yes, they are big.]*

Instructor (in regular voice):  If I make a simple statement, answer any way you wish.

Instructor (pretending to be the child):  I'm tired of wearing my seat belt.
*Child (pretending to be the parent):  [You must wear it for safety.]*
Instructor (pretending to be the child):  I want a sandwich.
*Child (pretending to be the parent):  [We'll be eating lunch soon.]*
Instructor (pretending to be the child):  We are going on a picnic.
*Child (pretending to be the parent):  [I can hardly wait.]*

Instructor (in regular voice):  If I make an exclamation, you make a exclamation, too!

Instructor (pretending to be the child):  Ouch! My seat belt is pinching me!
*Child (pretending to be the parent):  [Sorry! I'll loosen it for you!]*
Instructor (pretending to be the child):  Stop! There is a place to buy a drink!
*Child (pretending to be the parent):  [Quick! I'll get in the right lane!]*
Instructor (pretending to be the child):  Yippee!  We are at the park!
*Child (pretending to be the child):  [Whew! I'm glad!  That traffic was horrible!]*

# Lesson 144

-Story narration: "The Three Billy Goats Gruff"
-Poem review: "The Year" (Lesson 131)

⇨ Note to Instructor: Review "The Year" today.
⇨ Note to Instructor: Read aloud the story below. Use a soft, high voice for Little Billy Goat Gruff, a medium voice for Middle-sized Billy Goat Gruff, and a great, big, loud voice for Great Big Billy Goat Gruff. Use a growling, roaring, bellowing voice for the huge, ugly, mean troll. Have the child tell the story back to you; use the suggested questions at the story's end to prompt the child, if necessary. When the child has completed his oral narration, repeat the first sentence or the first two sentences of his narration back to him as a dictation exercise. Then, complete the narration yourself by writing the child's remaining sentences.

## The Three Billy Goats Gruff

Once upon a time three billy goats lived on a hillside. They were Little Billy Goat Gruff, Middle-sized Billy Goat Gruff, and Great Big Billy Goat Gruff.

The three billy goats grazed on their hillside until all the fresh green grass was gone. They decided to cross the stream at the bottom of the hill and go over into the green meadow on the other side. There was plenty of good fresh grass in the meadow, but to cross the stream, they had to go over a rickety-rackety bridge. Under the rickety-rackety bridge lived a huge, ugly, mean, and selfish troll.

The littlest Billy Goat Gruff was the first to cross the bridge. "Trip-trap! Trip, trap!" went the little goat over the bridge.

"Who's that trip-trapping over my bridge?" growled the huge, ugly, mean, and selfish troll.

"It is I, the Little Billy Goat Gruff," said the little goat in a little voice.

"I'm coming to eat you up!" said the troll.

" I'm so little," said the Little Billy Goat Gruff, "I'd hardly be a mouthful for you. Wait for my big brother. He is much fatter than I."

"Be gone, then," snarled the huge, ugly, mean, and selfish troll.

The next day, Middle-sized Billy Goat Gruff started over to the meadow. "TRIP-TRAP! TRIP-TRAP!" went the middle-sized Billy Goat Gruff across the bridge.

"Who's that trip-trapping over my bridge?" roared the troll.

"It is I, Middle-sized Billy Goat Gruff," said the middle-sized goat in a middle-sized voice.

"I'm coming to eat you up!" shouted the huge, ugly, mean, and selfish troll.

"Don't eat me," pleaded the middle-sized billy goat. "Wait for my brother. He is much fatter than I!"

"Be gone, then," growled the troll.

The next day, Great Big Billy Goat Gruff started across the bridge to join his brothers in the meadow. "**TRIP-TRAP! TRIP-TRAP!**" went the Great Big Billy Goat Gruff across the rickety-rackety bridge.

"Who's that trip-trapping over my bridge?" screeched the huge, ugly, mean, and selfish troll.

"**IT IS I, THE GREAT BIG BILLY GOAT GRUFF**," said Great Big Billy Goat Gruff in his great, big, billy goat voice.

"I'm coming to eat you up!" bellowed the huge, ugly, mean, and selfish troll, and he climbed onto the rickety-rackety bridge.

"**COME ON, THEN**," said Great Big Billy Goat Gruff.

The Great Big Billy Goat Gruff ran at the huge, ugly, mean, and selfish troll and tossed him into the air with his great big billy goat horns. He tossed the troll so far up the river that the troll never found his way back down.

Now every morning the three Billy Goats Gruff trip-trap across the rickety-rackety bridge to eat sweet green grass or wallow in the fresh meadow. At night, they trip-trap back across the rickety-rackety bridge to sleep peacefully on their hillside.

⇨   Note to Instructor: Ask the child to tell you the story back in his own words. If the child has trouble remembering, use these questions.

How many billy goats were there? *There were three billy goats.*

What did each look like? *One was little, one was medium-sized, and one was really big.*

Who did Little Billy Goat Gruff meet when he crossed the bridge? *He met the troll.*

What did the troll want to do to Little Billy Goat Gruff? *He wanted to eat him.*

Why didn't the troll eat him? *Little Billy Goat Gruff said that his brother was bigger and the troll should eat him.*

What did the troll want to do to Medium-sized Billy Goat Gruff? *He wanted to eat him.*

*Why didn't the troll eat him?* Medium-sized Billy Goat Gruff said his brother was bigger and the troll should eat him.

What did the troll want to do to Great Big Billy Goat Gruff? *He wanted to eat him.*

What did Great Big Billy Goat Gruff say to the troll? *He said, "Come on, then!"*

What did Great Big Billy Goat Gruff do to the troll? *He tossed him up the river with his horns.*

# Lesson 145

-Quotations
-Four types of sentences
-Parts of speech
-Conjunctions
-Dictation exercise: "I Am Coming to Eat You"
-Poem review: "The Caterpillar" (Lesson 2)
\* In Lesson 149, the child will need five or six postcard stamps and postcards to address to relatives. Plan now to have these on hand.

⇨ Note to Instructor: Review "The Caterpillar" today.

Instructor: Look back at the story of the Three Billy Goats Gruff with me. Can you point out some quotations? Look at the quotation marks on either side of these quotations. These are the actual words that the goats and the troll used. Here is an indirect quotation from the story: The troll said that he would eat the billy goats. Can you find the troll's exact words and read them for me?

*Child: "I'm coming to eat you up."*

Instructor: What is your favorite quotation from the story?

⇨ Note to Instructor: Help the child find the answers to the following questions in the story. Depending on the child's reading ability, either you or the child should read the story aloud as you complete the rest of the lesson.

Instructor: Now can you find me an **exclamation**? Remember, it will end with an exclamation point. Can you find a **question** that ends with a question mark? Can you find a **command**? The troll gives **commands** to the billy goats, doesn't he? Can you find a **statement**? Any sentence which tells you what happens next is a **statement**. **Statements** end with periods. Now can you find a sentence that has items in a list, separated by commas?

⇨ Note to Instructor: If the child cannot locate the sentence, point out the phrase "the huge, ugly, mean, and selfish troll."

Instructor: Is the word "troll" a **noun**, a **verb**, an **adjective**, a **conjunction**, or an **interjection**?

⇨ Note to Instructor: If necessary, remind the child that a noun is the name of a person, place, thing, or idea.

Instructor: "Troll" is a **noun**. Is the troll a person, place, thing, or idea? I think he is either a person or a thing! The words "huge, ugly, mean, and selfish" describe the troll. What do we call words that describe a **noun**?

*Child: An adjective describes a noun.*

Instructor: "Huge, ugly, mean, and selfish" are all **adjectives**. Can you find three **action verbs** in the story of the Billy Goats Gruff?

⇨ Note to Instructor: Action verbs in the story include grazed, decided, cross, went, growled, said, snarled, roared, snorted, shouted, pleaded, screeched, bellowed, tossed, and ran. "Trip-trap" is also used as a verb.

Instructor: Can you find a **linking verb**? Look for: am, is, are, was, and were.

⇨ Note to Instructor: Linking verbs are found in the first paragraph ("They **were** Little Billy Goat Gruff..."), the second paragraph, ("There **was** plenty of good fresh grass..."), the third paragraph ("The littlest Billy Goat Gruff **was** the first..."), the fifth paragraph ("It **is** I..."), etc.

Instructor: Now let's look for **conjunctions**. Remember, **a conjunction joins words or groups of words together.** Look for the words *and, but, or.*

### Dictation Exercise

Choose one or more of the following sentences. Tell the child that these are direct quotations and should have quotation marks around them.

"I'm coming to eat you up!"
"I'd hardly be a mouthful for you."
"Wait for my big brother. He is much fatter than I."

# Lesson 146

-Picture narration: "Planting Seeds"

How many people are in this picture? Yes, there are two people in this picture. They are father and son. The father's special, proper name is Mr. Jacob Kim. The son's special, proper name is Michael Kim. They are wearing the same kind of sweater. Is it a soft sweater or a rough, itchy sweater? I think it is a soft sweater. "Soft" is an **adjective** that describes sweater.

Mr. Kim and Michael are leaning over a table. Mr. Kim is touching something. What is Mr. Kim touching? It is a pot with dirt in it. Is it a large pot or a small pot? It is a small pot. "Small" is an **adjective** that describes pot. What is next to the pot? It is an orange. Do you like oranges? I bet this is a delicious orange. "Delicious" is an **adjective** that describes orange.

What else do you see on the table? I see orange slices, orange peels, and seeds. What kind of seeds do you think those are? They must be orange seeds. Mr. Kim peeled an orange and he and Michael ate it. Do you see the orange slice in Michael's hand? They did not eat the seeds, though. Instead, they put the seeds on the table.

Do you see the window behind Mr. Kim and Michael? What is sitting on the windowsill? It is a watering can. It is used to water plants. Now look out the window. What is happening outside? It is snowing. Do you think it is cold or warm outside? It must be very cold. During what season does it snow? It snows in winter. What are the winter months? The winter months are December, January, and February. It looks like a very heavy snow. "Heavy" is an **adjective** that describes snow.

Let's look again at Mr. Kim and Michael. What do you think they are doing with orange seeds, a watering can, and a pot filled with dirt? They are planting seeds. If they water the seeds, soon a little plant will start to grow. Eventually, it will grow into an orange tree. Why do you think Mr. Kim and Michael aren't planting seeds outside? It is too cold. The seeds can't grow during the winter unless they are kept warm inside.

I hope the seeds grow into a nice big tree with juicy oranges on it!

# Lesson 147

-Introducing adverbs
-Dictation exercise: "I Ate My Supper"
-Poem review: "The Year" (Lesson 131)
* The child will need a book, magazine, or newspaper for the enrichment activity.


⇨ Note to Instructor: Review "The Year" today.

**Instructor: An adjective is a word that describes a noun.** When you describe a **noun**, you tell more about it. The word "baby" is just a **noun**. But if you describe a baby as hungry, fat, happy, and squirmy, you can picture that baby in your mind! Just as we use descriptive words to tell more about **nouns**, we also use descriptive words to tell more about **verbs**. A word that describes a verb is called an **adverb**. Can you hear the word "verb" in the word "adverb?" That will help you to remember that **an adverb is a word that describes a verb.** Imagine that the hungry, fat, happy, squirmy baby is crying. How is he crying? Loudly? Softly? Angrily? Frantically? Demandingly? All of those words are **adverbs**. Each **adverb** describes the **verb** "crying." Each **adverb** tells you more about how the baby is crying. Most **adverbs** end with the letters "-ly." Here is the definition of an **adverb: An adverb is a word that describes a verb, an adjective, or another adverb.** I will say that again for you, and then we will repeat it together three times. **An adverb is a word that describes a verb, an adjective, or another adverb.** Together (three times): **An adverb is a word that describes a verb, an adjective, or another adverb.**

Instructor: Today we will talk about **adverbs** that describe **verbs**. I will give you some **verbs**. Let's try to think of **adverbs** that describe them. first, we will talk about the verb "work." Think of a word that describes how you can work.

⇨ Note to Instructor: Suggestions for adverbs include carefully, carelessly, slowly, eagerly, reluctantly, cheerfully, grumpily, thoughtfully, energetically.

Instructor: Let's think of **adverbs** to describe the **verb** "eat."

⇨ Note to Instructor: Suggestions for adverbs include neatly, sloppily, hungrily, carefully, slowly, eagerly, messily, politely, greedily, daintily, gratefully.

Instructor: Let's think of **adverbs** to describe the **verb** "dance."

⇨ Note to Instructor: Suggestions for adverbs include rhythmically, gracefully, skillfully, awkwardly, clumsily, slowly, quickly, energetically, nimbly, happily, joyfully, frantically, merrily.

Instructor: Answer the following questions by using **adverbs**. Try to answer me in complete sentences! If I say, "How did the child cry?" you should answer, "The child cried noisily," or "The child cried angrily." How did the dancer dance?

*Child: The dancer danced [gracefully].*

Instructor: How did the careless driver drive?

*Child: The careless driver drove [dangerously].*

Instructor: How did the little girl write her name?

*Child: The little girl wrote her name [neatly].*

Instructor: How did John do his work?

*Child: John did his work [quickly].*

Instructor: How did the boy carry his kitten?

*Child: The boy carried his kitten [carefully.]*

Instructor: How did the woman decorate the cake?

*Child: The woman decorated the cake [beautifully].*

⇨ Note to Instructor: Additional adverbs that you may use to prompt the child in any of the above sentences include cheaply, recklessly, clearly, dearly, diligently, beautifully, happily, strangely, unexpectedly, loudly, swiftly, softly, sweetly, gently, smoothly, bitterly, sadly, angrily, quietly, easily, immediately.

Instructor: I will say the definition of an **adverb** again for you, and then we will repeat it together three more times. **An adverb is a word that describes a verb, an adjective, or another adverb.** Together (three times): **An adverb is a word that describes a verb, an adjective, or another adverb.**

## Dictation Exercise

Choose one or more of the following sentences. If you choose the sentence with commas, remember to pause when you reach each comma.

I ate my supper gratefully.

I drank my milk thirstily and ate my sandwich carefully.

I ate my lunch hungrily, asked for my dessert politely, and waited for it patiently.

## Enrichment Activity

Send the child on an "adverb hunt." Use a chapter from one of his favorite books, or a newspaper or magazine article that includes descriptions. Have him circle or write down every adverb he finds.

# Lesson 148

-Adverbs
-Dictation exercise: "Whole Duty of Children"
-Poem review: "The Little Bird" (Lesson 139)
* In Lesson 149, the child will need five or six first class postcard stamps and postcards to address to relatives. Plan now to have these on hand. You will also need the addresses of several friends and family members.

⇨ Note to Instructor: Review "The Little Bird" today.

Instructor: I will say the definition of an adverb again for you, and then we will repeat it together three more times. **An adverb is a word that describes a verb, an adjective, or another adverb.**

Together (three times): **An adverb is a word that describes a verb, an adjective, or another adverb.**

Instructor: We have practiced finding **adverbs** that describe **verbs**. Let's practice that one more time. Can you list **adverbs** that describe the **verb** "talk?"

⇨ Note to Instructor: Suggestions for adverbs include loudly, softly, incessantly, rarely, clearly, happily, swiftly, sweetly, gently, sadly, quietly.

Instructor: **An adverb is a word that describes a verb.** Now let's talk about the second part of that definition: An adverb is a word that describes an adjective. Imagine that you see a black horse, galloping across a field. You might say, "That is a beautiful horse." But if the horse is the most beautiful horse you have ever seen, you might say, "That is a very beautiful horse." "Very" tells you just how beautiful the horse is. "Very" is an **adverb** because it describes the word "beautiful." It doesn't describe the horse. It is not a "very horse"! It is "very beautiful." I will read some sentences to you. Let's try together to find the **adjective** in each sentence and the **adverb** that describes it. "It is an extremely hot day." "Day" is a **noun.** What kind of day is it?

*Child: It is a hot day.*

Instructor: "Hot" is an **adjective** that describes the **noun** "day." "It is an extremely hot day." What word tells you *how* hot it is?

*Child: Extremely.*

Instructor: "Extremely" is an **adverb** that describes the **adjective** "hot." Listen to this sentence. "This is a perfectly beautiful flower!" What word describes the **noun** "flower?"

*Child: Beautiful.*

284

Instructor: "Beautiful" is an **adjective** that describes "flower." "This is a perfectly beautiful flower." How beautiful is the flower?

*Child: The flower is perfectly beautiful.*

Instructor: "Perfectly" is an **adverb** that describes <u>how</u> beautiful the flower is. It describes the **adjective** "beautiful." Here is one last sentence: "The baby is unusually noisy today." What is the baby?

*Child: The baby is noisy.*

Instructor: "Noisy" is an **adjective** that describes the baby. How noisy is the baby?

*Child: The baby is unusually noisy.*

Instructor: "Unusually" is an **adverb** that tells you more about the **adjective** "noisy." It doesn't describe the baby – the baby isn't an "unusually baby"! "Unusually" describes "noisy." Let's repeat the definition of an **adverb** together again: **An adverb is a word that describes a verb, an adjective, or another adverb.** We have talked about **adverbs** that describe **verbs**, and **adverbs** that describe **adjectives**. Sometimes, **adverbs** describe other **adverbs**! Listen to this last sentence: "The dog howled incredibly loudly."

In this sentence, "loudly" is an **adverb**. It tells you more about the **verb** "howled." How did the dog howl?

*Child: The dog howled loudly.*

Instructor: There is another **adverb** in this sentence. "Incredibly" describes "loudly." It tells you just how loudly the dog howled! "Incredibly" is an **adverb** that describes another **adverb**—"loudly." Let's repeat our definition together one last time: **An adverb is a word that describes a verb, an adjective, or another adverb.**

Together: **An adverb is a word that describes a verb, an adjective, or another adverb.**

## Dictation Exercise

Dictate as much of the following poem as fits the child's writing ability. Show the poem to the child. Remind him that each line of poetry and each word in a poem's title begins with a capital letter. Point to the end of each line. Explain that punctuation at the end of a line of poetry doesn't follow any particular rule. Show the child that there are commas at the end of each line, and a period at the end. Then dictate the poem, giving the child any necessary help in spelling, and remind him of the proper punctuation for the end of each line.

Whole Duty of Children
*Robert Louis Stevenson*

A child should always say what's true,
And speak when he is spoken to,
And behave mannerly at table,
At least as far as he is able.

# Lesson 149

-Addresses
-Copywork: "Addressing Postcards"
-Poem review: "Days of the Week" (Lesson 35)
* The child will need five or six first class stamps and postcards for this lesson as well as the addresses for family members and close friends.

⇨ Note to Instructor: Review "Days of the Week" today.

Instructor: **An adverb is a word that describes a verb, an adjective, or another adverb.** Let's say that together three times.

Together (three times): **An adverb is a word that describes a verb, an adjective, or another adverb.**

Instructor: Adverbs describe verbs, adjectives, and other adverbs; adjectives describe nouns. Do you remember the definition of an adjective? Let's say it together three times: **An adjective is a word that describes a noun.**

Together (three times): **An adjective is a word that describes a noun.**

Instructor: Today we are going to practice writing names and addresses. Do you remember talking about the first, middle, and last names of people in our family? These special names are **proper nouns.** Let's write down the first, middle, and last names of three people in our family. We will be sending postcards to them a little later on.

⇨ Note to Instructor: Write down the first, middle, and last names of these family members. You could also include close friends to whom the child might wish to send a postcard. Leave enough space under each name to write an address. If you don't know the middle name, write the person's "title of respect" (Mr. John Knowles, for example), and remind the child that abbreviated titles of respect begin with a capital letter and end with a period.

Instructor: We will write the names and addresses of these people on postcards. Postcards are like little letters. There is just enough room to write a sentence or two! Each postcard needs a full address, so that the post office can deliver it to the right house. I will write down our address so that we can review the different parts of an address.

⇨ Note to Instructor: As you write your address for the child, remind him what each part stands for. Review street or house number, street name, city name, and the proper state abbreviation. Remind him that state abbreviations are two capitalized letters with no period after them. Write your zip code, and remind him that a zip code is a special number that helps the post office find where you live.

Instructor: Now, I will write for you the addresses of some of the people whose names we've written down.

⇨ Note to Instructor: Write three to five addresses underneath the names you have previously written. As you write, explain each abbreviation and part of the address to the child.

## Copywork

If the postcards for this lesson do not already have address lines on them, draw lines for the child to write on (see Lesson 137). Ask the child to address as many postcards as his writing ability allows. Try to have the child address at least three postcards. He will be adding messages to these postcards in a later lesson. The instructor may write the return address.

## Enrichment Activity

The child who writes easily may address the additonal postcards.

# Lesson 150

-Writing postcards
-Nouns
-Adjectives
-Copywork: "My Postcard"
-Poem review: "The Goops" (Lesson 100)
* The child will need the postcards from the previous lesson.

⇨   Note to Instructor: Review "The Goops" today.

Instructor: Today we are going to write messages on our postcards. To write these messages, we will need nouns and adjectives. Let's review the definition of a noun. **A noun is the name of a person, place, thing, or idea.** Repeat that definition for me.

*Child:* **A noun is the name of a person, place, thing, or idea.**

Instructor: **An adjective is a word that describes a noun.** Let's repeat that together three times.

Together (three times): **An adjective is a word that describes a noun.**

Instructor: Your postcard message can be about a person, a place, or a thing. You can also write a message about an animal. Remember, the names of animals are **nouns** too! I would like you to tell me the name of a friend, brother, or sister; the name of a place where you have been recently; the name of a thing, like a toy or book, that you have enjoyed; and the name of an animal, either a pet or an animal you find interesting.

⇨   Note to Instructor: Help the child come up with these nouns. If he has trouble thinking of a place, suggest the grocery store, a playground, a place of worship, or some other place that you have visited in the past two weeks. Write the nouns that the child suggests on a piece of paper, so that he can look at them.

Instructor: Now I want you to think of an **adjective** that best describes each one of these **nouns**.

⇨   Note to Instructor: Your goal is to help the child think through a sentence that he will write on each postcard. The sentence should contain a noun and a word or phrase that describes the noun. You may use the following questions to help the child think of a descriptive word or phrase: What is the most important thing about this person? What is the most interesting thing about this place? Why do you like to play with this toy or read this book? What will help another person picture the animal in their mind? Focus on the person, place, thing, or animal that he is best able to describe. Help him formulate a sentence that tells another person why he finds this particular noun so interesting. Your goal is for the child to complete at least one sentence that he would like to share with someone else and will enjoy sending through the mail on a postcard. This sentence might be, "My baby sister is cute!" "We went to a fun playground." "I like my new Legos™ because it is fun to build with them." "Our dog has five tiny puppies." "My baby sister has a new tooth!" Any of these sentences would be a good piece of news for a postcard. So would, "We played at a playground with a great curvy slide," or "I read an exciting book last week. It was called _____." Write the child's final, favorite sentence or sentences on a sheet of paper.

## Copywork

Ask the child to copy his favorite sentence or sentences from your paper onto his postcards. Give him any help necessary to make this legible! You may want to allow him to use a pen, or trace over his pencil writing afterwards yourself; pencil sometimes smears in the mail. Mail the postcards with first-class stamps; they will arrive sooner!

## Enrichment Activity

The child may wish to write and send additional postcards.

# Lesson 151

-Dates
-Months of the year
-Seasons
-Days of the week
-Copywork: "Remembering the Days of the Week"
\* The child will need construction paper and art supplies for the enrichment activity.


Instructor: What is today's date? Let's write it now.

⇨ Note to Instructor: Write today's date. Point out the comma between the day of the month and the year.

Instructor: Each part of this date gives us information. The month tells us the season. Let's review the poem "The Year," which tells us what happens in each month.

⇨ Note to Instructor: Ask the child to recite "The Year." Prompt him, if necessary.


The Year
*Sara Coleridge, adapted by Sara Buffington*


January brings the snow,
Helps the skis and sleds to go.


February brings the rain,
Thaws the frozen lake again.


March brings breezes loud and shrill,
Stirs the dancing daffodil.


April brings the primrose sweet,
Scatters daisies at our feet.


May brings sunshine full and bright,
Sends the busy bees to flight.


June brings tulips, lilies, roses,
Fills the children's hands with posies.

Hot July brings stormy showers,
Lemonade, and lazy hours.

August brings the warmest air,
Sandy feet and sea-wet hair.

September brings the fruits so sweet,
Apples ripe from summer heat.

October brings the colored trees,
Scampering squirrels and cooling breeze.

Dull November brings the blast,
Then the leaves are whirling fast.

Chill December brings the sleet,
Blazing fire, and Christmas treat.[1]

[1] Alternate last line:"Blazing fire, and winter treat."

Instructor: The year has four seasons: Winter, spring, summer and fall. What are the winter months? Can you tell me in a complete sentence?
⇨ Note to Instructor: Prompt child for the answers to the following questions, if necessary.
Child: The winter months are December, January, and February.
Instructor: What are the spring months?
Child: The spring months are March, April, and May.
Instructor: What are the summer months?
Child: The summer months are June, July, and August.
Instructor: What are the fall months?
Child: The fall months are September, October, and November.
Istructor: The second part of the date tells you what day of the month it is. Let's review the poem "The Months" that tells us about the number of days in each month.
⇨ Note to Instructor: Ask the child to recite this poem alone.

The Months
*Mother Goose rhyme*


Thirty days hath September,
April, June, and November;
All the rest have thirty-one,
Except for February alone,
Which has four and twenty-four
Till leap year gives it one day more.


Instructor: The last part of the date is the year. What is the year of today's date? In what year were you born? How old are you? Do you know on what day of the week you were born? In old times, people thought that the day on which you were born made you act in a certain way! That's just a fairy tale, but it made a fun poem.

⇨   Note to Instructor: Ask the child to recite the poem "The Days of the Week" alone.


Days of the Week
*Mother Goose rhyme*
*adapted by Sara Buffington*


Monday's child is fair of face,
Tuesday's child is full of grace;
Wednesday's child is ever so sweet,
Thursday's child is tidy and neat;
Friday's child is prone to a giggle,
Saturday's child is easy to tickle;
But the child that is born on restful Sunday
Is happy and cheerful, and loves to play.


**Dictation Exercise**
Ask the child to write out the days of the week from memory. You may remind him of the days as he writes. Help him with the spelling of difficult names.

## Enrichment Activity

Have the child make a seven-page "My Week" booklet. The book could contain what the child does each day of the week. Instructor or child will write the name of one day of the week at the top of each sheet of paper. He can draw pictures or write sentences. Start this activity today, and finish it when the child has time. Have the child paste or draw a picture of himself on the cover.

# Lesson 152

-The four kinds of verbs
-Dictation exercise: "Dinosaurs"
-Poem review: "Mr. Nobody" (Lesson 81)
 * The instructor will need three light colors of construction paper, glue or tape, and a marker for the enrichment activity.

⇨ Note to Instructor: Review "Mr. Nobody" today.

Instructor: Today we are going to review the definition of a verb and talk about the different kinds of verbs. What is the definition of a verb? **A verb is a word that does an action, shows a state of being, links two words together, or helps another verb.** Let's say that together three times.

Together (three times): **A verb is a word that does an action, shows a state of being, links two words together, or helps another verb.**

Instructor: The easiest **verbs** to recognize are **action verbs**, because they tell about something you can see happening. I will give you some **action verbs**. Act them out for me! Run, skip, fall, roll, sing, sleep, read, laugh, talk, bark, mew, roar, growl, squeak.

⇨ Note to Instructor: Use as many of these verbs as you choose. Allow the child to act out each verb.

Instructor: The second part of your definition is, **"A verb shows a state of being."** Remember, we said that **state of being verbs** are words that don't show any action—they only show that you exist (Lessons 105 and 106)! When you sit perfectly still, you are not jumping, running, crawling, meowing, or giggling. But you are still here! You just are. These are the **verbs** which tell us that something "just is." The **state of being verbs** are: Am, is, are, was, were, be, being, been. Let's chant those together three times.

Together (three times):
Am [clap]
Is [clap]
Are, was, were. [clap]
Be [clap]
Being [clap]
Been. [clap] [clap]

Instructor: These are short sentences with **state of being verbs**: "She is." "You are." "They were." Another kind of **verb** called a **linking verb** connects or links a **noun** or **pronoun** to another word

(Lesson 107). I will give you a few sentences with **nouns** and **linking verbs**. You add a word after the **linking verb** that tells me more about the **noun**. "The worm was…" Can you tell me how the worm felt to your hand when you touched it?

*Child: The worm was slimy [or cold, etc.].*

Instructor: The **linking verb** "was" connects "worm" with a word that tells us more about the worm. Can you tell me something about a huge eighteen-wheeler truck if I say, "The truck is _____." Tell me how big the truck is, or what color it is.

*Child: The truck is huge [or another appropriate word].*

Instructor: The **linking verb** "is" connects the truck with the word _____. Now finish this sentence: "Blowing bubbles in the yard is…"

*Child: Blowing bubbles in the yard is [fun, messy]!*

Instructor: The **linking verb** "is" connects "blowing bubbles" with the word _____. What are the bubbles like? Begin your sentence with, "The bubbles are…"

*Child: The bubbles are [round, shiny, tiny, enormous, etc.]*

Instructor: The linking verb "are" connects "bubbles" and _____.

Listen again to the definition of a verb: **A verb is a word that does an action, shows a state of being, links two words together, or helps another verb.** We have talked about **verbs** that do actions, show state of being, and link words together. Let's finish by talking about **verbs** that help other **verbs**. We call these **helping verbs**. Let's say them together three times.

Together (three times):

Am [clap]

Is [clap]

Are, was, were. [clap]

Be [clap]

Being [clap]

Been. [clap] [clap]

Have, has, had [clap]

Do, does, did [clap]

Shall, will, should, would, may, might, must [clap] [clap]

Can, could!

Instructor: I will read you some sentences where a **helping verb** is helping an **action verb**. Tell me which **helping verb** you hear.

⇨ Note to Instructor: The helping verbs in the following sentences are italicized. If necessary, emphasize them slightly as you read.

Instructor: The Tyrannosaurus Rex *was* crashing through the underbrush.

*Child: Was*

Instructor: Tyrannosaurus *had been* sleeping. He woke up hungry!

*Child: Had, been*

Instructor: Tyrannosaurus thought, "I *am* hoping to find some prey!"

*Child: Am*

Instructor: He *was* hoping to find a nice Iguanodon or Allosaurus to eat.

*Child: Was*

Instructor: As he crashed along, he *could* hear something even bigger behind him.

*Child: Could*

Instructor: He thought, "It *might* be Gigantosaurus!"

*Child: Might*

Instructor: Tyrannosaurus decided that it *would* be smarter to return to his cave for another nap.

*Child: Would*

Instructor: Let's repeat the definition of a **verb** together two more times.

Together (two times): **A verb is a word that does an action, shows a state of being, links two words together, or helps another verb.**

## Dictation Exercise

Choose one or more of the following sentences.

Some dinosaurs were quite large.

Many dinosaurs were plant eaters, but some ate meat.

Tyrannosaurus Rex was hoping that he could find a nice dinosaur for a snack.

## Enrichment Activity

Repeat activity from Lesson 107: Help the child make a three-link paper chain from three different colors of construction paper that are light enough for the child to clearly see writing on them. The middle link should be yellow or white. While the links are flat, before putting the chain together: 1. Write a linking verb on the yellow or white link. 2. Write a noun or pronoun on another color link. 3. Write an adjective on the third strip of paper. Glue or tape the chain together, showing that the yellow (or white) linking verb "links" a noun or pronoun with an adjective to make a sentence. You could repeat this project writing a noun instead of an adjective for the third link in the chain.

# Lesson 153

-Adverbs
-Adjectives
-Dictation exercise: "My Kitten"
-Poem review: "The Year" (Lesson 131)
* The child will need art supplies for the enrichment activity. The instructor will need a volume "C" encyclopedia.

⇨  Note to Instructor: Review "The Year" today.

Instructor: When we talked about **nouns,** we learned that **a noun is the name of a person, place, thing, or idea.** When we talked about **adjectives,** we learned that **an adjective is a word that describes a noun.** I am going to give you a **noun** that names an animal: "kitten." The **noun** that names "kitten" doesn't tell me anything about the kitten. I don't know what color it is. I don't know how big it is. I don't know what it feels like to touch. I don't know if it is friendly or wild. I need other words to tell me these things. I am going to ask you to pretend you have a kitten. It can look like a real kitten, or like an imaginary kitten that you would never see in real life. I am going to let you  describe this kitten using **adjectives. An adjective is a word that describes a noun.** Let's begin with color words. Color words are **adjectives,** because they help describe **nouns.** What color is your pretend kitten?

*Child: My kitten is [color].*

Instructor : I am going to write a sentence that will have all of your adjectives in it. I will begin it, "My [color]…"

⇨  Note to Instructor: Begin writing a sentence when the child gives you words. You will make a complete sentence about this kitten, writing each part of the sentence as the child decides on it. Do not write the word "kitten" yet, since we will be adding other adjectives. You may use more than one adjective, verb, or adverb if the child wishes. Encourage the child to picture in his mind this extraordinary kitten.

Instructor: What size is the kitten? Is it big, enormous, gigantic, large, or tiny? These size words are **adjectives** that describe the size of the kitten. Choose an **adjective** to describe this kitten and tell me what it is.

*Child: My kitten is [adjective of size].*

Instructor: Now we know the kitten's size and its color. I will add your new **adjective** to the sentence I am writing. "My [color], [size]…"

⇨ Note to Instructor: Remember to add commas after these adjectives, since there will be more than two.

Instructor: Now I know the color and size of the kitten, but I need you to think of an another **adjective**. This time think of an **adjective** of touch that would describe your kitten—what does this kitten feel like when you hold it? Is it soft, furry, wet, sticky, curly, or fuzzy?

*Child: My kitten is [adjective of touch].*

Instructor: I will add that to your sentence. Now it reads: "My [color], [size], [adjective of touch] kitten..." Repeat that part of the sentence for me.

*Child: "My [color], [size], [adjective of touch] kitten..."*

Instructor: Now I know the color and size of the kitten and I know how it feels, but I don't know what it does. Now I need an **action verb** to tell me what this kitten does. Is it a kitten that runs, rolls, falls, jumps, eats, sleeps, skates, floats, plays, barks, mews, or roars?

*Child: [action verb]*

Instructor: Here is what I have written: My [color], [size], [adjective of touch] kitten [action verb]..." Read that much of the sentence back to me.

*Child: My [color], [size], [adjective of touch] kitten [action verb]...*

Instructor: Now I know the color and size of the kitten and I know how it feels, and I do know what it does. But I don't know <u>how</u> it does the action. I need an **adverb** to tell me <u>how</u> the kitten does his action. Remember: **An adverb is a word that describes a verb, an adjective, or another adverb.** <u>How</u> does the kitten [action verb]?

⇨ Note to Instructor: You may offer the child any of these options: loudly, softly, angrily, frantically, carefully, quickly, slowly, eagerly, hungrily, carefully, slowly, eagerly, messily, greedily, daintily, gratefully, skillfully, awkwardly, clumsily, energetically, happily, joyfully, frantically, merrily, dangerously, beautifully, recklessly, clearly, beautifully, unexpectedly, loudly, swiftly, softly, sweetly, gently, smoothly, quietly, easily, immediately.

*Child: [adverb]*

Instructor: Here is the sentence I have written: My [color], [size], [adjective of touch] kitten [action verb] [adverb]. Read that sentence back to me. Now I know what your kitten is like!

## Dictation Exercise

Read the sentence about the kitten back to the child. It will be long and possibly contain hard-to-spell words. Give patient help, as necessary, especially with spelling. You may wish to review dictation techniques in Lesson 122.

## Enrichment Activity

Draw, in color, a picture of this imaginary kitten. Look up "cat" in an encyclopedia and talk about adjectives and adverbs that describe the many varieties of cats.

# Lesson 154
-Story narration: "The Storm," by Sara Buffington

⇨ Note to Instructor: Read aloud the story below. Have the child tell the story back to you; use the suggested questions at the story's end to prompt the child, if necessary. When the child has completed his oral narration, repeat the first sentence or the first two sentences of his narration back to him as a dictation exercise. You write this dictation down for him.

## The Storm

The two little boys eagerly pressed their round faces against the large window. They longed to go outside and play. The older boy sweetly asked their mother, "Mommy, may we go outside and play? We would love to ride our bikes today."

The mother joined her sons at the window and gazed at the sky. "Look at the sky," she said softly. "Do you see the low, dark, grey clouds? That means a storm is coming. Let's stay inside this afternoon."

Just then they heard a long, rumbling sound. "I know that sound," the younger boy said quietly. "That's thunder."

They looked cautiously at the dark sky. More loud rumbles of thunder boomed overhead. The two boys looked at their mother anxiously. So she turned on a bright lamp and said cheerfully, "Let's play a game of Chutes and Ladders™. We can sit here near the window so we can play and watch the storm."

They were having great fun playing the board game, and barely heard the pitter-patter of little drops of rain on the roof. But soon the pitter-patter sound changed into a loud, continuous thumping. The rain was pouring! They looked out the window and saw sheets of rain battering their car, yard, and street. "Mommy, do you see the little waterfalls running from the roof?" said the older boy. "They are forming big puddles on the ground!"

A flash of bright light pierced the sky. It was lightning! After a few seconds, they heard a crackling sound, quickly followed by a huge boom. The dazzling lightning and rumbling thunder startled the boys. But they were not scared. They were inside a dry, safe room.

The lightning flashed and the thunder rolled. The little boys gazed out of the window. It was exciting to watch the storm, but they were glad to be inside!

"Plink! Plunk! Plink!" They heard a sound like tiny pebbles hitting the roof. The boys peered out through the window and saw little white balls of ice steadily falling from the sky. "That's hail," their mother explained. "The rain freezes in the sky and then it falls to the ground." The boys thought that hail was strange, but fun. Imagine, ice falling from the sky in the middle of summer!

After a while, the noisy hail stopped. The thunder gradually moved away. The lightning flashed, but it was pale and distant. The rain faded into a light drizzle. The sky grew lighter and lighter. Soon, the sun came out and shone down on the wet grass and enormous puddles.

"Boys," their mother said, "You may go outside and play now."

"Hurrah!" the boys cheered. "But let's watch another summer storm tomorrow!"

⇨ Note to Instructor: Ask the child to tell you the story back in his own words. If the child has trouble remembering, use these questions:

Why did the boys want to go outside? *They wanted to ride their bikes.*

Why didn't their mother let them go outside? *She saw a storm coming.*

What sound did they hear that first warned them of the storm? *They heard the thunder.*

What was the next thing they heard after the thunder? *They heard the rain fall.*

What did they see when they looked outside? *They saw lightning and rain.*

What fell from the sky that made a "plink" sound on the roof? *Hail fell from the sky.*

How did they know when the storm was over? *The thunder and lightning stopped, the rain and hail stopped, the sky got lighter, and the sun came out.*

Do you think the boys liked watching the storm? *Yes, they liked watching the storm, but they were glad they watched it from inside the house.*

# Lesson 155

-Adjectives
-Adverbs

Instructor: Can you repeat the definition of an **adverb** for me?

*Child:* **An adverb is a word that describes a verb, an adjective, or another adverb.**

⇨ Note to Instructor: If the child cannot remember the definition, repeat it with him three times.

Instructor: Can you repeat the definition of an **adjective** for me?

*Child:* **An adjective is a word that describes a noun or pronoun.**

⇨ Note to Instructor: If the child cannot remember the definition, repeat it with him three times.

Instructor: Let's look back at the story "The Storm" together (Lesson 154). We will see whether we can find the **adjectives** and **adverbs** in this story.

⇨ Note to Instructor: Expect this activity to take the remainder of your lesson time. See the key for the instructor that follows. Ask the child to identify only those adverbs ending in "-ly." When appropriate, point out the noun or pronoun which each adjective describes, and the verb or adjective described by each adverb (you do not need to point this out for every adjective and adverb!). Some adjectives and adverbs (such as "their" and "outside" are not labelled because they have not yet been taught). The purpose of the exercise is to begin to make the child aware of these descriptive words in stories. You need not cover the whole story; spend an appropriate amount of time for your child's attention span.

## Key for the Instructor

      adj.  adj.      adv.          adj.             adj.
The two little boys eagerly pressed their round faces against the large window. They
                        adj.       adv.
longed to go outside and play. The older boy sweetly asked their mother, "Mommy, may we go outside and play? We would love to ride our bikes today."

The mother joined her sons at the window and gazed at the sky. "Look at the sky,"
      adv.             adj. adj.  adj.
she said softly. "Do you see the low, dark, grey clouds? That means a storm is coming. Let's stay inside this afternoon."
                 adj.   adj.                    adj.
Just then they heard a long, rumbling sound. "I know that sound," the younger boy
      adv.
said quietly. "That's thunder."

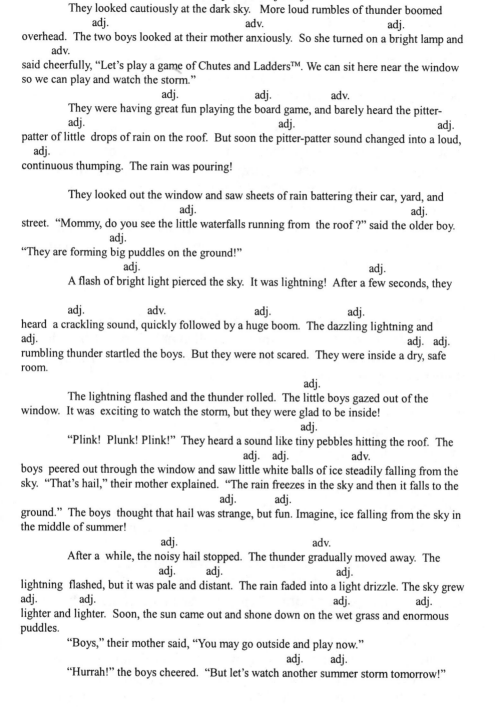

     adv.      adj.    adj.  adj.
  They looked cautiously at the dark sky. More loud rumbles of thunder boomed
     adj.          adv.        adj.
overhead. The two boys looked at their mother anxiously. So she turned on a bright lamp and
  adv.
said cheerfully, "Let's play a game of Chutes and Ladders™. We can sit here near the window
so we can play and watch the storm."
       adj.      adj.      adv.
  They were having great fun playing the board game, and barely heard the pitter-
     adj.             adj.         adj.
patter of little drops of rain on the roof. But soon the pitter-patter sound changed into a loud,
  adj.
continuous thumping. The rain was pouring!


  They looked out the window and saw sheets of rain battering their car, yard, and
          adj.                adj.
street. "Mommy, do you see the little waterfalls running from the roof?" said the older boy.
       adj.
"They are forming big puddles on the ground!"
      adj.               adj.
  A flash of bright light pierced the sky. It was lightning! After a few seconds, they

  adj.     adv.        adj.      adj.
heard a crackling sound, quickly followed by a huge boom. The dazzling lightning and
adj.                           adj.  adj.
rumbling thunder startled the boys. But they were not scared. They were inside a dry, safe
room.
                 adj.
  The lightning flashed and the thunder rolled. The little boys gazed out of the
window. It was exciting to watch the storm, but they were glad to be inside!
                 adj.
  "Plink! Plunk! Plink!" They heard a sound like tiny pebbles hitting the roof. The
                adj.  adj.      adv.
boys peered out through the window and saw little white balls of ice steadily falling from the
sky. "That's hail," their mother explained. "The rain freezes in the sky and then it falls to the
           adj.    adj.
ground." The boys thought that hail was strange, but fun. Imagine, ice falling from the sky in
the middle of summer!
       adj.           adv.
  After a while, the noisy hail stopped. The thunder gradually moved away. The
       adj.  adj.       adj.
lightning flashed, but it was pale and distant. The rain faded into a light drizzle. The sky grew
adj.   adj.               adj.      adj.
lighter and lighter. Soon, the sun came out and shone down on the wet grass and enormous
puddles.
  "Boys," their mother said, "You may go outside and play now."
                 adj.  adj.
  "Hurrah!" the boys cheered. "But let's watch another summer storm tomorrow!"

# Lesson 156

-Introducing articles
-Dictation exercise: "A Helicopter"
-Poem review: "Hearts Are Like Doors" (Lesson 27)
* The instructor will need a story book, magazine article, or newspaper column for the enrichment activity.

⇨ Note to Instructor: Review "Hearts Are Like Doors" today.

Instructor: We have learned about many different kinds of words. We have learned about **nouns, verbs, adjectives, adverbs, interjections**, and **conjunctions**. **Conjunctions** are the shortest of all of those words! Do you remember what a **conjunction** does? It joins words or groups of words together. The **conjunctions** are "and, but, or." How many letters are in the **conjunction** "and?" How about "but?" How about "or?"

⇨ Note to Instructor: If necessary, write "and, but, or" and let the child count the letters.

Instructor: Now we are going to learn about words that are even shorter than **conjunctions**! These words are called **articles**. **The articles are *a, an*, and *the*.** Let's say that together three times: **The articles are *a, an*, and *the*.**

Together (three times): **The articles are *a, an*, and *the*.**

Instructor: You use **articles** whenever you talk about **nouns**. You use them automatically—you don't even realize that you're using them.

⇨ Note to Instructor: Point to a chair.

Instructor: What is this?

*Child: A chair [or the chair].*

⇨ Note to Instructor: Most children will automatically use an article. If your child simply says "chair," say, "a chair" and have him repeat it after you.

Instructor: "A" [or "the"] is an **article**. We usually use "a" or "an" when we are talking about any old **noun**, and "the" when we are talking about specific **nouns**. Repeat this sentence after me: "There is a window."

*Child: There is a window.*

Instructor: That could be any window in this house—or in someone else's house. It is not a specific window. It is "*a* window."

⇨ Note to Instructor: Point to a window as you say the next sentence.

Instructor: Repeat this sentence after me: "There is the window."

*Child: There is the window.*

Instructor: "The window" is a specific window—that window right there! We use "the" whenever we are talking about a specific **noun**. When we are talking about any old **noun**, we use "a" or "an." "A" and "an" mean the same thing, but we use "an" before words that begin with vowels. When you were learning to read, do you remember learning the names of the vowels? The vowels are *a, e, i, o, u.* Let's say the vowels together:

Together: A, e, i, o, u.

Instructor: *A, e, i, o, u* are vowels. Say that with me.

Together: A, e, i, o, u are vowels.

Instructor: All the other letters of the alphabet are called consonants. Say that with me.

Together: All the other letters of the alphabet are called consonants.

Instructor: We use "a" before a word that begins with a consonant. If I say, "I will give you a banana," I use "a" before "banana" because "banana" begins with "b." "B" is a consonant. We use "an" before a word that begins with a vowel. If I say, "I will give you an apple," I use "an" before "apple" because "apple" begins with "a." "A" is a vowel. Now I am going to play the "A-An" riddle game with you. I will ask you a question. When you give me the answer, you will use "an" before words that begin with *a, e, i, o, u.* You will use "a" before all the words that begin with consonants—all the other letters of the alphabet. What is a huge, grey animal with a long trunk?

*Child: An elephant.*

Instructor: What has a shell on the outside and a yellow yolk on the inside?

*Child: An egg.*

Instructor: What is something that holds ice cream? We carry it around in our hand while we're eating the ice cream, and then eat it along with the last bit of ice cream.

*Child: An ice cream cone [or a cone].*

Instructor: What is a cat's baby called?

*Child: A kitten.*

Instructor: What fruit has the same name as its color?

*Child: An orange.*

Instructor: What has scales and swims in lakes, rivers, or the ocean?

*Child: A fish.*

Instructor: What do you hold up over your head when it rains?

*Child: An umbrella.*

Instructor: You use "an" before words that begin with vowels, and "a" before words that begin with consonants. Let's repeat the definition of an **article** three more times: **The articles are *a, an,* and *the.*** Together (three times): **The articles are *a, an,* and *the.***

## Dictation Exercise:

Choose one or more of the sentences below. Ask the child to choose whether "a" or "an" goes before the nouns. If you dictate the sentences with commas, remember to pause at each comma.

We  visited (a or an) zoo and saw (a or an) animal.
My sister and I saw (a or an) airplane, (a or an) helicopter, and (a or an) jet.
At the market we bought (a or an) apple, (a or an) orange, (a or an) banana, and (a or an) bunch of grapes.

## Enrichment Activity

Find the articles "a" and "an" in a story, magazine, or news column. Make a list of several articles along with the word that follows them.

# Lesson 157

-Articles
-Capitalization review
-Poem review: "The Caterpillar" (Lesson 2)

⇨ Note to Instructor: Review "The Caterpillar" today.

⇨ Note to Instructor: Introduce the idea that you capitalize titles of poems, stories, and books.

Instructor: Let's name the **articles. The articles are *a, an,* and *the.*** Say that with me three times.

Together (three times): **The articles are *a, an,* and *the.***

Instructor: We use "the" when we talk about specific **nouns**. We use "a" or "an" to talk about just any **nouns**. "A" comes before words that begin with a consonant, and "an" comes before words that begin with a vowel. What sits in a tree and says, "Who, who, who?"

*Child: An owl.*

⇨ Note to Instructor: Write down "an owl" and show it to the child.

Instructor: "Owl" starts with "o," and "o" is a vowel; so we use the **article** "an." What has four legs and barks?

*Child: A dog.*

⇨ Note to Instructor: Write down "a dog" and show it to the child.

Instructor: "Dog" starts with "d," and "d" is a consonant; so we use the article "a." I will write out another phrase that has "dog" in it. Do you recognize it?

⇨ Note to Instructor: Write "Go, Dog, Go" on the paper.

Instructor: This is the title of a book. Have you ever read this book? In this title, the word "dog" starts with a special kind of letter. What is it?

*Child: A capital letter.*

Instructor: The words "Go" and "Dog" are both capitalized because they are part of a title. The first word and every important word in a book title is capitalized. What is your favorite book?

⇨ Note to Instructor: Write down the title of the child's favorite book. Capitalize the first word and every other important word (generally, all words except for the articles *a, an,* and *the* and the conjunctions and prepositions of fewer than five letters). Point out the capital letters.

Instructor: Let's go back and look at the title of the last story we read. What is it called?

⇨ Note to Instructor: Look together at "The Storm" (Lesson 154). Point out the capital letters in the title.

Instructor: "The" is the first word of the title, so it is capitalized. "Storm" is an important word, so we capitalize it as well. Titles of stories are capitalized, just like titles of books. Titles of poems are capitalized, too. Let's look back at the last poem we memorized.

⇨ Note to Instructor: Look together at "The Little Bird" (Lesson 139). Point out the capital letters.

Instructor: The titles of poems, stories, and books are capitalized. Let's review some of the other places we use capital letters. Repeat after me: Capitalize **proper names** of people and places.

*Child: Capitalize proper names of people and places.*

Instructor: Names like "George Washington" and "Minnesota" are **proper names**, so they are capitalized. Repeat after me: Capitalize the names of days of the week.

*Child: Capitalize the names of days of the week.*

Instructor: What day of the week is it? Write it down and capitalize it.

⇨ Note to Instructor: Help the child spell the day of the week correctly.

Instructor: What month is it? Write it down and capitalize it. You should capitalize the months of the year.

⇨ Note to Instructor: Help the child spell the month correctly.

Instructor: What season is it? Is this winter, spring, summer, or fall? Remember: you should *not* capitalize the name of a season! Write down the name of the season that we are now in, but don't capitalize it.

⇨ Note to Instructor: Help the child identify the season and write it down.

Instructor: You should capitalize the name of a holiday. "Thanksgiving" and "Independence Day" are both holidays. They should begin with capital letters. Which one would you like to write down?

⇨ Note to Instructor: Help the child spell whichever holiday he chooses. If necessary, remind him that both words in "Independence Day" are capitalized.

Instructor: Always capitalize the word "I." Write the sentence, "Mom and I made cookies." Remember to capitalize the word "I."

⇨ Note to Instructor: Give all necessary help.

Instructor: You should always capitalize initials and put periods after them. Write down your own initials.

⇨ Note to Instructor: Give all necessary help.

Instructor: And remember—always capitalize the first word in a sentence!

**Enrichment Activity**

Dictate the following book titles to the child, and help him capitalize and spell them correctly.

Goodnight, Moon
The Hungry Caterpillar
Are You My Mother?
Cars and Trucks and Things That Go
Stuart Little
A Little Princess

# Lesson 158

-Introducing prepositions
-Dictation exercise: "Over My Head"
-Poem review: "The Little Bird" (Lesson 139)

⇨ Note to Instructor: Review "The Little Bird" today.

⇨ Note to Instructor: IMPORTANT! Over the next fifteen lessons, the child will be memorizing a very long list of prepositions. As he continues into later grades, he will find a memorized list of prepositions invaluable. As he learns about subjects, objects, and other ways that words function within sentences, he will need to be able to eliminate prepositional phrases before he can identify the central elements in sentences (since the object of a preposition is *never* the subject, direct object, or indirect object). The inability to recognize prepositions and their objects is one of the greatest stumbling blocks for students in middle-grade grammar. If he takes the time now to learn the prepositions by heart, his later grammar learning will become much simpler. (The student will learn the <u>definition</u> of a preposition as well, but learning the definition is not enough. He should <u>also</u> memorize the list, since not all prepositions follow the definition exactly.)

Instructor: Let's review **articles** one more time. **The articles are *a, an,* and *the*.** Say that with me three times.

Together (three times): **The articles are *a, an,* and *the*.**

Instructor: **Articles** are short words. **Conjunctions**—"and, but, or" —are short words. **Interjections** are short words too. Do you re-member **interjections? An interjection is a word that ex-presses sudden or strong feeling,** like "Wow!" or "Great!" Can you say those two **interjections** for me?

*Child: Wow! Great!*

Instructor: I'm glad you're enjoying your grammar so much, because we are going to learn a new part of speech! **A preposition is a word that shows the relationship of a noun or pronoun to another word in the sentence.** Let's work on that definition together. Repeat the first part with me three times: **A preposition is a word...**

Together (three times): **A preposition is a word...**

Instructor: Now let's say the second part three times: **...that shows the relationship...**

Together (three times): **...that shows the relationship...**

Instructor: Now I will say those two parts of the definition together. **A preposition is a word that shows the relationship...** Let's try to repeat that together three times.

Together (three times): **A preposition is a word that shows the relationship...**

Instructor: Now let's repeat the next part three times. **...of a noun or pronoun...**

Together (three times): **...of a noun or pronoun...**

Instructor: I will say the whole definition so far. **A preposition is a word that shows the relationship of a noun or pronoun...** Can we say that together three times?

Together (three times): **A preposition is a word that shows the relationship of a noun or pronoun...**

Instructor: Now for the last part! **...to another word in the sentence.** Let's say that three times.

Together (three times): **...to another word in the sentence.**

Instructor: Whew! That was a very long definition. Here is the whole thing: **A preposition is a word that shows the relationship of a noun or pronoun to another word in the sentence.** Let's say that whole thing together three times.

Together (three times): **A preposition is a word that shows the relationship of a noun or pronoun to another word in the sentence.**

Instructor: You have worked so hard on the definition that you need a break! Lie down on the floor and stretch. Now you are on the floor. What is the relationship between you and the floor? You are *on* the floor. "On" is a **preposition.** It is showing the relationship between a pronoun—"you"—and another word in the sentence—"the floor." Now I think that you should shake out your arms. Sit up and hold your arms up, up, up. Look up at your hands. Where are your hands?

*Child: Above my head* or *Over my head* or *Up in the air* or *In the air.*

⇨ Note to Instructor: You can prompt the child with one of the above, if necessary.

Instructor: "Above" [or whatever preposition the child uses] is a **preposition.** It tells about the relationship between your hands and your head (or your hands and the air). Now you can put your hands down. I think you should take a real break. I think you should crawl beneath the table and hide. Where are you?

*Child: Under the table*

Instructor: You are under the table! Under is a **preposition.** It tells about the relationship between you and the table. Remember: **A preposition is a word that shows the relationship of a noun or pronoun to another word in the sentence.**

## Dictation Exercise

Choose one of the following sentences. Remember to pause at each comma.

My hands are over my head.

I am hiding under the table, and no one can see me.

I am stretching out on the floor for a rest because I have worked so hard.

# Lesson 159

-Prepositions
-Copywork: "Aboard the Ship"
-Poem review: "The Year" (Lesson 131)
* The instructor will need a plate, fork, knife, spoon, napkin, and glass.

⇨ Note to Instructor: Review "The Year" today.
⇨ Note to Instructor: You will need a plate, fork, knife, spoon, napkin, and glass for today's lesson.

Instructor: In the last lesson, we learned a very long definition. **A preposition is a word that shows the relationship of a noun or pronoun to another word in the sentence.** I will say the first part of that definition: **A preposition is a word that shows the relationship...** Repeat that with me three times.

Together (three times): **A preposition is a word that shows the relationship...**

Instructor: Now listen to the last part of the definition: **...of a noun or pronoun to another word in the sentence.** Let's say that three times.

Together (three times): **...of a noun or pronoun to another word in the sentence.**

Instructor: Here is the whole thing: **A preposition is a word that shows the relationship of a noun or pronoun to another word in the sentence.** Let's say that whole thing together three times.

Together (three times): **A preposition is a word that shows the relationship of a noun or pronoun to another word in the sentence.**

Instructor: Let's practice some more **prepositions** while we also practice setting the table. You have a plate, silverware, a glass, and a napkin. Answer this question in a complete sentence. Where will you put the plate?

⇨ Note to Instructor: For each of the following questions, have the child carry out the action he describes in his complete sentence.

*Child: I will put the plate on the table.*

Instructor: The word "on" tells you about the relationship between the plate and the table. "On" is a **preposition**. The fork goes beside the plate, on the left. Put the fork beside the plate, on the left. "Beside" is a **preposition**. It tells you about the relationship between the fork and the plate. The knife also goes beside the plate, on the other side. The knife and the fork have the same relationship to the plate. Both are *beside* it. Neither one is *on* the plate! The blade of the knife should be turned toward the plate. The blade of the knife has a very particular relationship to the plate! It is *toward* it—not *away from* it. Place the spoon beside the knife. What relationship does the spoon have with the knife?

*Child: The spoon is beside the knife.*

Instructor: Now, place the glass *on* the table, *above* the knife. The glass has a relationship to the table *and* a relationship to the knife. The preposition "on" tells about its relationship to the table. The preposition "above" tells about its relationship to the knife. Now we should place the napkin beside the fork, to the left. If you think that a paper napkin might blow away, you can also place it *under* the fork. Go ahead and do that now. "Under" is a preposition. It tells about the relationship between the fork and the napkin. There are many different prepositions to learn, so we are going to end today's lesson by chanting a few of them: Aboard, about, above, across. I will repeat that three times, and then we will say it together three times.

Instructor (three times): Aboard, about, above, across.

Together (three times): Aboard, about, above, across.

## Copywork

Copy as many of the following sentences as is appropriate.

The little boy went aboard the ship.
He wandered about the ship, looking at the rigging above him.
He leaned over the edge of the ship and looked across the water at the shore.

## Enrichment Activity

Using his body, furniture, toys, and/or a cardboard box, have the child act out a few of the following prepositions:

Above, among, behind, below, beneath, beside, between, in, inside, near, on, off, over, under, underneath, up, upon, with, within.

# Lesson 160
-Picture narration: "Bedtime"

⇨ Note to Instructor: The prepositions in the following dialogue are italicized. When appropriate, point out that the prepositions are telling more about the relationship between the nouns (people, places and things) in the picture.

How many people are *in* this picture? There are two people *in* this picture. They are mother and daughter. It is bedtime. What does the mother have *on* her lap? Yes, she has a book *on* her lap. *On* is a **preposition**, and it tells more about the relationship between the book and the mother's lap. Why do you think she has a book *on* her lap? She has been reading a bedtime story *to* her daughter. It is about three billy goats that try to cross a bridge with a troll *on* it. Do you know that story? The girl is asking her mother a question. Her mother has just finished reading the story. What do you think she is asking her mother to do? She is asking her mother to read her another story. I wonder if her mother will read her another story. Stories are fun to read, but it is more important for children to get their rest.

The little girl likes to sleep *with* stuffed animals. How many stuffed animals are *on* her bed? Yes, there are two stuffed animals *on* her bed. I see the dog. What stuffed animal is *beside* the dog? A teddy bear is *beside* the dog. "Beside" is a **preposition**, and it shows the relationship *between* the teddy bear and the dog. The teddy bear's name is Mr. Fiddlesticks. The girl has many toys. Do you see her other toys? Where are they? They are *on* the shelves. I see a lamp *on* the bottom shelf. What is *on* the lamp? There is a frog *on* the lamp. "On" is a **preposition**, and it shows the relationship between the frog and the lamp. What is *beside* the frog lamp? There are books *beside* the lamp. "Beside" is a **preposition**, and it shows the relationship *between* the books and the lamp. What is *above* the lamp? There are books *above* the lamp. "Above" is a **preposition**, and it shows the relationship *between* the books and the lamp. This girl must be smart. Smart, bright children read books and stories. What is *on* the other end of the middle shelf? It is a counting toy called an abacus. What is located *between* the books and the abacus? There is a globe *between* the books and the abacus. "Between" is a **preposition,** and it shows the relationship *between* the globe and the books and the abacus. I see an animal *on* the top shelf, do you? What is *below* the elephant? The globe is *below* the elephant. "Below" is a **preposition,** and it shows the relationship *between* the elephant and the globe. What is *against* the elephant's head? The vase is *against* the elephant's head. "Against" is a **preposition,** and it shows the relationship *between* the elephant and the vase. What is *in* the vase? A flower is *in* the vase. "In" is a **preposition**, and it shows the relationship *between* the vase and the flower. The little girl likes flowers. Do you see any other flowers in the room? There are flowers *on* her blanket. "On" is a **preposition**, and it shows the relationship *between* the flowers and the blanket.

I think the mother is going to say good-night so the girl can go to sleep. What do you think the girl will dream about tonight? I think she may dream about the story she heard or about a field full of flowers.

# Lesson 161

-Prepositions
-Poem review: "Work" (Lesson 15)

⇨ Note to Instructor: Review "Work" today.

Instructor: Let's keep working on our long **preposition** definition. **A preposition is a word that shows the relationship of a noun or pronoun to another word in the sentence.** I will say the first part of that definition: **A preposition is a word that shows the relationship...** Repeat that with me three times.

Together (three times): **A preposition is a word that shows the relationship...**

Instructor: Now listen to the last part of the definition: **...of a noun or pronoun to another word in the sentence.** Let's say that three times.

Together (three times): **...of a noun or pronoun to another word in the sentence.**

Instructor: Here is the whole thing: **A preposition is a word that shows the relationship of a noun or pronoun to another word in the sentence.** Let's say that whole thing together three times.

Together (three times): **A preposition is a word that shows the relationship of a noun or pronoun to another word in the sentence.**

Instructor: Let's work on our first list of **prepositions**. I will repeat it three times, and then we will say it together five times.

Instructor (three times): Aboard, about, above, across.

Together (five times): Aboard, about, above, across.

Instructor: Now I want you to make up some sentences that use these **prepositions.** I am going to give you two **nouns** and a **preposition**. Make up a sentence that uses the **preposition** to show the relationship between the two nouns. Here is an example. I might give you the **nouns** "worm" and "hole," and the **preposition** "in." You might answer, "The worm is in the hole." Or I might give you the **nouns** "bird" and "trees," and the **preposition** "above." You would say, "The bird is above the trees." Here are your first **nouns** and your first **preposition**: Captain, ship, aboard.

*Child: The captain is aboard the ship.*

Instructor: Book, bears, about.

*Child: The book is about the bears.*

Instructor: Sun, ground, above.

*Child: The sun is above the ground.*

Instructor: Goat, bridge, across.

*Child: The goat ran across the bridge.*

Instructor: Now we will work on the second part of the **preposition** list. Listen to me say it three times, and then we will try to say it together three times.

Instructor (three times): After, against, along, among, around, at.

Together (three times): After, against, along, among, around, at.

Instructor: Now I will say the whole list that we have learned so far. Aboard, about, above, across, after, against, along, among, around, at. I am going to say that list for you three times. I want you to say as much of it as you can along with me.

Instructor (slowly, three times, with child joining in): Aboard, about, above, across. After, against, along, among, around, at.

Instructor: Let's go on making up sentences together. I am going to give you two words or phrases that you can link together with your **preposition**: Puppy, ball, after.

⇨ Note to Instructor: Give the child any necessary help to formulate sentences like these.

*Child: The puppy ran after the ball.*

Instructor: Ladder, wall, against.

*Child: The ladder leans against the wall.*

Instructor: Train, tracks, along.

*Child: The train runs along the tracks.*

Instructor: Child, pillows, among.

*Child: The child wallowed among the pillows.*

Instructor: Monkey, mulberry bush, around.

*Child: All around the mulberry bush, the monkey chased the weasel!*

Instructor: Hungry man, table, at.

*Child: The hungry man sat at the table.*

Instructor: Good! Now let's do the whole list together, three more times.

Instructor (slowly, three times, with child joining in): Aboard, about, above, across. After, against, along, among, around, at.

322

## Dictation Exercise

Choose the title and one or more of the following sentences from the first stanza of "Bed in Summer" by Robert Louis Stevenson. Before dictating the stanza, show it to the child. Point out that the words in the title are capitalized. Show the child that the first word of every line is capitalized. Point out that there is no punctuation mark after the first line, a period after the second line, a comma after the third line, and a period after the last line. Remind the child of this punctuation while dictating.

Bed in Summer
*By Robert Louis Stevenson*


In winter I get up at night
And dress by yellow candle light.
In summer, quite the other way,
I have to go to bed by day.

## Enrichment Activity

Ask the child to make up additional sentences with several of the prepositions from this lesson, following the same pattern. You write each sentence on the top of an unlined piece of paper. Have the child draw the relationship between the nouns and prepositions in the sentence. Stick figures are fine! Then ask the child to write the preposition on the picture at the appropriate place. (For example, you might write, "The train runs along the tracks" at the top of the paper. After drawing the train and the tracks, the child could write "along" next to the tracks, or draw an arrow pointing to the train's wheels and write "along" beside the arrow.) As a variation, the child may simply choose to illustrate the sentences given in the lesson.

# Lesson 162

-Prepositions
-Dictation exercise: "Beneath the Pyramids"
-Poem review: "Days of the Week" (Lesson 35)


⇨ Note to Instructor: Review "Days of the Week" today.

Instructor: Let's review our **preposition** definition. **A preposition is a word that shows the relationship of a noun or pronoun to another word in the sentence.** I will say the first part of that definition: **A preposition is a word that shows the relationship...** Repeat that with me three times.

Together (three times): **A preposition is a word that shows the relationship...**

Instructor: Now listen to the last part of the definition: **...of a noun or pronoun to another word in the sentence.** Let's say that three times.

Together (three times): **...of a noun or pronoun to another word in the sentence.**

Instructor: Here is the whole thing: **A preposition is a word that shows the relationship of a noun or pronoun to another word in the sentence.** Let's say that whole thing together three times.

Together (three times): **A preposition is a word that shows the relationship of a noun or pronoun to another word in the sentence.**

Instructor: I will say the list of **prepositions** that we have learned so far. Aboard, about, above, across, after, against, along, among, around, at. I am going to say that list for you three times. I want you to say as much of it as you can along with me.

Instructor (slowly, threee times, with child joining in): Aboard, about, above, across, after, against, along, among, around, at.

Instructor: Now we will add four more **prepositions** to our list: Before, behind, below, beneath. Listen carefully while I say those **prepositions** three times. Then we will repeat them together three more times.

Instructor (three times): Before, behind, below, beneath.

Together (three times): Before, behind, below, beneath.

Instructor: Let's get up and walk around the room. First, I want you to walk *before* me. Where are you? You are in front of me. *Before* tells

324

more about our relationship. Now, let's change the relationship. Walk *behind* me. Where are you? You aren't in front of me any more! *Behind* tells me that our relationship has changed. Now lie down on the floor.

⇨ Note to Instructor: Stand over the child; the illustration will be clearer if you can straddle him.

Instructor: Where are you now? Our relationship has changed again! Now you are *below* me. And there is also something *beneath* you. What is beneath you?

*Child: The floor is beneath me.*

Instructor: The **preposition** *beneath* tells about the relationship between you and the floor. We have learned the **prepositions** before, behind, below, beneath. Let's repeat those together three more times.

Together (three times): Before, behind, below, beneath.

Instructor: Now I will repeat the whole list for you, from the beginning, five times. Join in with me as far as you are able.

Instructor (slowly, three times, with child joining in): Aboard, about, above, across, after, against, along, among, around, at. Before, behind, below, beneath.

## Dictation Exercise

Choose one or more of the following sentences.

At the library, I found many books.
Among the books, I found one about mummies.
Beneath the pyramids, mummies lie in special tombs.

## Enrichment Activity

Read the phrases below one at a time and ask him to make up the rest of the sentence.

| | |
|---|---|
| Aboard the ship... | Around the house... |
| Above the ground... | At bedtime... |
| Across the street... | Before breakfast... |
| After breakfast... | Behind the bookcase... |
| Along the path... | Between the pages... |
| Among my toys... | Beneath the tree... |

# Lesson 163

-Prepositions
-Dictation exercise: "Beneath the Castle Wall"
-Poem review: "The Goops" (Lesson 100)

⇨ Note to Instructor: Review "The Goops" today.

Instructor: Today we will try to say our whole **preposition** definition together. Listen carefully: **A preposition is a word that shows the relationship of a noun or pronoun to another word in the sentence.** Now, let's repeat that together three times.

Together (three times): **A preposition is a word that shows the relationship of a noun or pronoun to another word in the sentence.**

Instructor: I will say the list of **prepositions** that we have learned so far three times. Try to say them with me.

Instructor (slowly, three times, with child joining in): Aboard, about, above, across. After, against, along, among, around, at. Before, behind, below, beneath.

Instructor: Now let's add four more **prepositions** to this list. I will say them for you three times.

Instructor (three times): Beside, between, beyond, by.

Instructor: Let's say those four **prepositions** together three times.

Together (three times): Beside, between, beyond, by.

Instructor: Let's go back and look at the picture in Lesson 160. We will practice using these **prepositions** as we talk about this picture. Let's find some things that are *beside*. Where is the mother?

*Child: The mother is beside the bed.*

Instructor: Where is the teddy bear?

*Child: The teddy bear is beside the little girl.*

Instructor: Can you find some other things that are *beside?*

⇨ Note to Instructor: Possible answers include: The globe is beside the books. The puppy is beside the little girl. The chair is beside the bed. The vase is beside the elephant.

Instructor: Now let's find some things that are between. Where is the elephant?

*Child: The elephant is between the books and the flower.*

Instructor: Where is the puppy?

*Child: The puppy is between the mother and the little girl.*

Instructor: Can you find some other things that are between?

⇨ Note to Instructor: Possible answers include: The globe is between the

326

books and the abacus. The vase is between the elephant and the doll. The teddy bear is between the girl and the mother. The little girl is between the sheets and the blanket.

Instructor: "Beyond" means "on the other side" or "out of reach." The elephant is *beyond* the little girl's reach while she is lying in bed. What other objects in the room are *beyond* her reach?

⇨ Note to Instructor: Possible answers include: Any of the objects on the bookshelves.

Instructor: What do you think the little girl can see out of her window? We don't know, because the curtain is drawn. The scene on the other side of the window is *beyond* our view.

⇨ Note to Instructor: Ask the child what might be on the other side of the window (tree, yard, swing, sandbox, another house). Help him to say, "The tree is beyond the window."

Instructor: The preposition "by" often means the same thing as "beside." It means "close to" or "near." The mother is *by* the bed. The window is *by* the bookshelves. We have also seen "by" in another place. Let's go back and look at the poem called "Bed In Summer" (Lesson 161). Where do you see the word "by"? It tells us who wrote the poem. We often use "by" to indicate the author of a book or story or poem. It shows a relationship between a person and a poem or story. The person wrote the poem or story! That is a very important relationship. Now, let's say those four prepositions together three times more: Beside, between, beyond, by.

Together (three times): Beside, between, beyond, by.

Instructor: Now I will repeat the whole list for you, from the beginning, five times. Join in with me as far as you are able.

Instructor (slowly, three times, with child joining in): Aboard, about, above, across. After, against, along, among, around, at. Before, behind, below, beneath. Beside, between, beyond, by.


## Dictation Exercise (Adapted from classic poets)

Choose one or more of the following sentences. For this lesson, dictate ony these sentences. Do not dictate the author's name.

They camped beneath the castle wall.
*Adapted from "Marmion" by Sir Walter Scott*

The cold earth slept beneath the sinking moon.
*Adapted from "The Cold Earth Slept Below" by Percy Bysshe Shelley*

Beneath his sad brow, his eye flashed like a broad sword, drawn from the sheath.
*Adapted from "Excelsior!" by Henry Wadsworth Longfellow*

## Enrichment Activity
Read the first stanza of "The Daffodils" together. Help the child find each preposition. Point out that "o'er" is a poetic contraction of "over." Ask the child to copy and illustrate one or more lines.

The Daffodils
*William Wordsworth*

I wandered lonely as a cloud
That floats on high o'er vales and hills,
When all at once I saw a crowd,
A host, of golden daffodils;
Beside the lake, beneath the trees,
Fluttering and dancing in the breeze.

# Lesson 164

-Articles
-Commas in a series
-Conjunctions
-Prepositions
-Dictation exercise: "During My Lesson"


Instructor: Do you remember the "little words" that we studied? The **articles** "a," "an," and "the" are very short words! Let's say together: **The articles are *a, an,* and *the*.**
Together: **The articles are *a, an,* and *the*.**
Instructor: We use "the" to talk about specific **nouns**. We use "a" and "an" to talk about any old **noun**.
⇨    Note to Instructor: Point to a particular chair as you say the next sentence.
Instructor: If I say, "Sit in the chair," you know that you should sit in one specific chair. But if I say "Sit in a chair," you could choose any chair to sit in. Even though the articles "a" and "an" are so short, they have their own special rule. "An" comes before words that begin with vowels. Repeat after me: The vowels are *a, e, i, o, u.*
*Child: The vowels are a, e, i, o, u.*
Instructor: All the other letters of the alphabet are called consonants. The article "a" comes before words that begin with consonants. If I say, "I will give you a gift," I use "a" before "gift" because "gift" begins with the consonant "g." If I tell you, "Go get an eraser," I use "an" before "eraser" because "eraser" begins with the vowel "e." Now I am going to let you look at a tricky sentence which is almost like a word puzzle.


At the zoo, I saw an ape, an elephant, an itchy monkey, an ostrich, and an ugly baboon.


Instructor: Tell me the letters at the beginning of each animal's name.
*Child: a (ape), e (elephant), m (monkey ), o (ostrich), b (baboon)*
Instructor: Now, here is the tricky part. Do the little words "a" and "an" come just before each animal's name, or are they placed just before some <u>other</u> word?
⇨    Note to Instructor: Point to the article before each word. Then ask the child to name each word after the article. For "ape," "elephant," and "ostrich," remind the child that "a,""e," and "o" are vowels, and that the

article "an" should come before a word that begins with a vowel. For "monkey" and "baboon," remind the child that "m" and "b" are consonants, but that "itchy" and "ugly" are the words that follow the articles and so require the article "an."

Instructor: Look at the sentence again with me. There are five animals at the zoo. The names of the animals are all in a series or list. What punctuation mark separates the names?

*Child: A comma separates the names.*

Instructor: Remember, we use commas to separate items in a list. The last two items in this list of animals are an ostrich and an ugly baboon. Those two items are connected with the special word "and." "And" is a **conjunction**. Do you remember what a **conjunction** is?

⇨  Note to Instructor: Prompt the child, if necessary.

Instructor: **A conjunction joins words or groups of words together.** Let's say that together three times.

Together (three times): **A conjunction joins words or groups of words together.**

Instructor: Remember, "junction" means "joining." A road junction is a place where two roads join together. A **"conjunction"** in grammar is a place where two words or groups of words join together. Let's look again at the sentence about the zoo one more time. What is the very first word?

*Child: At.*

Instructor: What kind of word is "at"? You have memorized it in a list. Remember: Aboard, about, above…

*Child: At is a preposition.*

Instructor: **A preposition is a word that shows the relationship of a noun or pronoun to another word in the sentence.** The **preposition** "at" tells you about the relationship between five animals and a place. They are not in your bedroom! They are at the zoo. I will say the prepositions we have already learned for you three times. Join in with me.

Instructor (slowly, three times, with child joining in): Aboard, about, above, across. After, against, along, among, around, at. Before, behind, below, beneath. Beside, between, beyond, by.

Instructor: Now we are going to do a little march around the room, and while we march, we will say, "Down, during, except, for, from!" We will say that until we are out of breath and ready to stop.

⇨  Note to Instructor: March around the room saying, "Down, during, except, for, from!" as long as seems appropriate.

## Dictation Exercise

Choose one of the following sentences. Remember to pause after the comma.

During my lesson, I worked.
During my lesson, I worked for twenty minutes.
I went down the stairs for a drink of water during a break from my lesson.

# Lesson 165

-Prepositions
-Adverbs
-Dictation exercise: "In the Afternoon"
-Poem review: "Mr. Nobody" (Lesson 81)

⇨ Note to Instructor: Review "Mr. Nobody" today.

Instructor: I will say the whole definition of a preposition for you. Then we will say it together three times. **A preposition is a word that shows the relationship of a noun or pronoun to another word in the sentence.**

Together (three times): **A preposition is a word that shows the relationship of a noun or pronoun to another word in the sentence.**

Instructor: In the last lesson, we learned five new **prepositions**: Down, during, except, for, from. Let's say that list together three times.

Together (three times): Down, during, except, for, from.

Instructor: Now I will say the list of **prepositions** we have learned so far. Say them with me three times.

Together (three times): Aboard, about, above, across. After, against, along, among, around, at. Before, behind, below, beneath. Beside, between, beyond, by. Down, during, except, for, from.

Instructor: Let's add four more **prepositions** to that list. I will say them for you three times.

Instructor (three times): In, inside, into, like.

Instructor: We will practice making sentences with these **prepositions**. I will give you two parts of a sentence, and I want you to use the **preposition** to show the relationship between them. The parts are "The stars twinkled" and "the sky." I will say them again: "The stars twinkled" and "the sky." Now add the **preposition** "in."

*Child: The stars twinkled in the sky.*

Instructor: The stars twinkled in the sky. Now I am going to add one more word: An **adverb**! Remember, **An adverb is a word that describes a verb, an adjective, or another adverb.** Let's repeat that together.

Together: **An adverb is a word that describes a verb, an adjective, or another adverb.**

Instructor: Now I will add the **adverb** "brightly." In this sentence,

332

"The stars twinkled in the sky," my **adverb** will describe the verb "twinkled." Repeat this sentence after me: "The stars twinkled brightly in the sky."

*Child: The stars twinkled brightly in the sky.*

Instructor: I will give you two more sentence parts: "The sun climbed" and "the morning sky." Use the **preposition** "into" and show the relationship between "The sun climbed" and "the morning sky."

⇨ Note to Instructor: For the remainder of the lesson, remember to repeat the sentence parts and the preposition until the child can remember them and repeat them back to you. This assures you that the child is listening, and also gives the child practice retaining words in his mind.

*Child: The sun climbed into the morning sky.*

Instructor: Can you add the **adverb** "cheerfully" to your sentence? Remember, the adverb describes the verb "climbed."

*Child: The sun climbed cheerfully into the morning sky.*

Instructor: Put the sentence parts "The child stayed" and "the house" together using the **preposition** "inside."

*Child: The child stayed inside the house.*

Instructor: Now put the **adverb** "lazily" into your sentence. Remember, the **adverb** describes the **verb** "stayed."

*Child: The child stayed lazily inside the house.*

Instructor: Now put the sentence parts "The clouds floated in the sky" together with "whipped cream." Use the **preposition** "like."

*Child: The clouds floated in the sky like whipped cream.*

Instructor: Finally, add the **adverb** "gently" to your sentence. Remember, the **adverb** describes the **verb** "floated."

*Child: The clouds floated gently in the sky like whipped cream.*

Instructor: Repeat with me three times: In, inside, into, like.

Together (three times): In, inside, into, like.

Instructor: I will say the whole list of **prepositions** three times. See if you can say them along with me.

Instructor (slowly, three times, with child joining in): Aboard, about, above, across. After, against, along, among, around, at. Before, behind, below, beneath. Beside, between, beyond, by. Down, during, except, for, from. In, inside, into, like.

## Dictation Exercise

Choose one of the following sentences. Pause at each comma when you dictate.

In the afternoon, I went inside the house.

In the afternoon, I went inside the house, and I looked into the refrigerator.

In the afternoon, I went inside the house, looked into the refrigerator, and found a snack like the treat I had yesterday.

## Enrichment Activity

Ask the child to draw a picture of the scene described in the lesson. Include the cheerful sun, the house, the child resting in the house, and the whipped-cream clouds. He could paste cotton in the sky if he wishes. You may wish to use the picture to review the relationships described in the lesson.

# Lesson 166

-Prepositions
-Verbs
-Poem review: "Mr. Nobody" (Lesson 81)

⇨  Note to Instructor: Review "Mr. Nobody" today.

Instructor: In our last lesson, we learned the **prepositions** "In, inside, into, like." Say those for me.

*Child: In, inside, into, like.*

Instructor: I will say the whole long list of **prepositions** three times. I want you to see if you can say all of them with me!

Instructor (slowly, three times, with child joining in): Aboard, about, above, across. After, against, along, among, around, at. Before, behind, below, beneath. Beside, between, beyond, by. Down, during, except, for, from. In, inside, into, like.

Instructor: Now let's read a new poem together. I will read it as you follow along.

I Love You Well
*A Mother Goose rhyme*

I love you well, my little brother,
And you are fond of me;
Let us be kind to one another,
As brothers ought to be.
You shall learn to play with me,
And learn to use my toys;
And then I think that we shall be
Two happy little boys.

Instructor: Together, we will find the different kinds of **verbs** in this poem. I will remind you of the definition of a **verb**. **A verb is a word that does an action, shows a state of being, links two words together, or helps another verb.** Let's say that together three times.

Together (three times): **A verb is a word that does an action, shows a state of being, links two words together, or helps another verb.**

Instructor: Can we find **action verbs** in this poem? Remember,

**action verbs** tell about something that you can do.

➪ Note to Instructor: The action verbs in the poem are "love" (first line), "learn" (fifth line), "play" (fifth line), "learn" (sixth line), "use" (sixth line), and "think" (seventh line).

Instructor: The second part of your definition is "**A verb shows a state of being.**" Remember, the **state of being verbs** show that someone exists. Here is the list of **state of being verbs**: Am, is, are, was, were, be, being, been. Let's chant those together three times.

Together (three times): Am, is, are, was, were, be, being, been.

Instructor: Remember sentences with **state of being verbs** can be very short: "I was," or "He was." Another kind of **verb** called a **linking verb** connects a **noun** or **pronoun** with another word. There is a **linking verb** in the second line of this poem: "And you are fond of me." The **verb** "are" links "you" to "fond." "Fond" tells us a little bit more about the little brother in the poem. He likes his older brother! "Are" is the **linking verb**. Let's look at the poem again.

I Love You Well
*A Mother Goose rhyme*

I love you well, my little brother,
And you are fond of me;
Let us be kind to one another,
As brothers ought to be.
You shall learn to play with me,
And learn to use my toys;
And then I think that we shall be
Two happy little boys.

Instructor: Now look at te last wo lines of the poem: "And then I think that we shall be two happy little boys." There are two words between "we" and "two happy little boys." They *link* "we" and "two happy little boys." What are those two words?
*Child: Shall be*
Instructor: "Be" is a **linking verb**. It links "we" to the words that give more information about the little boys. They are happy! "Shall"

336

is a **helping verb**. Remember, some **verbs** help other **verbs**. "Shall" is helping the **linking verb** "be." Can you find another place in the poem where "shall" helps a **verb**?

*Child: Shall learn*

Instructor: Good! I will say the list of **helping verbs** for you.
Am [clap]
Is [clap]
Are, was, were. [clap]
Be [clap]
Being [clap]
Been. [clap] [clap]
Have, has, had [clap]
Do, does, did [clap]
Shall, will, should, would, may, might, must [clap] [clap]
Can, could!

Instructor: Let's say that together three times.
Together (three times):
Am [clap]
Is [clap]
Are, was, were. [clap]
Be [clap]
Being [clap]
Been. [clap] [clap]
Have, has, had [clap]
Do, does, did [clap]
Shall, will, should, would, may, might, must [clap] [clap]
Can, could!

### Enrichment Activity

Work on memorizing the poem "I Love You Well."

# Lesson 167

-Prepositions
-Dictation exercise: "King of the Stuffed Animals"
-Poem review: "The Little Bird" (Lesson 139)

⇨ Note to Instructor: Prepare for today's lesson by setting a chair in the middle of the room. This will be a "throne." You may throw a blanket over it or put a special cushion on it if you wish.

⇨ Note to Instructor: Review "The Little Bird" today.

Instructor: Go and get me one of your favorite stuffed animals. He will help us learn our new **prepositions** today! Today, he has been appointed "King of the Stuffed Animals." Set him on his throne! The King is *on* the throne. What is the relationship between the King and the throne?

*Child: The King is on the throne.*

Instructor: "On" is a **preposition** that tells us more about the relationship between the King and his throne. Oh! I hear a fierce growl outside the door! The lion, who is king of the jungle, isn't sure he likes the Stuffed Animal King. I think your King had better get off his throne! Set him on the floor, where he can pretend that he isn't really the King. He is *off* the throne. Now, what is the relationship between the King and his throne?

*Child: The King is off his throne.*

Instructor: He is *off* his throne, but he is still *near* it. "Off" and "near" are both **prepositions** that tell us more about the relationship between the King and his throne. He is off it, but he is still near it. Oh, dear, I hear the lion again! Perhaps the King should hide under his throne. Now his throne is *over* him! "Over" is also a **preposition**. The King has had many different kinds of relationships with his throne! He has been *on* the throne, *off* the throne, and *near* the throne. Now the throne is *over* him!

⇨ Note to Instructor: You may pause at this point and allow the child to create other relationships between the King and his throne: under, behind, below, beneath, above.

Instructor: There is one more **preposition** that we need to know today. It is the preposition "of." Your stuffed animal is the King *of* the Stuffed Animals. "Of" describes the relationship between the King and the Stuffed Animals! "Of" is a very useful **preposition**. The King's throne is made *of* wood (or metal). "Of" tells about the relationship between the wood (or metal) and the chair. If the King had a crown, it

338

might be made of gold. "Of" tells about the relationship between the crown and the gold. Do you remember the definition of a **preposition**? **A preposition is a word that shows the relationship of a noun or pronoun to another word in the sentence.** We have talked about many different relationships today! Now say that definition together with me three times.

Together (three times): **A preposition is a word that shows the relationship of a noun or pronoun to another word in the sentence.**

Instructor: Let's repeat the **prepositions** that we used today three times: Near, of, off, on, over.

Together (three times): Near, of, off, on, over.

Instructor: Now listen to the entire list of **prepositions** that we have learned so far: Aboard, about, above, across. After, against, along, among, around, at. Before, behind, below, beneath. Beside, between, beyond, by. Down, during, except, for, from. In, inside, into, like. Near, of, off, on, over. I will say that whole list three times, and I want you to try to say it along with me.

Instructor (slowly, three times, with child joining in): Aboard, about, above, across. After, against, along, among, around, at. Before, behind, below, beneath. Beside, between, beyond, by. Down, during, except, for, from. In, inside, into, like. Near, of, off, on, over.

## Dictation Exercise

Choose one or more of the following sentences to dictate. Pause at the comma.

[Stuffed animal's name] is king of the stuffed animals.
He sits on his throne and rules over them.
But when the lion is near, [stuffed animal's name] jumps off his throne.

## Enrichment Activity

Make the King of the Stuffed Animals a crown of gold paper. Point out that "of" expresses the relationship between the crown and the gold paper.

# Lesson 168

-Prepositions

-Dictation exercise: "Through the Rain"

Instructor: Listen while I recite the entire list of **prepositions** that we have learned so far: Aboard, about, above, across. After, against, along, among, around, at. Before, behind, below, beneath. Beside, between, beyond, by. Down, during, except, for, from. In, inside, into, like. Near, of, off, on, over. I will say that whole list three times, and I want you to try to say it along with me.

Instructor (slowly, three times, with child joining in): Aboard, about, above, across. After, against, along, among, around, at. Before, behind, below, beneath. Beside, between, beyond, by. Down, during, except, for, from. In, inside, into, like. Near, of, off, on, over.

Instructor: Today, we are learning four very interesting, new **prepositions**. The first **preposition** is "past." Let's take a little walk around the house together, and talk about the things that we walk past.

⇨ Note to Instructor: You can also walk around the yard, if you prefer. Each time you pass something that can be named, say, "We just walked past the door." "We just walked past the sofa." "We just walked past your bed." Continue walking and talking until you are ready to return to the lesson area.

Instructor: The **preposition** "past" tells about the relationship between you and an object you leave behind you. Once you leave it, it is "past" you. The next **preposition** on today's list is "since." This word tells us about time. Repeat these sentences after me: "I have not eaten breakfast since this morning."

*Child: I have not eaten breakfast since this morning.*

Instructor: I have not taken a bath since yesterday.

*Child: I have not taken a bath since yesterday.*

Instructor: We have been talking about **prepositions** *since* Lesson 158!

*Child: We have been talking about prepositions since Lesson 158!*

⇨ Note to Instructor: "Since" also acts as an adverb and as a conjunction. Distinguishing between the uses of "since" is too complicated for a young child. Do not ask the child to make up sentences with "since"; most children will naturally use it as an adverb or conjunction, rather than a preposition. (See a dictionary for examples of each usage.)

Instructor: The next **preposition** is "through." Let's take another little walk through the kitchen. We will start on one side of the kitchen and go all the way through the kitchen to the other side. "Through" means "from one side to the other." We go *through* tunnels and doors. No one wants to stay *in* a tunnel or a door! You go from one side of it to the other—and out! The last preposition is "throughout." If I say, "It rained throughout the day," did the rain ever stop?

*Child: No.*

Instructor: "We searched for the library book throughout the house." Did we search the whole house?

*Child: Yes.*

Instructor: We searched the house from top to bottom! "Throughout" is another way of saying "the whole thing, from beginning to end." Now I will say our four new **prepositions** three times.

Instructor (three times): Past, since, through, throughout.

Instructor: Say those prepositions with me three times.

Together (three times): Past, since, through, throughout.

Instructor: I am going to write these **prepositions** for you to see.

⇨ Note to Instructor: Let the child watch as you print the four new prepositions (past, since, through, throughout).

Instructor: Now, I am going to read some sentences and play a trick on you. When I get to one of these prepositions, I am going to say the word *preposition* instead! I want you to decide which new preposition would fit in that place. Then you repeat the sentence back to me and say a real preposition.

⇨ Note to Instructor: You may need to repeat each sentence more than once.

Instructor: I always walk slowly when I walk *preposition* the toy store window.

*Child: I always walk slowly when I walk <u>past</u> the toy store window.*

Instructor: When Grandma burned the supper, the smoke spread *preposition* the house.

*Child: When Grandma burned the supper, the smoke spread <u>throughout</u> the house.*

⇨ Note to Instructor: If the child uses the preposition "through," ask, "Did the smoke fill the house, or did it just go in one door and out another?"

Instructor: I have grown an inch *preposition* last year.

*Child: I have grown an inch <u>since</u> last year.*

Instructor: The children playing cops and robbers ran screaming *preposition* the house.

*Child: The children playing cops and robbers ran screaming <u>through</u> the house.*

Instructor: Let's say "Past, since, through, throughout" together three more times.

Together (three times): Past, since, through, throughout.

**Dictation Exercise** (Adapted from classic poets)

Choose one of the following sentences.

I see the lights gleam through the rain and mist.
*From "The Day is Done" by Phoebe Cary*

Sound the trumpet, beat the drum, throughout all the world around.
*From "The Masque" by John Dryden*

Wild winter wind, storm throughout the night, and dash the black clouds against the sky.
*From "Safe" by Augusta Webster*

# Lesson 169

## -Cumulative poem review

⇨  Note to Instructor: Review all poems memorized up to this point.

| Lesson | Poem | Author |
|---|---|---|
| 2 | "The Caterpillar" | Christina G. Rossetti |
| 15 | "Work" | Anonymous |
| 27 | "Hearts Are Like Doors" | Anonymous |
| 35 | "Days of the Week" | Mother Goose rhyme adapted by Sara Buffington |
| 43 | "The Months" | Mother Goose rhyme |
| 81 | "Mr. Nobody" | Anonymous |
| 100 | "The Goops" | Gelett Burgess |
| 131 | "The Year" | Sara Coleridge, adapted by Sara Buffington |
| 139 | "The Little Bird" | Mother Goose rhyme |

⇨  Note to Instructor: You may also read back through the poems which were not memorized.

| | |
|---|---|
| "Dancing" | Lesson 58 |
| "Monday, Mommy Baked a Cake" | Lesson 59 |
| "The Star" | Lesson 86 |
| "Sunflowers" | Lesson 91 |
| "The Wind" | Lesson 115 |
| "Let Dogs Delight to Bark and Bite" | Lesson 126 |
| "How Creatures Move" | Lesson 129 |
| "Bed in Summer" (one stanza) | Lesson 161 |
| "The Daffodils" (one stanza) | Lesson 163 |
| "I Love You Well" | Lesson 166 |

# Lesson 170

-Letter writing
    -Writing a friendly letter
-Prepositions


Instructor: Today, we are going to work on a letter to a friend. But first, we need to review our **preposition** list! I will say it for you once, and then we will try to say it together three more times. Aboard, about, above, across. After, against, along, among, around, at. Before, behind, below, beneath. Beside, between, beyond, by. Down, during, except, for, from. In, inside, into, like. Near, of, off, on, over. Past, since, through, throughout.

Instructor (slowly, three times, with child joining in): Aboard, about, above, across. After, against, along, among, around, at. Before, behind, below, beneath. Beside, between, beyond, by. Down, during, except, for, from. In, inside, into, like. Near, of, off, on, over. Past, since, through, throughout.

Instructor: After we write our letter, we will send it *to* a friend. Can you guess what kind of word *to* might be?

⇨   Note to Instructor: If necessary, prompt child by saying: What is the relationship between your letter and the friend?

Instructor: "To" is a **preposition**. It tells us more about the relation-ship between the letter and your friend. Your friend will receive the letter. "To" and "toward" have the same meaning. You will send the letter *to* your friend, and it will move *toward* him through the mail. Answer me in a complete sentence. To whom will you send your letter?

⇨   Note to Instructor: The child will write a friendly letter in this lesson. Help him decide on a recipient. Then ask the child to put this name into a complete sentence.

*Child: I will send my letter to [name of friend].*

Instructor: The other **prepositions** we will add to our list are the **prepositions** *under* and *underneath*. Both words mean the same thing. Do you remember when the King of the Stuffed Animals hid under his throne? We could also say, "He hid underneath his throne," and it would mean the same thing. Listen to me say those four **prepo-sitions** three times, and then we will say them three times together.

Instructor (three times): To, toward, under, underneath.

Together (three times): To, toward, under, underneath.

Instructor: Now let's work on our letter to [name of friend]. You will tell me what you want to say to your friend, and I will write the letter out for you. Then you will copy part of the letter onto your own paper. You will finish copying the letter tomorrow.

➱ Note to Instructor. Make suggestions about content: tell about a school project, a model the child has recently made, a science observation, an interesting person or fact from history, or a recent family activity. Write the letter out for the child, following the form below. Aim for four or five sentences in the body of the letter. Indent the first line of the paragraph and simply explain to the child that the first line of the letter should begin about the width of two fingers from the margin.

**Date** (Today's date, written on the right-hand side of the paper)

**Greeting** (Dear ____,)
(Remember that a comma comes after the greeting. Remind the child that a title of respect which is abbreviated begins with a capital letter and has a period following it).

**Body of the Letter** (This week, we went to see a play…)

**Closing** (You may use "Love," "Sincerely," or "Yours truly." Remember that a comma comes after the closing. The closing should be in line with the date above.)

**Writer's Name** (Child signs his own name.)

**Copywork**
Ask the child to copy the first half of his letter.

# Lesson 171

-Addressing an envelope

* The child will need a business size envelope and a first class stamp.

Instructor: Before we continue copying our letter, let's review our **preposition** list. I will say it for you once, and then we will try to say it together three more times. Aboard, about, above, across. After, against, along, among, around, at. Before, behind, below, beneath. Beside, between, beyond, by. Down, during, except, for, from. In, inside, into, like. Near, of, off, on, over. Past, since, through, throughout. To, toward, under, underneath.

Instructor (slowly, three times, with child joining in): Aboard, about, above, across. After, against, along, among, around, at. Before, behind, below, beneath. Beside, between, beyond, by. Down, during, except, for, from. In, inside, into, like. Near, of, off, on, over. Past, since, through, throughout. To, toward, under, underneath.

Instructor: Repeat after me: **A preposition is a word that shows the relationship of a noun or pronoun to another word in the sentence.**

*Child:* **A preposition is a word that shows the relationship of a noun or pronoun to another word in the sentence.**

Instructor: Today, I want you to finish copying out your letter, as neatly as you can.

⇨ Note to Instructor: Give the child time to complete his copying of the letter.

Instructor: Now, I will write your name and address on a piece of paper. You will copy this name and address into the left-hand corner of an envelope. I will also write the name and address of your friend. You will copy this name and address in the center of the envelope.

⇨ Note to Instructor: Draw light lines on the envelope, as illustrated on the next page, to help guide the child's writing. As he writes, point out the abbreviations. Remind him that a zip code helps the post office send the envelope to the right place. Remind him to use a period after titles of respect and other appropriate abbreviations.

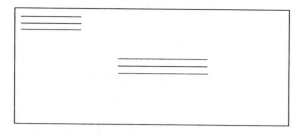

When the child is finished copying the letter and the envelope, help him fold the letter neatly, put it in the envelope, and mail it. Remember that letters this size should be folded into thirds. First, fold up the bottom third, and then fold down the top third.

## Enrichment Activity

The child who enjoys letter-writing may write another letter to a different person.

# Lesson 172

-Prepositions

Instructor: Today, we are going to learn the very last of the **prepositions**! First, let's review the **prepositions** we have already learned. I will say them for you once, and then we will try to say them together three more times. Aboard, about, above, across. After, against, along, among, around, at. Before, behind, below, beneath. Beside, between, beyond, by. Down, during, except, for, from. In, inside, into, like. Near, of, off, on, over. Past, since, through, throughout. To, toward, under, underneath.

Instructor (slowly, three times, with child joining in): Aboard, about, above, across. After, against, along, among, around, at. Before, behind, below, beneath. Beside, between, beyond, by. Down, during, except, for, from. In, inside, into, like. Near, of, off, on, over. Past, since, through, throughout. To, toward, under, underneath.

Instructor: We are going to add the last **prepositions** to this list. I will say these last six **prepositions** for you three times, and then we will say them three more times together.

Instructor (three times): Until, up, upon. With, within, without.
Together (three times): Until, up, upon. With, within, without.

Instructor: "Until" means "Up to the time of." If we read until lights out time, we read up to the time of lights out. If we swim until five o'clock, we swim up to the time of five o'clock. Put the **preposition** "until" together with the phrases, "We will do our school" and "lunch."

*Child: We will do our school until lunch.*

Instructor: "Up" is an easy **preposition**. If I tell you to "Climb up the stairs," will you know what to do? What if I tell you that the eensy-weensy spider went up the waterspout? Do you know what the spider is doing? "Upon" is another easy **preposition**. It has the same meaning as "on." "Put the plate upon the table" means the same thing as "Put the plate on the table." I will give you two sentences with "on" in them. Replace the **preposition** "on" with the **preposition** "upon." "Put your shoes on your feet.

*Child: Put your shoes upon your feet.*

Instructor: Put your hands on your head?

*Child: Put your hands upon your head.*

Instructor: Now you have learned the **prepositions** "until, up, upon." The **preposition** "with" means "together." Do you like ice cream with hot fudge sauce?

*Child: Yes!*

Instructor: Finish the following sentences for me: "I like to play with..."

*Child: I like to play with [toys, my friends, my brother].*

Instructor: I prefer to eat my hot dogs with...

*Child: I prefer to eat my hot dogs with [mustard].*

Instructor: "Within" is the next **preposition**. It means "inside." If I tell you that you will find great wisdom within your grammar book, it means that wisdom is inside your grammar book! If I say, "We will be finished with this lesson within the hour," it means that we are only doing grammar during this hour. It will not go over into the next hour! Put these two phrases together for me, using the **preposition** "within": "It is thundering, so stay" and "the house."

*Child: It is thundering, so stay within the house.*

Instructor: And now we have reached our very last **preposition**! "Without" means that you do not have something. If I tell you, "Sleep in your room without a light," do you have a light?

*Child: No, I do not have a light.*

Instructor: If you ask to buy an expensive toy, and I say, "No, you will have to do without the toy!" are you going to get the toy?

*Child: No, I will not get the toy.*

Instructor: If I say, "You have done all of your work without complaint!" have you complained today?

*Child: No, I have not complained.*

Instructor: Now, I will say those last six **prepositions** again: Until, up, upon. With, within, without. Say them with me three more times. Together (three times): Until, up, upon. With, within, without.

Instructor: Now it is time to do the whole list! I will say them for you once, and then we will try to say them together three more times. Aboard, about, above, across. After, against, along, among, around, at. Before, behind, below, beneath. Beside, between, beyond, by. Down, during, except, for, from. In, inside, into, like. Near, of, off, on, over. Past, since, through, throughout. To, toward, under, underneath. Until, up. upon. With, within, without.

Instructor (slowly, three times, with child joining in): Aboard, about, above, across. After, against, along, among, around, at. Before, behind, below, beneath. Beside, between, beyond, by. Down, during, except, for, from. In, inside, into, like. Near, of, off, on, over. Past, since, through, throughout. To, toward, under, underneath. Until, up, upon. With, within, without.

Instructor: I will read the following poem to you. Follow along with me as I read.

Foreign Lands
*Robert Louis Stevenson*

Up into the cherry tree
Who should climb but little me?
I held the trunk with both my hands
And looked abroad on foreign lands.

I saw the next door garden lie,
Adorned with flowers, before my eye,
And many pleasant places more
That I had never seen before.

I saw the dimpling river pass
And be the sky's blue looking-glass;
The dusty roads go up and down
With people tramping into town.

If I could find a higher tree
Farther and farther I should see,
To where the grown-up river slips
Into the sea among the ships,

To where the roads on either hand
Lead onward into fairy land,
Where all the children dine at five,
And all the playthings come alive.

Instructor: I will point out some **prepositions** in the poem "Foreign Lands." Each **preposition** shows a relationship between two words. I am going to ask you to tell me which two words are related. In the third line, "I held the trunk with both my hands," the **preposition** "with" shows a relationship between what two words?

⇨ Note to Instructor: If the child cannot answer, read the line again, emphasizing the words in bold print: "I held the **trunk** with both my **hands**."

*Child: "Trunk" and "hands." ["both" is also acceptable]*

Instructor: In the third stanza, the child in the tree sees "people tramping into town." The **preposition** "into" shows a relationship between what two words?

⇨ Note to Instructor: If necessary, read the line again: "**People** tramping into **town**."

*Child: "People" and "town."*

Instructor: In the fourth stanza, the child sees that the "river slips into the sea." The preposition "into" shows a relationship between what two words?

⇨ Note to Instructor: If necessary, read the line again: "**River** slips into the **sea**."

*Child: "River" and "sea."*

## Enrichment Activity
The child may memorize the poem.

# Lesson 173
-Story narration: "The Three Bears" retold by Sara Buffington

⇨ Note to Instructor: Read aloud the story below. Have the child tell the story back to you; use the suggested questions at the story's end to prompt the child, if necessary. When the child has completed his oral narration, repeat the first two or three sentences of his narration back to him as a dictation exercise. Then, complete the narration yourself by writing the child's remaining sentences.

## The Three Bears

Once upon a time there were three bears who lived together in a charming cottage in the woods. They were Great Big Papa Bear, Medium-sized Mama Bear, and Itty-bitty Baby Bear. They had just fixed their breakfast of porridge, but it was too hot to eat. So they decided to take a walk in the woods. They hoped that the porridge would be cool enough to eat when they got home. So they opened the charming blue door of their charming wood cottage, walked down their charming walkway lined with charming red roses, and left.

While the bears were off on their woodland walk, a little girl named Goldilocks happened by the cottage. She was a pretty girl, named for her long, golden locks of hair, but she was also very naughty. So when she saw the charming cottage of the bear family, she said to herself, "Oh! That is the most charming wood cottage with the most charming red roses and the most charming blue door. I must go inside and look around." It never occurred to her to ask for permission or to knock on the door. As I already explained, she was a naughty, rude, little girl.

Inside she found three bowls of porridge: one big, one medium-sized, and one very small. She tasted the porridge in the big, blue bowl.

"Ow!" she cried out. "That porridge is too hot!"

Then she tasted the porridge in the medium-sized, red bowl.

"Yuck!" she whined. "That porridge is too cold!"

Then she tasted the very small, yellow bowl of porridge.

"Mmm!" she exclaimed. "This porridge is neither too hot nor too cold. This is just right." And she gobbled up the whole bowl.

Now, she was very full from eating the porridge, so she decided to take a rest. Near the fireplace, she saw three rocking chairs: one big, one medium-sized, and one very small. First she sat in the big rocking chair. It had a big, blue cushion on it.

"Oh!" she complained. "That cushion is too hard!" So she jumped off the rocking chair and threw the big, blue cushion on the floor. Then she sat in the medium-sized rocking chair. It had a medium-sized, red cushion on it.

"Hmph!" she grumbled. "That cushion is too soft!" So she jumped off the rocking chair and threw the medium-sized, red cushion on the floor.

Then she sat in the very small rocking chair. It had a very small, yellow cushion on it. "Ah!" she sighed. "This cushion is neither too hard nor too soft. This cushion is just right." So she rocked and she rocked and she rocked until she broke the very small rocking chair!

She was very tired from all that rocking, so she climbed up the stairs to the bedroom. There she found three beds: one big, one medium-sized, and one very small. First she lay down in the big bed with the blue blanket.

"Ooh!" she groaned. "That blanket is too thick!" So she tossed the blanket aside and hopped out of bed. Then she lay down in the medium-sized bed with the red blanket on it.

"Brrr," she shivered. "That blanket is too thin!" So she tossed that blanket aside and hopped out of bed.

Then she lay down in the very small bed with the yellow blanket on it. "Mmm," she murmured. "This blanket is neither too thick nor too thin. This blanket is just right." And she fell fast asleep.

Just then the bear family came back from their walk. Great Big Papa Bear lumbered over to his porridge bowl. He bellowed in his big, gruff, booming voice:

## "Somebody has been eating my porridge!"

Medium-sized Mama Bear padded over to her porridge bowl. She exclaimed in her medium-sized, surprised voice:

"Somebody has been eating my porridge!"

Then Itty-bitty Baby Bear scampered over to his porridge bowl. He cried in his high, shrill, squeaky voice:

"Somebody has been eating my porridge, and has eaten every last drop!"

Then the Bear family went over to the rocking chairs. They needed to sit down to recover from the shock of their porridge having been eaten. Great Big Papa Bear saw his big, blue cushion lying on the

353

floor.  He boomed in his great, big voice:

## "Somebody has been sitting in my chair!"

Then Medium-sized Mama bear noticed her medium-sized, red cushion lying on the floor.  She cried out in her medium-sized voice:

"Somebody has been sitting in my chair!"

Then Itty-bitty Baby Bear saw his broken rocking chair.  He squealed in his very small, but very high-pitched, voice:

"Someone has been sitting in my chair, and has broken the leg off!"

The Bears were so upset that they decided they had better go lie down for a rest.  Itty-bitty Baby Bear was the most upset, and he cried all the way up the stairs.  When they got to the bedroom, Great Big Papa Bear saw his blue blanket crumpled at the end of his big bed.  He thundered:

## "Somebody has been sleeping in my bed!"

Then Medium-sized Mama Bear saw her red blanket hanging off the end of her medium-sized bed.  She exclaimed in her medium-sized voice:

"Somebody has been sleeping in my bed!"

Then Itty-bitty Baby Bear saw that his bed linens were rumpled, too.  And there, on the pillow, sleeping deeply, lay Goldilocks.  Itty-bitty Baby Bear (who was already quite upset, as you can imagine) cried out in his high, squeaky, piercing voice:

"Somebody has been sleeping in my bed, and she is still in it!"

Upon hearing Itty-bitty Baby Bear's shrill voice, Goldilocks bolted wide awake.  There she saw a most terrifying sight: a whole bear family leaning over her bed and looking very annoyed!  She let out a little scream, dashed out of bed, flew down the stairs and out of the charming wood cottage with the charming blue door.  The bears never saw her again.

The bears, exhausted by the whole experience, lay down for a long nap.  What else was there to do about the matter?  And just as they had thought, when they awoke they felt a lot better.  As for Goldilocks, I don't know what happened to her afterwards.  But I feel sure that the next time she saw a charming cottage, she went right past it, walking on her merry way.

⇨ Note to Instructor: Ask the child to tell you the story back in his own words. If the child has trouble remembering, use these questions:

Who lived in the cottage? *The three bears lived in the cottage.*

Where did they go? *They went for a walk in the woods.*

What happened while they were gone? *Goldilocks went into their cottage.*

What did Goldilocks do first? *She ate the porridge.*

After she ate the porridge, what did she do? *She rocked in the rocking chairs.*

What happened to Itty-bitty Baby Bear's chair? *She broke it.*

After she rocked in the chairs, what did she do? *She lay down in the beds.*

When the bears came home, how did they react to seeing their porridge eaten and their chair cushions on the floor? *They were very upset.*

Which bear was the most upset? *Baby Bear was the most upset.*

Where did the bears find Goldilocks? *She was sleeping in Baby Bear's bed.*

What did Goldilocks do when she saw the Bears? *She ran out of the house.*

What did the bears do after Goldilocks left? *They took a nap.*

# Lesson 174

-Introducing synonyms
-Dictation exercise: "Roller Coasters"
* The child will need either a dictionary or thesaurus for the enrichment activity.

⇨ Note to Instructor: Chant the preposition list twice today (this should take about ninety seconds): Aboard, about, above, across. After, against, along, among, around, at. Before, behind, below, beneath. Beside, between, beyond, by. Down, during, except, for, from. In, inside, into, like. Near, of, off, on, over. Past, since, through, throughout. To, toward, under, underneath. Until, up, upon. With, within, without.

Instructor: Today we are going to learn about a fun kind of word: **synonyms**! **Synonyms** are words that mean the same thing. I'm going to read you part of the story of The Three Bears again. Listen to the words that I emphasize.

⇨ Note to Instructor: Emphasize the words in bold print.

Goldilocks tasted the porridge in the big, blue bowl.
"Ow!" she cried out. "That porridge is too hot!"
Then she tasted the porridge in the medium-sized, red bowl.
"Yuck!" she **whined**. "That is too cold!"
She sat in the big rocking chair. It had a big, blue cushion on it.
"Oh!" she **complained**. "That cushion is too hard!" So she jumped off the rocking chair and threw the big, blue cushion on the floor. Then she sat in the medium-sized rocking chair. It had a medium-sized, red cushion on it.
"Hmph!" she **grumbled**. "That cushion is too soft!" So she jumped off the rocking chair and threw the medium-sized, red cushion on the floor.

Instructor: When Goldilocks didn't like the porridge and the chairs at the house of The Three Bears, she *complained, whined,* and *grumbled.* Those three words all have the same meaning. They are **synonyms**. **Synonyms are words that have the same meaning.** Listen to me repeat that definition, and then we will say it together three times: **Synonyms are words that have the same meaning.**
Together (three times): **Synonyms are words that have the same meaning.**
Instructor: You can remember that **synonyms** have the same meaning

356

by thinking to yourself: "SSSSynonyms have the sssssame meaning."
We will read several lists of **synonyms** together. For each list, I will
give you a sentence. I want you to say the sentence back to me three
times, each time choosing a different **synonym**. I will do the first one
for you. Here is the list of **synonyms**.

happy
glad
joyful
pleased
delighted

Instructor: Here is the sentence.

The father was *happy* to see his son.

You would say back to me: "The father was *glad* to see his son. The
father was *pleased* to see his son. The father was *delighted* to see his
son." Now let's read the second list of **synonyms** together.

cold
chilly
freezing
icy
frosty
wintry

Instructor: Here is the sentence.

In January, the nights are *cold*.

⇨   Note to Instructor: Allow the child to look at the list of synonyms while
repeating this sentence three times, substituting a different synonym for
"cold" each time. Follow the same procedure for the following lists and
sentences.

The traveller gazed in amazement at the <u>big</u> mountain.
big, large, grand, majestic, huge, immense, colossal, gigantic

I am so late that I must <u>run</u> home.
run, sprint, jog, dash, speed, dart, zip, hasten

I should not <u>talk</u> when my mother is talking to me!
talk, chatter, speak, converse, prattle

Roller coasters are so exciting that they make me <u>shout</u>!
shout, yell, shriek, scream, screech, squeal, holler, whoop

**Dictation Exercise**
Choose one of the sentences above. Read it to the child twice, each time using a different synonym. Let the child choose the synonyms he would like to hear. Then you dictate one of the sentences for him to write from memory. For good writers, you may repeat this process with another sentence.

**Enrichment Activity**
Ask the child to rewrite the following paragraph, substituting a synonym for each italicized word. You may wish to help him use a thesaurus or dictionary, such as *Roget's Children's Thesaurus* (Scott Foresman–Addison Wesley, 1994) or *Merriam-Webster's Elementary Dictionary* (2000).

One morning, a *good little* girl decided to go for a *walk*. She found a *house* in the *woods*. When she *went in,* she saw *food* on the table. It looked *good!* She *ate* some and then felt *sleepy*. She *lay down* and *slept* until three bears *disturbed* her! She *woke up* and *ran away* into the *woods*.

# Lesson 175

-Introducing antonyms
-Dictation exercise: "Brush Your Teeth"
* The child will need art supplies for the enrichment activity.

⇨ Note to Instructor: Chant the preposition list twice today (this should take about ninety seconds): Aboard, about, above, across. After, against, along, among, around, at. Before, behind, below, beneath. Beside, between, beyond, by. Down, during, except, for, from. In, inside, into, like. Near, of, off, on, over. Past, since, through, throughout. To, toward, under, underneath. Until, up, upon. With, within, without.

Instructor: In the last lesson, we learned the definition of a **synonym.** Listen to me repeat that definition, and then we will say it together three times. **Synonyms are words that have the same meaning.**

Together (three times): **Synonyms are words that have the same meaning.**

Instructor: Remember, "SSSSynonyms have the sssssame meaning." **Antonyms are opposites.** Let's say that together three times: **Antonyms are opposites.**

Together (three times): **Antonyms are opposites.**

Instructor: Now I want you to do the opposite of everything I say. Stand up! What are you doing?

⇨ Note to Instructor: If necessary, prompt the child to do the action indicated in the child's dialogue below.

*Child: I am sitting down.*

Instructor: Smile! What are you doing?

*Child: I am frowning.*

Instructor: Laugh! What are you doing?

*Child: I am crying.*

Instructor: Wake up! What are you doing?

*Child: I am sleeping.*

Instructor: Now we will play a game called "Contradictions." You have been *contradicting.* "Contradiction" is when you say the opposite of what someone says to you. I will say a sentence, and I want you to say the sentence back to me—with an opposite meaning. For example, if I say to you, "I am so happy!" I want you to say, "I am so sad!" Here is the first sentence: "That cat is so fat!"

⇨ Note to Instructor: If necessary, prompt the child to substitute the antonym given. However, the suggested dialogue for the child is only one option—if the child chooses another word of opposite meaning, accept it.

*Child: That cat is so thin!*

Instructor: The glass is certainly full.

*Child: The glass is certainly empty.*

Instructor: It is cold in here!

*Child: It is hot in here.*

Instructor: I like my food raw.

*Child: I like my food cooked* or *I hate my food raw.*

Instructor: Time to work!

*Child: Time to play!*

Instructor: This chair is too hard!

*Child: This chair is too soft!*

Instructor: Go out!

*Child: Come in!*

Instructor: You just used two **antonyms**. "Come" is the opposite of "go." "In" is the opposite of "out." That was very good!

⇨ Note to Instructor: Wait to see if the child offers: *That was very bad.* If not, repeat, "That was very good!" several times with emphasis, until he contradicts you.

## Dictation Exercise

Choose one or more of the following sentences. Remember to pause at commas.

Brush your teeth up and down.

I have a little shadow that goes in and out with me.

When she was good, she was very, very, good, but when she was bad, she was horrid.

## Enrichment Activity

Ask the child to draw pictures illustrating the following pairs of antonyms:

fat/thin
happy/sad
wide/narrow
tall/short
in/out
up/down

# Lesson 176
-Picture narration: "Playing Together"

Let's look at the picture of the children playing together. How many people are in the picture? There are two people in the picture. There is a baby and a boy. The boy and the baby are brother and sister. The brother's name is Timothy. The sister's name is Beth. They both have the same mother and father. Timothy is a boy, a son, and a brother. Beth is a girl, a daughter, and a sister. "Brother" and "sister" are opposites. They are **antonyms**. "Boy" and "girl" are opposites. They are **antonyms** too.

Timothy and Beth are opposites in other ways. Right now, they do not look very much alike! Timothy is tall. What is the opposite of "tall"? "Short" is the opposite of "tall." These two words are antonyms. Timothy is tall and Beth is short. Beth is also younger that Timothy. What word is the opposite of "young"? "Old" is the opposite of "young." They are **antonyms**. Timothy is older and Beth is younger.

Look at Timothy's face. He looks happy and cheerful. "Happy" and "cheerful" mean the same thing. Those two words are **synonyms**. Timothy is having fun playing with his sister Beth. He is a very good older brother because he is kind and patient with her. Do you see how he is pointing to the block? He is trying to teach her to say "block." His mother and father are very proud of Timothy for being so helpful with his younger sister.

What does Beth have in her hair? She has two bows in her hair. They are small and little. "Little" and "small" have the same meaning. They are **synonyms**. Beth is enjoying her playtime with Timothy. She wants to continue playing with the blocks. Timothy is pointing to a block. What shape is it? It is square. What do you think they might play with after they finish playing with the blocks? They might play with the ball on the floor. What shape is the ball? It is round. "Round" and "square" are **antonyms**.

Timothy knows that being a big brother is an important job. Beth likes to copy everything he does! So he tries to be sweet and kind —because Beth is learning from him all the time.

# Lesson 177

-Four types of sentences
-Poem review: "The Year" (Lesson 131)

⇨　Note to Instructor: Review "The Year" today.

⇨　Note to Instructor: Write the title "Types of Sentences" on the top of a sheet of lined paper.

Instructor: Do you remember what a **sentence** is? I will help you begin: A sentence is a group...

*Child:* **A sentence is a group of words that expresses a complete thought.**

⇨　Note to Instructor: If the child cannot complete the definition, tell him the definition and ask him to repeat it with you three times.

Instructor: There are four types of **sentences**. The first type of **sentence** is a **statement**. **Statements give information.** Take a minute now and write that down on your paper: **Statements give information.**

⇨　Note to Instructor: Help the child spell the words correctly. Remind him that sentences begin with a capital letter and end with a punctuation mark.

Instructor: **Statements give information.** They tell you something. **Statements** end with periods. Let's imagine that you have a very hungry, friendly baby puppy outside! The puppy whined and barked because it was so hungry, so you went out and took care of it. What did you do for the puppy?

*Child: I fed the puppy.*

Instructor: "I fed the puppy" is a **statement**. It gives information. The second type of **sentence** is a **command**. **Commands give an order or make a request.** They usually end with a period. Take a minute to write that definition down on your paper: **Commands give an order or make a request.**

⇨　Note to Instructor: Although it is ideal to have the child write down each definition, you may assist him if he is not ready to write out all four sentence definitions. Note that there is no dictation exercise following this lesson.

Instructor: If you and I heard a hungry, friendly, imaginary baby puppy howling and barking at our door, what **command** might I give you so that you would take care of it?

*Child: Feed the puppy.*

Instructor: The third type of **sentence** is a **question**. **A sentence that asks something is called a question. Questions** end with question marks. Write that definition down on your paper: **A**

**sentence that asks something is called a question.**

⇨ Note to Instructor: Help the child with spelling, especially if he has not yet learned that "u" always follows "q." Ask him to practice making question marks on the line beneath the definition.

Instructor: What question might your mother ask you when you came in from feeding the puppy?

*Child: Have you fed the puppy? (or Did you feed the puppy?)*

Instructor: The fourth type of **sentence** is the **exclamation. An exclamation shows sudden or strong feeling.** It ends with an exclamation point. Write the definition of an **exclamation** down on your paper, and put an exclamation point after it: **An exclamation shows sudden or strong feeling.**

⇨ Note to Instructor: Ask the child to practice making neat exclamation points on the line beneath the definition.

Instructor: What if you went out to feed the hungry, little puppy and discovered that it was a huge, hungry wolf? You might shout something to tell me that there was a wolf outside. What would you shout?

*Child: Help! There's a wolf outside!*

Instructor: That would certainly show strong feeling!

# Lesson 178

-Verbs

-Dictation exercise: "The Platypus"

\* The instructor will need twenty-five index cards for the enrichment activity.


⇨   Note to Instructor: Chant the preposition list twice today (this should take about ninety seconds): Aboard, about, above, across. After, against, along, among, around, at. Before, behind, below, beneath. Beside, between, beyond, by. Down, during, except, for, from. In, inside, into, like. Near, of, off, on, over. Past, since, through, throughout. To, toward, under, underneath. Until, up, upon. With, within, without.

Instructor: Let me repeat the definition of a **verb** for you. **A verb is a word that does an action, shows a state of being, links two words together, or helps another verb.** Can you say that definition back to me?

⇨   Note to Instructor: If the child cannot repeat the definition back to you, say it with him three times.

Instructor: I will give you some names of animals. Put an **action verb** with each one to tell me what sound each animal makes. Cows.

*Child: Cows moo.*

Instructor: Dogs…

*Child: Dogs bark.*

Instructor: Bears…

*Child: Bears growl.*

Instructor: Kittens…

*Child: Kittens meow.*

Instructor: A platypus…I bet you don't know what a platypus says. What is a platypus? A platypus is a small, furry mammal that lays eggs. It lives in the waters of Australia, and it has a bill like a duck. Why am I telling you this? I want you to listen to the sentence, "A platypus is a small, furry mammal." Does that sentence have an **action verb** in it?

⇨   Note to Instructor: You may say each word of the sentence to the child and ask, "Can you do this? Can you *a?* Can you *platypus?* Can you *is?*" and so on.

Instructor: What is the sentence about?

*Child: A platypus.*

Instructor: What does the sentence tell you about the platypus?

*Child: The platypus is a small, furry mammal.*

Instructor: The **verb** "is" links the word "platypus" to words that tell us more about the platypus. Remember, the **linking verbs** we have learned are the same as **state of being verbs**, but they are followed by information. It wouldn't be very interesting to say, "The platypus is." You want to know more about it! Remember, **state of being verbs** become **linking verbs** if they link a word to other words which give more information about it. Repeat those **verbs** after me: Am, is, are, was, were. Be, being, been.

⇨ Note to Instructor: If the child cannot say the list, repeat it with him five times.

Instructor: There are four kinds of **verbs**: **action verbs**, **state of being verbs**, **linking verbs**, and **helping verbs**. Let's say the list of **helping verbs** together, beginning with "Am, is, are, was, were." Together: Am, is, are, was, were. Be, being, been. Have, has, had. Do, does, did. Shall, will, should, would, may, might, must. Can, could!

⇨ Note to Instructor: If the child cannot repeat the list with you, say it with him twice more.

Instructor: I know what a platypus says. A platypus can growl like a puppy and can cluck like a hen! Listen to me say that sentence one more time:

⇨ Note to Instructor: Emphasize the words in bold print.

Instructor: A platypus **can** growl like a puppy and **can** cluck like a hen. What kind of **verb** is **can**?

*Child: Can is a helping verb.*

Instructor: "Can" is helping the verb "growl." What kind of **verb** is growl? Is growling something you can do? Yes, you can growl. Growl is an **action verb**. What kind of **verb** is cluck?

*Child: Cluck is an action verb.*

Instructor: Now you have reviewed all four kinds of **verbs** *and* you have learned all sorts of interesting information! Did you know that a platypus is half the size of a cat and likes to eat frogs?

## Dictation Exercise

Choose one or more of the following sentences. If you choose the third sentence, remember to pause at each comma.

The platypus is a furry mammal that lays eggs.
The platypus can growl like a puppy and can cluck like a hen.
The platypus eats frogs, tadpoles, and small fish. It lives in a burrow underground.

## Enrichment Activity

You will need 25 index cards. On the first five, write the linking verbs (one on each card): Am, is, are, was, were. On eight more cards, write the following eight words and phrases (one on each card):

The platypus
Forests
Red Riding Hood
Baby mice
Bulldozers
A pretzel
A clown
Beetles

On the last twelve cards, write the following words and phrases (one on each card):

furry
crunchy
squirmy
shady
creepy
adorable
powerful
stupid
silly
dangerous
orange
green

Help the child to combine the "subject cards" (nouns) with the "descriptive cards" (adjectives) using the linking verb cards to connect them. As you form each sentence, point out the linking verb to the child, and remind the child that the linking verb is connecting the two parts of the sentence together. Allow humorous combinations.

# Lesson 179

-Adverbs
-Adjectives
-Dictation exercise: "The Friendly Cow"

⇨ Note to Instructor: Chant the preposition list twice today (this should take about ninety seconds): Aboard, about, above, across. After, against, along, among, around, at. Before, behind, below, beneath. Beside, between, beyond, by. Down, during, except, for, from. In, inside, into, like. Near, of, off, on, over. Past, since, through, throughout. To, toward, under, underneath. Until, up, upon. With, within, without.

Instructor: Do you remember the definition of an **adjective**? I will start you on it: An adjective is a word...

Child: **An adjective is a word that describes a noun or pronoun.**

⇨ Note to Instructor: If the child cannot repeat this definition, say it with him three times.

Instructor: Do you remember the definition of an **adverb**? I will start you on it: An adverb is a word...

Child: **An adverb is a word that describes a verb, an adjective, or another adverb.**

⇨ Note to Instructor: If the child cannot repeat this definition, say it with him three times.

Instructor: The names of animals are **nouns**, and **adjectives** describe **nouns**. I will give you the name of an animal, and I want you to think of some **adjectives** that describe it. Cow.

⇨ Note to Instructor: You may suggest black, white, red, friendly, large, small, tame, or wild.

Instructor: In the last lesson, you told me that a cow moos. Now put your **adjective** together with the **noun** and **verb** to make a sentence.

Child: *The [adjective] cow moos.*

Instructor: Tell me an **adverb** that describes how the cow moos.

⇨ Note to Instructor: You may suggest loudly, softly, hungrily, forlornly, melodiously, lovingly, or lazily.

Instructor: Now put that all together into one sentence.

Child: *The [adjective] cow moos [adverb].*

Instructor: The dog barks. Give me an **adjective** that describes the dog.

⇨ Note to Instructor: You may suggest furry, bouncy, sleek, hungry, strong, scruffy, flea-bitten, dirty, loving, or faithful.

Instructor: Now put the **adjective** into your sentence.

*Child: The [adjective] dog barks.*

Instructor: Tell me an **adverb** that describes how the dog barks.

⇨ Note to Instructor: You may suggest loudly, suddenly, angrily, incessantly, ferociously, warningly, or bravely.

Instructor: Now put that all together into one sentence.

*Child: The [adjective] dog barks [adverb].*

Instructor: A kitten meows. Give me an **adjective** that describes the kitten.

⇨ Note to Instructor: You may suggest tiny, fluffy, clean, soft, cuddly, sweet, grey, black, helpless, or playful.

Instructor: Put the **adjective** into your sentence.

*Child: The [adjective] kitten meows.*

Instructor: Tell me an **adverb** that describes how the kitten meows.

⇨ Note to Instructor: You may suggest softly, weakly, innocently, frequently, timidly, or persistently.

Instructor: Now put that all together into one sentence.

*Child: The [adjective] kitten meows [adverb].*

Instructor: Can you find the **adjective** in the following sentence? "The gentle wind blows through the trees."

⇨ Note to Instructor: You may prompt the child by asking, "What kind of wind?"

*Child: Gentle.*

Instructor: "Gentle" describes the **noun** "wind." "Wind" is a thing. Can you find the **adjective** in this sentence? Beautiful flowers bloom in the garden.

⇨ Note to Instructor: You may prompt the child by asking, "What kind of flowers?"

*Child: Beautiful.*

Instructor: "Beautiful" describes the **noun** "flowers." "Flowers" are things. Can you find the **adverb** in this sentence? The stars are twinkling brightly in the sky.

⇨ Note to Instructor: You may prompt the child by asking, "The stars are twinkling how?"

*Child: Brightly.*

Instructor: "Brightly" describes the **action verb** "twinkling." Now I will give you a sentence with both an **adjective** and an **adverb** in it. The **adjective** will describe a **noun**—a person, place, thing, or idea. The **adverb** will describe an **action verb**. I will say the sentence twice for you:

Instructor (twice): The weary runner sprinted bravely down the track.

370

Instructor: Can you find the **adjective**?

⇨ Note to Instructor: You may prompt the child by asking, "Who is the sentence about? It is about a runner. "Runner" is a noun. What kind of runner?"

*Child: Weary.*

Instructor: Can you find the **adverb**?

⇨ Note to Instructor: You may prompt the child by asking, "What did the runner do? Sprinted. "Sprinted" is an action verb. The runner sprinted how?"

*Child: Bravely.*

## Dictation Exercise

Choose one or more of the following sentences (adapted from "The Cow" by Robert Louis Stevenson). Remember to pause at each comma.

The friendly cow, all red and white, I love with all my heart.
She gives me cream with all her might, to eat with apple tart.
She wanders lowing here and there, and yet she cannot stray.
She walks among the meadow grass and eats the meadow hay.

# Lesson 180

-Interjections
-Prepositions
-Dictation exercise: "Ow! Yuck! Oh!"
-Poem review: "The Goops" (Lesson 100)
* The child will need drawing supplies for the enrichment activity.

⇨ Note to Instructor: Review "The Goops" today.

Instructor: I want you to read the following sentences from "The Three Bears" with me. I will read out loud as you follow along.

Goldilocks said to herself, "Oh! That is the most charming wood cottage with the most charming red roses and the most charming blue door."

"Ow!" she cried out. "That porridge is too hot!"

"Yuck!" she whined. "That porridge is too cold!"

"Mmm!" she exclaimed. "This porridge is neither too hot nor too cold. This is just right."

"Oh!" she complained, "That cushion is too hard!"

"Hmph!" she grumbled. "That cushion is too soft!"

"Ah!" she sighed. "This cushion is neither too hard nor too soft. This cushion is just right."

"Ooh!" she groaned. "That blanket is too thick!"

"Brrr," she shivered. "That blanket is too thin!"

"Mmm," she murmured. "This blanket is neither too thick nor too thin. This blanket is just right."

Instructor: Goldilocks talks to herself quite a lot! These short words express strong feeling. Do you remember what we call a word that expresses sudden or strong feeling?

*Child: An interjection.*

Instructor: Repeat that definition for me in a complete sentence: **An interjection is a word that expresses sudden or strong feeling.**

Child: **An interjection is a word that expresses sudden or strong feeling.**

Instructor: Let's read a few more sentences about Goldilocks from the story of The Three Bears.

She tasted the porridge in the big, blue bowl.
The chair had a big, blue cushion on the seat.
She threw the big, blue cushion under the chair.
Goldilocks liked the little bed with the yellow blanket.
Goldilocks saw a whole bear family beside her bed!

Instructor: Can you find the preposition in each sentence? Remember, **A preposition is a word that shows the relationship of a noun or pronoun to another word in the sentence.** Go through the **preposition** list in your mind and see whether you can find those words in these sentences. What is the **preposition** in the first sentence?

*Child: In.*

⇨ Note to Instructor: If the child cannot find the preposition, ask, "What word shows the relationship between the porridge and the big blue bowl?"

Instructor: "In" shows the relationship between the porridge and the big, blue, bowl. What is the **preposition** in the second sentence?

⇨ Note to Instructor: If the child cannot find the preposition, ask, "What word shows the relationship between the cushion and the seat?"

*Child: On.*

Instructor: "On" shows the relationship between the cushion and the seat. What is the **preposition** in the third sentence?

⇨ Note to Instructor: If the child cannot find the preposition, ask, "What word shows the relationship between the cushion and the chair?"

*Child: Under.*

Instructor: "Under" shows the relationship between the cushion and the chair. What is the **preposition** in the fourth sentence?

⇨ Note to Instructor: If the child cannot find the preposition, ask, "What word shows the relationship between the little bed and the yellow blanket?"

*Child: With.*

Instructor: "With" shows the relationship between the little bed and the yellow blanket. What is the **preposition** in the fifth sentence?

⇨ Note to Instructor: If the child cannot find the preposition, ask, "What word shows the relationship between the bear family and the bed?"

*Child: Beside.*

Instructor: "Beside" shows the relationship between the Bear family and the bed.

**Dictation Exercise**

Choose one or more of these sentences that Goldilocks exclaims.

Ow! That porridge is too hot!
Yuck! That porridge is too cold!
Oh! That cushion is too hard!
Ah! This cushion is neither too hard nor too soft!
Oh! That is the most charming wood cottage with the most charming red roses and the most charming blue door!

**Enrichment Activity**

Have the child draw pictures of one or more of the following scenes and label each with the correct preposition:

the porridge in the big, blue bowl
the big, blue cushion on the seat of the chair
the big, blue cushion under the chair
the little bed with the yellow blanket
the whole bear family beside Goldilocks in the bed

# Lesson 181

- Quotations
    - Direct quotations
    - Indirect quotations
- Dictation exercise: "Who's That Trip-trapping?"

⇨  Note to Instructor: Chant the preposition list twice today (this should take about ninety seconds): Aboard, about, above, across. After, against, along, among, around, at. Before, behind, below, beneath. Beside, between, beyond, by. Down, during, except, for, from. In, inside, into, like. Near, of, off, on, over. Past, since, through, throughout. To, toward, under, underneath. Until, up, upon. With, within, without.

Instructor: I am going to read you some quotes. See if you can tell me who says each one of these sentences.

⇨  Note to Instructor: When reading these quotes, use a deep voice for the **Papa Bear** and the **Biggest Billy Goat Gruff,** a medium voice for the Mama Bear and the Medium-sized Billy Goat Gruff, and a little squeaky voice for the Baby Bear and the Little Billy Goat Gruff. The font size will remind you which is which. Do not show the child the quotes until you are finished. The purpose of the lesson is to fix in the child's mind that a direct quotation uses the <u>exact</u> words of the speaker.


"Mmm. This blanket is neither too thick nor too thin. This blanket is just right." (Goldilocks)

"Oh, Mommy dear, we sadly fear, our mittens we have lost!" (The Three Little Kittens)

"I'm coming to eat you up!" (The Troll)

**"Somebody has been eating my porridge!"** (Papa Bear)

"Somebody has been eating my porridge!" (Mama Bear)

"Don't eat me. I'm just medium-sized. Wait for my brother. He is much fatter than I!" (The Medium-Sized Billy Goat Gruff)

"What! Lost your mittens, you naughty kittens! Then you shall have no pie!" (Mother Cat)

"Somebody has been eating my porridge, and has eaten every last drop!" (Baby Bear)

" I'm so little that I'd hardly be a mouthful for you. Wait for my big brother. He is much fatter than I." (The Littlest Billy Goat Gruff)

"Who's that trip-trapping over my bridge?" (The Troll)

"Somebody has been sitting in my chair!" (Mama Bear)

"Someone has been sitting in my chair, and has broken the leg off!" (Baby Bear)

**"Somebody has been sleeping in my bed!"** (Papa Bear)

## "Come on, then, and try to eat me!" (The Great Big Billy Goat Gruff)

"Somebody has been sleeping in my bed, and she is still in it!" (Baby Bear)

⇨ Note to Instructor: After you have read the quotes to the child and he has had a chance to identify them, show him the book. Point out the quotation marks on either side of the quotes.

Instructor: Each one of these sentences is a direct quotation. These are the <u>exact</u> words spoken by the characters in the stories. A direct quotation has quotation marks on either side of it. An indirect quotation tells you what someone says but doesn't use their exact words. Look at the difference between these two sentences.

⇨ Note to Instructor: Show the child the following two sentences.

The Little Billy Goat Gruff said, "Wait for my big brother. He is much fatter than I."
The Little Billy Goat Gruff told the troll to wait for his big brother.

Instructor: Do you see the difference between the direct and indirect quotation? The direct quotation uses the actual words spoken by the Little Billy Goat Gruff, but the indirect quotation just tells you the information that the Little Billy Goat Gruff said. Look at the next two sentences. Can you tell me which is the direct quotation, and which is the indirect quotation?

The Three Little Kittens told their mother that they had lost their mittens.
The Three Little Kittens said, "Oh, Mommy dear, we sadly fear, our mittens we have lost!"

Instructor: Can you tell me which of these sentences is a direct quotation? Which is an indirect quotation?

The Troll said, "I'm coming to eat you up!"
The Troll said that he would eat up the Biggest Billy Goat Gruff.

Instructor: Remember, a direct quotation uses the actual words spoken by someone. It has quotation marks on either side of the actual words.

## Dictation Exercise

Tell the child that each of the following sentences is a direct quotation and should have quotation marks on either side of it. If necessary, have the child practice making quotation marks before doing the dictation exercise. Choose one or more of the following quotes.

"I'm coming to eat you up!"

"Who's that trip-trapping over my bridge?"

"Someone has been sitting in my chair, and has broken the leg off!"

# Lesson 182

-Nouns
-Pronouns
-Dictation exercise: "Paul Revere"
-Poem review: "The Little Bird" (Lesson 139)

⇨ Note to Instructor: Review "The Little Bird" today.

Instructor: Can you tell me the definition of a **noun**?

*Child:* **A noun is the name of a person, place, thing, or idea.**

Instructor: Listen carefully to this sentence. It has all four kinds of **nouns** in it: "The little girl, filled with excitement, peered into the kitchen to see her birthday cake on the counter." This sentence contains the name of a person, a place, a thing, and an idea. What kind of person is named in this sentence?

*Child: A little girl.*

⇨ Note to Instructor: Repeat the sentence as needed.

Instructor: What place is named in the sentence? The little girl peered into it.

*Child: The kitchen.*

Instructor: What thing is named in the sentence? The little girl wanted to see it!

*Child: The birthday cake.*

Instructor: What idea is named in the sentence? The little girl felt it as she peered into the kitchen.

*Child: Excitement.*

Instructor: Remember, an idea is something that you can think about in your mind, but can't see or touch. You can feel excitement in your mind but you can't see it or touch it. Now let's talk about another type of word. Listen to the sentence again. "The little girl, filled with excitement, peered into the kitchen to see <u>her</u> birthday cake on the counter." Do you remember what the word "her" is?

⇨ Note to Instructor: If necessary, prompt the child for the answer.

*Child: "Her" is a pronoun.*

Instructor: **A pronoun is a word used in the place of the noun.** Repeat that definition with me.

Together: **A pronoun is a word used in the place of the noun.**

Instructor: I will read the **pronouns** to you while you listen.

378

*I, me, my, mine.*
*You, your, yours.*
*He, she, him, her, it, his, hers, its.*
*We, us, our, ours.*
*They, them, their, theirs.*

Instructor: Listen to me while I say the sentence again. "The little girl, filled with excitement, peered into the kitchen to see her birthday cake on the counter." This time, I will put a **pronoun** in place of one of the nouns. "The little girl peered into the kitchen, full of excitement, to see <u>it</u> on the counter." Which **noun** did I replace with a **pronoun**?
*Child: The birthday cake*
Instructor: "It" is a **pronoun** that stands for the **noun** "cake." Listen one more time: "Filled with excitement, <u>she</u> peered into the kitchen to see her birthday cake on the counter." Which **noun** did I replace with a **pronoun**?
*Child: The little girl.*
Instructor: "She" is a **pronoun** that stands for the noun "girl." I am going to read you several sentences, and I want you to repeat them back to me. Here is the sentence: "Sam forgot to water the flowers." Repeat it back to me.
*Child: Sam forgot to water the flowers.*
Instructor: Sam forgot to water <u>them</u>.
*Child: Sam forgot to water them.*
Instructor: The girls will wrap a present for their brother.
*Child: The girls will wrap a present for their brother.*
Instructor: They will wrap a present for <u>him</u>.
*Child: They will wrap a present for him.*
Instructor: What noun did we replace with the pronoun "him"?
*Child: Their brother.*
Instructor: The woman cooked a huge meal.
*Child: The woman cooked a huge meal.*
Instructor: <u>She</u> cooked it.
*Child: She cooked it.*
Instructor: Who is "she"?
*Child: The woman.*
Instructor: What is "it"?
*Child: The meal.*
Instructor: The man gave money to the poor people.
*Child: The man gave money to the poor people.*

Instructor: He gave it to <u>them</u>.
*Child: He gave it to them.*
Instructor: Who is "he"?
*Child: The man.*
Instructor: What is "it"?
*Child: The money.*
Instructor: Who is "them"?
*Child: The poor people.*

## Dictation Exercise

Choose one or more of the following pairs of sentences.

The mother cat licked the kittens. She licked them.
The children played with the puppy. They played with it.
Paul Revere rode his horse to warn the people. He rode it to warn them.

# Lesson 183

-Contractions
-Copywork: "Contractions"

⇨ Note to Instructor: Chant the preposition list twice today (this should take about ninety seconds): Aboard, about, above, across. After, against, along, among, around, at. Before, behind, below, beneath. Beside, between, beyond, by. Down, during, except, for, from. In, inside, into, like. Near, of, off, on, over. Past, since, through, throughout. To, toward, under, underneath. Until, up, upon. With, within, without.

Instructor: I will tell you a story today, and you will say one line of it over and over again with me. Once upon a time, an old woman made a man out of gingerbread. She put him in the oven, but when he started to bake he jumped up and ran away. Do you know what he said when he ran? Say it with me.

Together: Run, run, as fast as you can. You can't catch me. I'm the gingerbread man.

Instructor: You are using contractions when you say the gingerbread man's line. "Can't" and "I'm" are contractions. They are short forms of the words "cannot" and "I am." A contraction is made up of two words, put together into one word, with some letters left out. A punctuation mark called an apostrophe is put in the place of the missing letters. Now say: Run, run, as fast as you can. You <u>cannot</u> catch me. <u>I am</u> the gingerbread man.

Child: *Run, run, as fast as you can. You cannot catch me. I am the gingerbread man.*

Instructor: The gingerbread man passed a cow, and the cow said, "You'll be a lovely meal! Stop and let me eat you!" The cow was using a contraction, too. "You'll" is short for "You will." Say, "<u>You will</u> be a lovely meal."

Child: *You will be a lovely meal.*

Instructor: And the gingerbread man said—say it with me—

Together: Run, run, as fast as you can. You can't catch me. I'm the gingerbread man.

Instructor: The gingerbread man passed two farmers, and the farmers said, "Wouldn't it be nice to eat that gingerbread man?" They could have said, "<u>Would</u> <u>not</u> it be nice to eat that gingerbread man?" But they were in a hurry. They called out, "Stop so we can eat you!" And the gingerbread man said:

Together: Run, run, as fast as you can. You can't catch me. I'm the gingerbread man.

Instructor: Then the gingerbread man came to a stream. He couldn't cross it, but a fox came along and said, "I'll carry you across." "I'll" is a contraction of what two words?

*Child: I will.*

⇨ Note to Instructor: Prompt child for the answer, if necessary.

Instructor: So the gingerbread man jumped on the fox's back. But when the fox plunged into the water, the gingerbread man started to get wet. He climbed up on the fox's nose and...what happened then?

*Child: The fox ate him.*

Instructor: And then the fox licked his lips and said, "I'm so glad I had that lovely snack." "I'm" is a contraction of what two words?

*Child: I am.*

⇨ Note to Instructor: Prompt child for the answer, if necessary. In the following exercise, if the child is unable to think of the correct contraction, say it for him and ask him to repeat it after you.

Instructor: I will say two or three words for you, and I want you to make each set of words into a contraction.

Instructor: He is.

*Child: He's*

Instructor: She is

*Child: She's*

Instructor: It is

*Child: It's*

Instructor: We will

*Child: We'll*

Instructor: You are

*Child: You're*

Instructor: I cannot

*Child: I can't*

Instructor: She will not

*Child: She won't*

Instructor: He does not

*Child: He doesn't*

Instructor: They were not

*Instructor: They weren't*

## Copywork

Ask the child to copy the following list onto his own paper in two straight columns.

| | |
|---|---|
| are not | aren't |
| were not | weren't |
| has not | hasn't |
| have not | haven't |
| does not | doesn't |
| did not | didn't |
| should not | shouldn't |
| could not | couldn't |
| would not | wouldn't |
| do not | don't |
| cannot | can't |
| is not | isn't |
| was not | wasn't |

## Enrichment Activity

Use the list above as a diagnostic quiz. The purpose of this quiz is to find out what you need to reteach. Read the child the words in the left hand column and ask him to write the contractions from memory.

# Lesson 184

-Poem memorization: "All Things Beautiful"

⇨  Note to Instructor: Read the entire poem aloud to the child. Then read only the first two stanzas three times. Repeat this process later in the day.

All Things Beautiful
*Cecil Alexander*

All things bright and beautiful,
All creatures great and small,
All things wise and wonderful,
The Lord God made them all.

Each little flower that opens,
Each little bird that sings,
He made their glowing colors,
He made their tiny wings.

The purple-headed mountain,
The river running by,
The sunset, and the morning,
That brighten up the sky;

The cold wind in the winter,
The pleasant summer sun,
The ripe fruits in the garden,
He made them every one.

The tall trees in the greenwood,
The meadows where we play,
The rushes by the water,
We gather every day;

He gave us eyes to see them,
And lips that we might tell
How great is God Almighty,
Who has made all things well.

# Lesson 185

-Introducing written composition: ordering ideas
-"My Morning," Part I
-Poem review: "All Things Beautiful" (Lesson 184)

➪ Note to Instructor: Read "All Things Beautiful" once through. Read the first two stanzas twice. Then read the third and fourth stanzas three times in a row.

➪ Note to Instructor: Before a child can write a composition, he must be able to put his ideas into order. "Ideas" are abstractions, and many young children have difficulty dealing with abstractions. We will not ask the young child to order ideas yet, but we will begin to prepare him to order his ideas by practicing the skills of ordering on something concrete: morning chores and activities. By teaching the child to pay attention to the order in which he carries out his morning duties, you are preparing his mind to pay attention to the order of ideas—a skill which will continue to develop as he matures.

Instructor: Today, we are going to begin working on a composition about what you do in the morning. We are going to practice putting into the right order the actions that you take every morning. When you got up this morning, did you put your clothes on over top of your pajamas? No. First, you took *off* your pajamas. Then, you put *on* your clothes. Did you put on your socks *after* you put on your shoes? No. You put on your socks first, and you put on your shoes second.

I am going to help you learn how to write a composition. In our composition, you will tell the things that you do in the morning in the right order. I want you to tell me everything that you do in the mornings.

➪ Note to Instructor: If you prefer, you can choose one particular morning and list the events that took place on it.

Instructor: I want you to tell me in complete sentences, beginning with "I," what you do in the mornings. Begin with, "I got up at…"

➪ Note to Instructor: This is just the first step in the composition process. You should write down, in list form, each sentence that the child says. Make sure that each sentence is a complete sentence with a capital letter and a punctuation mark ("I made up my bed," not "made bed"). Talk about each sentence as you write. When you have finished, go back through and number the sentences in the order in which the actions occurred.

# Lesson 186

-Written composition: forming paragraphs
-"My Morning," Part II
-Copywork: the composition
-Poem review: "All Things Beautiful" (Lesson 184)

⇨ Note to Instructor: Read "All Things Beautiful" once through. Read the first two stanzas twice. Then read the third and fourth stanzas three times in a row.

Instructor: Today we will look back at our sentences describing your morning chores. I will read the sentences to you in order. Let's make sure that you have put all of the events of your day in the proper order.

⇨ Note to Instructor: Aim to have six sentences in the final composition. If the child has many more events than this, you will want to eliminate some (see Enrichment Activity below). Ask the child to help you identify which events are more important and which are less important. Once you have settled on the final sentences which will be in the composition, explain to the child that you will use the ordering words "first," "next," "then," and "after that" to help put the events into their proper order. You will then rewrite the sentences on the list into one coherent paragraph. The first sentence should be indented and should begin with the word "First." The following sentences should begin with the words "next," "then," or "after that." Don't worry too much about varying the sentence style. When a child is beginning to write, it is acceptable for each sentence to follow the same pattern! When you have finished writing the paragraph for the child, decide on a title for the composition. Capitalize the first word and each important word in this title and center it on the top line of the paper.

## Copywork

Ask the child to copy the title and the first half of his composition onto his own paper. Remind him to indent the first line, to capitalize his title and the first word in each sentence, and to use proper punctuation.

## Enrichment Activity

A child who writes easily may wish to write a longer composition.

# Lesson 187

-Written composition: copying the final work
   -"My Morning," Part III
-Copywork: the composition
-Poem review: "All Things Beautiful" (Lesson 184)
* The child may need art supplies.

⇨ Note to Instructor: Read "All Things Beautiful" once through. Read the first four stanzas one more time. Then read the fifth and sixth stanzas three times in a row.

⇨ Note to Instructor: Chant the helping verb list three times.

Am [clap]
Is [clap]
Are, was, were. [clap]
Be [clap]
Being [clap]
Been. [clap] [clap]
Have, has, had [clap]
Do, does, did [clap]
Shall, will, should, would, may, might, must [clap] [clap]
Can, could!

## Copywork

The child should finish copying his composition. He may illustrate any part of it that he wishes.

# Lesson 188

-Picture narration: "Morning Time"

Let's look at the picture together. It is a picture of a boy. His name is Hector. It is morning, and he just woke up half an hour ago. He climbed out of bed and changed out of his pajamas. He put his pajamas in the clothes hamper and then got dressed in his clothes for the day. What clothes did he put on? He put on shorts and a short-sleeved shirt. It must be summer! He is wearing his shorts and shirt now. Then he went to the kitchen to eat his breakfast. He knows that eating breakfast is very important. It gives him strength to study and play each day. After breakfast, he went to the bathroom and brushed his teeth. He also combed his hair. Do you think he did a good job? I think he did a good job. He even remembered to comb the back of his head.

Then Hector went back to his bedroom. What is he doing now? He is making his bed. He pulled up the blankets and placed his toys neatly at the top of his bed. Do you see his toys? What kind of toys are they?

Hector wants to go outside and ride his bike today, but he still has things to do. Look at his face. He is thinking about how much fun it will be to ride his bike. Can you think of anything he needs to do before he can go outside? He needs to put on his socks and shoes. Do you see them lying near the bed? Point to the socks and shoes. Do you think Hector has fed his dog, Lucky? How do you know? There is no food inside Lucky's food bowl and Lucky looks very hungry. See how he is staring expectantly at Hector? He is hoping Hector will remember to feed him. I am sure Hector will remember. He is a very responsible child and he always does all of his chores before he goes out to play.

# Lesson 189

-Prepositions
-Dictation exercise: "Rain"
-Poem review: "All Things Beautiful" (Lesson 184)

⇨ Note to Instructor: Read "All Things Beautiful" once through. Read the first four stanzas one more time. Then read the fifth and sixth stanzas three times in a row.

Instructor: Repeat after me: **A preposition is a word that shows the relationship of a noun or pronoun to another word in the sentence.**

*Child:* **A preposition is a word that shows the relationship of a noun or pronoun to another word in the sentence.**

Instructor: I will say our list of **prepositions**, and then we will say them together two more times. Aboard, about, above, across. After, against, along, among, around, at. Before, behind, below, beneath. Beside, between, beyond, by. Down, during, except, for, from. In, inside, into, like. Near, of, off, on, over. Past, since, through, throughout. To, toward, under, underneath. Until, up. upon. With, within, without.

Together (twice): Aboard, about, above, across. After, against, along, among, around, at. Before, behind, below, beneath. Beside, between, beyond, by. Down, during, except, for, from. In, inside, into, like. Near, of, off, on, over. Past, since, through, throughout. To, toward, under, underneath. Until, up, upon. With, within, without.

Instructor: I will read you some sentences. Wherever there is a **preposition**, I will say the word *preposition*. I want you to repeat the sentence back to me, and put a real **preposition** in that blank. For example, if I say, "Mandy is *preposition* her desk," you will say back to me, "Mandy is *at* her desk.

⇨ Note to Instructor: The child's answers are suggested, but any appropriate preposition from the list is acceptable. If the child is unable to answer, begin to repeat the list back to him, one preposition at a time, asking him to try each preposition. (Generally this will spark his imagination so that you will not have to continue on through the whole list.)

Instructor: There is a ceiling *preposition* Mandy's head.
*Child: There is a ceiling <u>above</u> Mandy's head.*
Instructor: The dog chased the cat *preposition* the house.
*Child: The dog chased the cat <u>into</u> [or out of] the house.*

Instructor: The baby threw its pacifier *preposition* the sofa.
*Child: The baby threw its pacifier <u>under</u> [or behind] the sofa.*
Instructor: When Luis vacuumed, he found balls of dust *preposition* his bed.
*Child: When Luis vacuumed, he found balls of dust <u>under</u> his bed.*
Instructor: We will do school *preposition* lunchtime.
*Child: We will do school <u>until</u> [or after] lunchtime.*
Instructor: Take your hat *preposition* when you come inside.
*Child: Take your hat <u>off</u> when you come inside.*
Instructor: The train sped *preposition* the tunnel.
*Child: The train sped <u>through</u> the tunnel.*
Instructor: I like pancakes *preposition* maple syrup.
*Child: I like pancakes <u>with</u> maple syrup.*
Instructor: Do not cram your mouth *preposition* too much food!
*Child: Do not cram your mouth <u>with</u> too much food!*

## Dictation Exercise

Show the child the following poem by Robert Louis Stevenson. Point out that there is a comma after each line (except for the last line which ends in a period). Dictate the poem, title first, and then one line at a time. Require the child to center the title "Rain," on his paper, but unless he writes easily, <u>you</u> write "Robert Louis Stevenson." Remind him that each line should begin at the left-hand margin of his paper, and that the first letter of each line of a poem should be capitalized.

Rain
*Robert Louis Stevenson*

The rain is raining all around,
It falls on field and tree,
It rains on the umbrellas here,
And on the ships at sea.

## Enrichment Activity

Ask the child to memorize "Rain."

# Lesson 190

-Synonyms
-Antonyms
-Dictation exercise: "The Troll"
-Poem review: "All Things Beautiful" (Lesson 184)

⇨ Note to Instructor: Read "All Things Beautiful" three times through.
Instructor: Do you remember that "ssssynonyms have the sssssame meaning"? Listen to me repeat the definition of a **synonym**, and then we will say it together: **Synonyms are words that have the same meaning.**
Together: **Synonyms are words that have the same meaning.**
Instructor: **Antonyms are opposites.** Let's say that together three times: **Antonyms are opposites.**
Together (three times): **Antonyms are opposites.**
Instructor: Now, we will read several lists of synonyms together. For each list, I will give you a sentence. I want you to say the sentence back to me three times, each time choosing a different **synonym** for the word I emphasize.
⇨ Note to Instructor: In the following exercises, allow the child to look at the list of synonyms given as he repeats the sentence three times, substituting different synonyms for the italicized word you emphasize.
Instructor: I will do the first one for you. Let's read the list of synonyms:

Together: pretty, beautiful, lovely, gorgeous
Instructor: Here is the sentence. "The sunset was *pretty*." You would say back to me, "The sunset was *beautiful*. The sunset was *lovely*. The sunset was *gorgeous*." Read those sentences.

*Child reads:* The sunset was <u>beautiful</u>. The sunset was <u>lovely</u>. The sunset was <u>gorgeous</u>."

Instructor: Now, let's read a second list of synonyms together:

Together: ugly, frightful, horrible, unsightly, dreadful, hideous
Instructor: Here is the sentence for you to practice substituting different synonyms for a word: "The troll who lived under the bridge was certainly *ugly*." I want you to say the sentence back to me three times, each time choosing a different **synonym** for the word "ugly."

*Child: the troll was [synonym]. The troll was [synonym]. The troll was [synonym].*
Instructor: If you were a troll, you might not see the troll as ugly. You might see him as handsome. Here are some **antonyms** for "ugly." They are the <u>opposite</u> of ugly. Remember, **antonyms are opposites**. Read these **antonyms** for "ugly" with me.

Together: Beautiful, handsome, lovely, pretty, comely, good-looking, attractive
Instructor: Here is a sentence that you will say back to me three times: The troll who lived under the bridge was certainly *good-looking.*" Each time, choose a different word from the list we just read.
*Child: The troll was [synonym]. The troll was [synonym]. The troll was [synonym].*

Instructor: Let's read another list of synonyms:

Together: bite, chew, gnash, chomp, nibble, munch.
Instructor: Here is the sentence to say back to me three times, using a different **synonym**: "The troll wanted to *bite* the Great Big Billy Goat Gruff."
*Child: The troll wanted to [chew] the Great Big Billy Goat Gruff. The troll wanted to [gnash] the Great Big Billy Goat Gruff. The troll wanted to [chomp] the Great Big Billy Goat Gruff.*

Instructor: Let's practice a few more **antonyms**. For each sentence that I say to you, tell me the opposite. I am sad.
*Child: I am happy.*
Instructor: I am awake.
*Child: I am asleep.*
Instructor: This room is quiet.
*Child: This room is noisy.*
Instructor: The sun is up.
*Child: The sun is down.*
Instructor: The sky is light.
*Child: The sky is dark.*
Instructor: You have done an excellent job of contradicting me!

## Dictation Exercise
Dictate one or more of the following pairs of sentences to the child.
Tell the child that you will stop at a period for the count of five, and
that you will draw your breath before beginning the next sentence.

The troll liked goats.  He relished them.
The goats would taste delicious.  They would taste yummy.
The goats tricked the foolish troll.  They outwitted him and got away.

## Enrichment Activity
Ask the child to make up sentences using the following synonym sets:

Set 1
warble, sing, carol, whistle, trill, twitter, tweet (think birds!)

Set 2
wiggly, squirmy, jumpy, jerky, twitchy, fidgety

Set 3
fancy, colored, decorated, befrilled, flowery, ornate, embellished

# Lesson 191

-Parts of speech review

-Poem review: "All Things Beautiful" (Lesson 184)

⇨ Note to Instructor: Read "All Things Beautiful" out loud once. Ask child to recite the poem from memory. Stop and read out loud three times any stanza that he finds difficult.

⇨ Note to Instructor: Read the following paragraph aloud together. Together:

Robin Hood crept carefully through the forest. He was looking for a rich traveller with much gold. Robin Hood could take his gold, and give it to an old, poor woman. The old woman would thank him and weep with joy. "Oh!" she would say. "I am a happy woman!"

⇨ Note to Instructor: Tell the child that every word in the above paragraph is one of the following:

noun
pronoun
adjective
verb (action, linking, helping)
adverb
preposition
article
conjunction
interjection

⇨ Note to Instructor: Allow the child to look at this list as he identifies each word in the paragraph. A key for the instructor follows.

## Key for the Instructor

| | |
|---|---|
| Robin Hood | noun (proper name) |
| crept | verb |
| carefully | adverb |
| through | preposition |
| the | article |
| forest | noun |
| He | pronoun |
| was | helping verb |

| | |
|---|---|
| looking | action verb |
| for | preposition |
| a | article |
| rich | adjective |
| traveller | noun |
| with | preposition |
| much | adjective |
| gold. | noun |
| Robin Hood | noun (proper name) |
| could | helping verb |
| take | action verb |
| his | pronoun |
| gold | noun |
| and | conjunction |
| give | action verb |
| it | pronoun |
| to | preposition |
| an | article |
| old, | adjective |
| poor | adjective |
| woman. | noun |
| The | article |
| old | adjective |
| woman | noun |
| would | helping verb |
| thank | action verb |
| him | pronoun |
| and | conjunction |
| weep | action verb |
| with | preposition |
| joy. | noun (idea) |
| "Oh!" | interjection |
| she | pronoun |
| would | helping verb |
| say. | action verb |
| "I | pronoun |
| am | linking verb |
| a | article |
| happy | adjective |
| woman!" | noun |

396

# Lesson 192
-Written composition: ordering ideas
  -"Giving Directions," Part I
-Poem review: "All Things Beautiful" (Lesson 184)

⇨ Note to Instructor: Read "All Things Beautiful" out loud once. Ask child to recite the poem from memory. Stop and read out loud three times any stanza that he finds difficult.

⇨ Note to Instructor: The child will continue practicing ordering events by working on a composition which gives step-by-step directions on how to do something. Choose something fairly simple and concrete: making toast, brushing teeth, feeding or bathing a pet, getting a drink from the refrigerator, feeding or bathing the baby, making a bed, or some other action that the child performs regularly. In today's lesson, help the child describe the action, step-by-step, as though he were telling someone unfamiliar with the action how to perform it. Write down the steps for the child in list form. Each step should be written as a complete sentence. If you begin a description and it becomes too complicated or frustrating, stop and try describing a simpler activity. When the child has finished telling you the sentences and you have written them down, read them back to the child. Make sure that they are in the proper order. Number them.

# Lesson 193

-Written composition: forming paragraphs
  -"Giving Directions," Part II
-Copywork: the composition
-Poem review: "All Things Beautiful" (Lesson 184)

⇨ Note to Instructor: Read "All Things Beautiful" out loud once. Ask child to recite the poem from memory. Stop and read out loud three times any stanza that he finds difficult.

Instructor: Today we will look back at our sentences that give directions. I will read the sentences to you in order. Let's make sure that you have put all of the directions in the proper order.

⇨ Note to Instructor: Aim to have six to seven sentences in the final composition. If the child has many more sentences than this, you will want to eliminate some (see Enrichment Activity below). Ask the child to help you identify which directions are unnecessary. Once you have settled on the final sentences which will be in the composition, explain to the child that you will use the ordering words "first," "next," "then," and "after that" to help put the directions into their proper order. You will then rewrite the sentences on the list into one coherent paragraph. The first sentence should be indented and should begin with the word "First." The following sentences should begin with the words "next," "then," or "after that." Don't worry too much about varying the sentence style. When a child is beginning to write, it is acceptable for each sentence to follow the same pattern! When you have finished writing the paragraph for the child, decide on a title for the composition. Capitalize the first word and each important word in this title and center it on the top line of the paper.

## Copywork

Ask the child to copy the title and the first half of his composition onto his own paper. Remind him to indent the first line, to capitalize his title and the first word in each sentence, and to use proper punctuation.

## Enrichment Activity

A child who writes easily may wish to write a longer set of directions or a second set describing a different activity.

# Lesson 194

-Written composition: copying the final work
  -"Giving Directions," Part III
-Copywork: the composition
-Poem review: "All Things Beautiful" (Lesson 184)

➪   Note to Instructor: Read "All Things Beautiful" out loud once. Ask child to recite the poem from memory. Stop and read out loud three times any stanza that he finds difficult.

Instructor: Today we will finish copying your composition. Then I will ask you to read it me, and I will follow your directions.

## Copywork

Ask the child to finish copying his composition. When he is completely done, have him read the composition out loud to you as you follow the directions (if this is possible).

# Lesson 195
-Cumulative poem review

Instructor: Today we are going to review all of the poems you have memorized so far.

When we recite a poem, we begin with the title and author. I will give you the title and author for each poem. Say the title and author back to me, and then recite the poem. Remember, stand up straight! Don't fidget while you're reciting! And speak in a nice, loud, slow voice.

⇨ Note to Instructor: You may prompt as necessary. If the child repeats the poem accurately, move on to the next poem. If he stumbles, ask him to repeat the line he cannot remember three times.

| Lesson | Poem | Author |
|--------|------|--------|
| 2 | "The Caterpillar" | Christina G. Rossetti |
| 15 | "Work" | Anonymous |
| 27 | "Hearts Are Like Doors" | Anonymous |
| 35 | "Days of the Week" | Mother Goose rhyme adapted by Sara Buffington |
| 43 | "The Months" | Mother Goose rhyme |
| 81 | "Mr. Nobody" | Anonymous |
| 100 | "The Goops" | Gelett Burgess |
| 131 | "The Year" | Sara Coleridge, adapted by Sara Buffington |
| 139 | "The Little Bird" | Mother Goose rhyme |
| 184 | "All Things Beautiful" | Cecil Alexander |

⇨ Note to Instructor: You may also read back through the poems which were not memorized.

| | |
|---|---|
| "Dancing" | Lesson 58 |
| "Monday, Mommy Baked a Cake" | Lesson 59 |
| "The Star" | Lesson 86 |
| "Sunflowers" | Lesson 91 |
| "The Wind" | Lesson 115 |
| "Let Dogs Delight to Bark and Bite" | Lesson 126 |
| "How Creatures Move" | Lesson 129 |
| "Bed in Summer" (one stanza) | Lesson 161 |
| "The Daffodils" (one stanza) | Lesson 163 |
| "I Love You Well" | Lesson 166 |
| "Foreign Lands" | Lesson 172 |
| "Rain" | Lesson 189 |

# Lesson 196

-Dictation exercise: review session 1

Instructor: For each of the next three lessons, I will dictate three sentences to you. These sentences will include many of the rules we have studied. Remember, I will pause briefly whenever I reach a comma. I will pause and count to five whenever I reach a period, and I will take a breath before beginning the next sentence.

⇨ Note to Instructor: Choose one of the following sets of sentences. If you see the child writing some part of the sentence incorrectly, stop him and remind him of the appropriate rule. He should do these sentences in pencil so that he can erase and make immediate corrections. Don't frustrate the child. Adjust your speed of dictation to the child's ability.

My brother and I play soccer. We play on Tuesdays, Thursdays, and Saturdays in the summer. In the fall, we play other teams.

My family and I camp at night in the park. We usually go on Friday nights and stay until Saturday afternoon. Spring, summer, and fall are good times to camp.

My baby sister and I climb on monkey bars at the park. She likes to swing, giggle, and then fall down on purpose. In the spring, we go on Mondays and Wednesdays, but in the fall, we go only on Saturdays.

# Lesson 197

-Dictation exercise: review session 2

Instructor: The dictation sentences in today's lesson will include many of the rules we have studied. Remember, I will pause briefly whenever I reach a comma. I will pause and count to five whenever I reach a period, and I will take a breath before beginning the next sentence. If one of the sentences is an exclamation, I will sound excited as I dictate it.

⇨ Note to Instructor: Choose one of the following sets of sentences. If you see the child writing some part of the sentence incorrectly, stop him and remind him of the appropriate rule. He should do these sentences in pencil so that he can erase and make immediate corrections. Make sure to read the exclamations with an excited voice. For long words help the child sound the words out syllable by syllable. Give all necessary help with spelling. Don't frustrate the child. Adjust your speed of dictation to the child's ability.

On July 4, 1776, the states declared independence. Mr. Ellis sets off fireworks on the Fourth of July. They fizzle and spark!

On July 4, 1776, the United States of America declared independence. The Fourth of July and Thanksgiving are my two favorite holidays! Mr. Ellis comes over to celebrate both holidays with us.

On the first Thanksgiving Day, the colonists thanked God for their new home. On July 4, 1776, the United States of America declared independence from Britain! Mr. Ellis comes to our house to celebrate both holidays with us.

# Lesson 198
-Dictation exercise: review session 3

Instructor: The dictation sentences in today's lesson will include many of the rules we have studied. Remember, I will pause briefly whenever I reach a comma. I will pause and count to five whenever I reach a period, and I will take a breath before beginning the next sentence.

⇨ Note to Instructor: Choose one of the following sets of sentences. If you see the child writing some part of the sentence incorrectly, stop him and remind him of the appropriate rule. He should do these sentences in pencil so that he can erase and make immediate corrections. Give all necessary help in spelling. Don't frustrate the child. Adjust your speed of dictation to the child's ability.

Would you like a cookie? Mrs. R. L. Brown made cookies for us. Aren't they wonderful?

Would you like a chocolate cookie? Mrs. R. L. Brown made cookies for her friends and gave us some. Aren't they rich, gooey, and wonderful?

Would you like a chocolate marshmallow cookie? Mrs. R. L. Brown made cookies for all her friends and gave us a whole bag. Aren't they rich, gooey, sticky, and wonderful?

# Lesson 199
## -Story narration: "The Donkey and the Salt"

➯ Note to Instructor: Read the following story aloud to the child, and then ask the child to tell it back to you in his own words. When the child is able to summarize the story in three or four sentences, write these sentences down for him in neat printing (or in writing that he can easily read). Read his version back to him and then file it in his notebook.

### The Donkey and the Salt

A merchant who lived long ago often heaped huge bags of salt upon his donkey's back and drove the donkey to the market. There, he would sell the salt for a good price. He was happy—but his donkey was discontent. The salt was tremendously heavy. And although the money that the merchant earned at the market bought the donkey good grain and sweet hay, the donkey complained about his work. "If only I didn't have to haul these bags of salt!" he moaned. "My life would be so much easier!"

On his way to the market one day, the donkey stumbled on a little bridge over a stream and fell into the water. As he lay in the water, the salt melted and ran away down the stream. "Get up," the merchant ordered. When the donkey scrambled to his feet, the bags were empty. He felt light and carefree! He switched his tail and trotted happily down the road, free of his burden.

The merchant was sad, for he made no money at the market. He returned home with empty hands. "What will I do?" he asked himself. "Without my market days, I will no longer be able to buy grain and hay for my donkey."

But the donkey was pleased with his day off. On his next trip to the market, he stumbled again—this time on purpose! He rolled into the water and waited for the salt to melt. When the bags were empty once more, he jumped to his feet and ambled cheerfully along. "Hurrah!" he thought to himself. "I am free of my burden again! Now I know the secret. I don't ever have to carry salt to the market again."

The merchant realized that his lazy donkey had fallen on purpose. So the next day, he loaded the donkey with bags of sponges. Sure enough, when the donkey went over the bridge, he jumped into the water and lay there, satisfied with his plan. But when he got to his hooves, his burden was harder to bear than usual. The sponges had soaked up the water, and the bags were as heavy as lead. He staggered wearily home under the load, wishing that he had been wiser. "I'll never again try to get out of working," he thought to himself. "Getting out of work is harder than just doing it in the first place."

Moral: Lazy people often end up working harder than anyone else!

# Lesson 200
-Parts of speech hunt

⇨ Note to Instructor: Read through the following list of grammatical terms with the child. Then go back to story "The Donkey and the Salt" in Lesson 199. As you read through the story together, ask the child to hunt for one of each of these grammatical terms. You might want to consider offering a small reward (such as raisins or chocolate chips) for each word that the child finds. Several answers are indicated in the "Partial Key" below; if necessary, you can drop hints. Encourage! This is a review, not a test.

## Grammatical Terms

noun
pronoun
adjective
action verb
linking verb
helping
adverb
preposition
article
conjunction
interjection
question
statement
exclamation
contraction
direct quotation
indented paragraph
the pronoun "I" (capitalized)

## Partial Key

| article | noun | | | action verb | adjective | noun |
|---|---|---|---|---|---|---|
| A | merchant who lived long ago often heaped | | | huge | | bags of salt |
| preposition | pronoun | | conjunction | | | preposition |
| upon | his | donkey's back and | | | drove the donkey | to |
| article | noun | | helping verb | action verb | | |
| the | market. | There, he would | | sell | the salt for a good price. He |

406

linking verb

was happy—but his donkey was discontent.

linking verb

adverb     adjective   conjunction

The salt was tremendously heavy.     And     although the money that the merchant earned at the market  bought the donkey good grain and sweet hay,

exclamation

the donkey complained about his work. "If only I didn't have to haul these bags of

exclamation

salt!" he moaned. "My life would be so much easier!"

statement

On his way to the market one day, the donkey stumbled on a little bridge

statement

over a stream and fell into the water. As he lay in the water, the salt melted and ran

command

away down the stream. "Get up," the merchant ordered. When the donkey scrambled to his feet, the bags were empty. He felt light and carefree! He switched his tail and trotted happily down the road, free of his burden.

indented paragraph

The merchant was sad, for he made no money at the market. He returned home with empty hands.

question                              direct quotation          pronoun "I"

"What will I do?" he asked himself. "Without my market days, I will no longer be able to buy grain and hay for my donkey."

But the donkey was pleased with his day off. On his next trip to the market, he stumbled again—this time on purpose! He rolled into the water and waited for the salt to melt. When the bags were empty once more, he jumped to his feet and

interjection

ambled cheerfully along. "Hurrah!" he thought to himself. "I am free of my burden

contraction

again! Now I know the secret. I don't     ever have to carry salt to the market again."

The merchant realized that his lazy donkey had fallen on purpose. So the next day, he loaded the donkey with bags of sponges. Sure enough, when the donkey went over the bridge, he jumped into the water and lay there, satisfied with his plan. But when he got to his hooves, his burden was harder to bear than . The sponges had soaked up the water, and the bags were as heavy as lead. He staggered wearily home under the load,

contraction

wishing that he had been wiser. "I'll     never again try to get out of working," he thought to himself. "Getting out of work is harder than just doing it in the first place."


# End of Second Grade

# Glossary of Terms and Definitions

## Terms

**action verb** – An action verb is a word that does an action.

**adjective** – An adjective is a word that describes a noun.

**adverb** – An adverb is a word that describes a verb, an adjective, or another adverb.

**antonym** – Antonyms are words that have opposite meanings.

**article** – The articles are *a*, *an*, and *the*.

**command** – A command gives an order or makes a request.

**common noun** – A common noun is the name of any person, place, thing, or idea.

**conjunction** – A conjunction is a word that joins words or groups of words together.

**exclamation** – An exclamation shows sudden or strong feeling.

**helping verb** – A helping verb is a verb that helps another verb.

**interjection** – An interjection is a word that expresses sudden or strong feeling.

**linking verb** – A linking verb is a word that links two words together.

**noun** – A noun is the name of a person, place, thing, or idea.

**preposition** – A preposition is a word that shows the relationship of a noun or pronoun to another word in the sentence.

**pronoun** – A pronoun is a word used in place of a noun.

**proper noun** – A proper noun is a word that names a particular person, place, thing, or idea.

**question** – A question asks something.

**sentence** – A sentence is a group of words that expresses a complete thought.

**state of being verb** – A state of being verb is a word that shows a state of being.

**statements** – A statement gives information.

**synonym** – Synonyms are words that have the same meaning.

**verb** – A verb is a word that does an action, shows a state of being, links two words together, or helps another verb.

## Memorized Definitions

A noun is the name of a person, place, thing, or idea.

A pronoun is a word used in place of a noun.

A verb is a word that does an action, shows a state of being, links two words together or helps another verb.

A sentence is a group of words that expresses a complete thought.

An adjective is word that describes a noun.

A conjunction is a word that joins words or groups of words together.

An interjection is a word that expresses sudden or strong feeling.

An adverb is word that describes a verb, an adjective, or another adverb.

A preposition is a word that shows the relationship of a noun or pronoun to another word in the sentence.

Synonyms are words that have the same meaning. Antonyms are opposites.

## Memorized Lists
### State of Being Verbs (and Linking Verbs)
am, is, are, was, were, be, being, been
### Helping Verbs
am, is, are, was, were, be, being, been, have, has, had, do, does, did, shall, will, should, would, may, might, must, can, could
### Articles
a, an, the
### Conjunctions
and, but, or
### Prepositions
aboard, about, above, across, after, against, along, among, around, at, before, behind, below, beneath, beside, between, beyond, by, down, during, except, for, from, in, inside, into, like, near, of, off, on, over, past, since, through, throughout, to, toward, under, underneath, until, up. upon, with, within, without

# Index

# D

# Q

# R

# S

# Y